Mindfulness-Based Practices in Therapy

Mindfulness-Based Practices in Therapy

A Cultural Humility Approach

Don Davis, Cirleen DeBlaere,
Joshua N. Hook, *and* Jesse Owen

AMERICAN PSYCHOLOGICAL ASSOCIATION
Washington, DC

Published by
American Psychological Association
750 First Street, NE
Washington, DC 20002
https://www.apa.org

Order Department
https://www.apa.org/pubs/books
order@apa.org

In the U.K., Europe, Africa, and the Middle East, copies may be ordered from Eurospan
https://www.eurospanbookstore.com/apa
info@eurospangroup.com

Typeset in Meridien and Ortodoxa by Circle Graphics, Inc., Reisterstown, MD

Printer: Sheridan Books, Chelsea, MI
Cover Designer: Beth Schlenoff, Bethesda, MD

Library of Congress Cataloging-in-Publication Data

Names: Davis, Donald D., 1950- author. | DeBlaere, Cirleen, author. | Hook, Joshua N., author. | Owen, Jesse, author.
Title: Mindfulness-based practices in therapy : a cultural humility approach / Don Davis, Cirleen DeBlaere, Joshua N. Hook, and Jesse Owen.
Description: Washington, DC : American Psychological Association, [2020] | Includes bibliographical references and index.
Identifiers: LCCN 2019023024 (print) | LCCN 2019023025 (ebook) | ISBN 9781433831478 (paperback) | ISBN 9781433831744 (ebook)
Subjects: LCSH: Mindfulness-based cognitive therapy.
Classification: LCC RC489.M55 D38 2020 (print) | LCC RC489.M55 (ebook) | DDC 616.89/1425—dc23
LC record available at https://lccn.loc.gov/2019023024
LC ebook record available at https://lccn.loc.gov/2019023025

http://dx.doi.org/10.1037/0000156-000

Printed in the United States of America

10 9 8 7 6 5 4 3 2 1

To Mom with thanks for teaching me to enjoy learning,
and thanks to my second mom for giving me someone
to enjoy learning with.

—DON DAVIS

To my mom, Mei-o DeBlaere, who taught me the value
of appreciating religious and spiritual diversity,
and to Dr. Roberta Seldman, who helped me to take
my first mindful steps as a therapist—love you both!

—CIRLEEN DEBLAERE

To Mark, who journeyed with me as I worked to clarify my values,
accept my struggles and difficulties, and live a full life.

—JOSHUA N. HOOK

To my Sensei, Ivan Almodovar, Sr., who first introduced me
to be mindful and, moreover, taught me to have
a purposeful and fulfilled life.

—JESSE OWEN

CONTENTS

PREFACE

As counselors and psychologists, our hope is that therapy is an environment in which clients can come and trust that we will do everything in our power to know them deeply. We want therapy to be a process whereby they can bring the segmented and disjointed parts of their lives to be shared, grieved, and eventually integrated. Healing in the area of cultural identity requires the type of space where a person can find refuge from the all too commonly felt need to segment the self and keep rigid boundaries related to cultural identities. Many therapists do not know how to engage cultural opportunities of this kind.

This problem seems especially evident when it comes to issues of faith or existential worldview. Mental health providers serve a wide variety of individuals and communities, ranging from those with to those without a strong faith in a religious or spiritual community. But many clients consider religion and spirituality to be an important part of their identity (up to 75% of individuals in the United States; Pew Research Center, n.d.). Furthermore, many others have had negative experiences with organized religion or do not attune to this aspect in their daily lives. Despite the importance of religion or spirituality for working with many marginalized groups, many therapists report feeling unprepared to address the spiritual diversity within their clientele. Moreover, some therapists may not know if mindfulness practices are consistent with clients' ways of being. Therefore, it may be difficult to implement a multicultural vision without addressing this gap.

We considered emerging conversations related to mindfulness as an opportunity to learn more about how to engage people's spiritual and existential identities. With the mindfulness movement, the mental health profession has become enamored with secularized practices that were originally refined within a variety of monastic traditions within Buddhism. The popularity of these practices has sparked multicultural conversations about how to make these practices increasingly accessible to the general public while also honoring the cultural and spiritual traditions from which these practices originated.

As therapists, our role is to be able to converse with people about what matters most to them. Many clients may draw on spiritual language to tell us about these matters, and it is our responsibility to prepare ourselves to meet these clients where they are.[1] We can assist our clients by learning other ways of being and, more specifically, by not adopting an "all knowing" stance. At the same time, we do not want to burden our clients by expecting them to educate us. Thus, we cultivate a motivation for lifelong learning beyond any one client, or belief system, or way of engaging in therapy. We push ourselves daily, weekly, and yearly to be in a growth mind-set, which is founded in a state of humility. Our clients need us to be able to listen like a trusted confidant—even, and maybe most importantly, when we may not have the cultural background or experiences to make that empathy process simple. Cultural humility is the guiding theoretical framework for our writing. To prepare ourselves for the work of therapy, humility reminds us of our limitations in knowledge more than our strengths or achievements. It can make us more receptive to addressing new and complex situations. It can keep our minds open to new options. These are skills that require refinement for anyone seeking to gain expertise at working in the area of cultural diversity.

Before moving forward, we want to acknowledge and thank several people. First, we thank Sarah Gazaway, the first author's (D.D.'s) graduate research assistant during the past 2 years. She played a crucial role in helping to keep this project moving forward. She gave feedback on manuscripts, helped reconcile the references, compiled helpful resources, and helped to coordinate the coauthors. This project could not have happened (or happened on time) without her tireless efforts. Second, we thank our mentors, Ev Worthington, Bonnie Moradi, and Karen Kitchener. We are also thankful for our colleagues who provided us with opportunities to dialogue about, as well as concrete examples of, the integration of mindfulness within their work with culturally marginalized groups. In particular, we thank Negar Fani, Carlton Green, Candice Hargons, and Nathan Mascaro.

[1]All clinical case material in the chapters is fictionalized.

I

CONCEPTUAL AND PERSONAL FOUNDATIONS

1

Cultural Humility and Mindfulness

Why This, Why Now?

All of us share in the experience of humanity while facing a changing world that sometimes looks and feels different based on our nationality, gender, race or ethnicity, sexuality, or religion. Technology has made the world smaller and more interconnected. Just think about the past few decades: Innovations in technology (e.g., smartphones, e-mail, social media) have put people in a new and rapidly changing social environment. We face constant exposure to a world of information and images that are only a click away. In a split second, we can interact with someone on the other side of the earth.

These staggering changes continue to accelerate perhaps faster than we are able to adjust to them (e.g., people sleeping with their cell phones and compulsively checking messages throughout the night), and the future developments are likely not even within our current scope of understanding. In this rapidly shifting context, qualities that include flexibility and having an awareness of one's limitations become increasingly important (Hess & Ludwig, 2017). It is difficult to live well—or help our clients live well—without embracing change to those aspects of life that are frequently changing and yet holding onto those cultural values and beliefs that ground us in our daily lives and within our communities.

This new world seems rich with opportunities and dangers. We have never had more potential for connection with others from different cultures and communities. This increased "connectedness," though, somehow seems to intensify the potential for loneliness. University students are showing up for

http://dx.doi.org/10.1037/0000156-001
Mindfulness-Based Practices in Therapy: A Cultural Humility Approach, by D. Davis, C. DeBlaere, J. N. Hook, and J. Owen

therapy in droves (Twenge, 2017). In the United States and many other parts of the world, social media perpetuates simmering hostilities between identity groups that can turn violent. Once (at least sometimes) obscured, we now see the ugly side of humanity in plain view—and constantly. We have less room to hide from the reality of life and human suffering. Our technology berates us with images of another school shooting, another killing of an African American person, another campus riot with echoes of racist chants coupled with flaming torches, traumatized students screaming at each other with no unity in sight, another woman subjected to the abuse of power—an endless torrent of human suffering. These dismal reminders of our society are not what define us, but they are part of us—all of us. It is the daily trauma that accentuates the lack of safety and uncertainty in the world, in our country, and in our neighborhoods.

Altogether, the increased potential for connection seems to strain our collective ability to engage cultural differences. In the old world, we might have been able to avoid some of our enemies. Now, social media keeps hostile connections alive. Each time our phone rings, we are trained to reach in our pockets and potentially see someone spewing vitriol. Sadly, many of our professional networks may not fare much better. The more people care about an issue, the more difficult it can be to practice cultural humility.

In our first book on cultural humility (Hook, Davis, Owen, & DeBlaere, 2017), we began with an invitation to explore the diversity of humanity and the many cultural stories that make people who they are. To open this book, we invite you to think about your desire for connection with other people. What are the sources of deepest meaning in your life or the people you care for? When have you felt alive, fulfilled, and connected? Who lets you lower your defenses? When have you felt deeply known and loved?

Before you read any further, check in with yourself about how you are doing in the face of all the things changing in your life. Right now—how are you doing? In training to be a psychologist, we learned to keep a professional distance from our clients. But we live in the same world. We are the same kind of humans. We are not too far removed from the same isolation and pain that brings them to our offices fatigued and depleted by their lives. We invite you to consider the parts of your life that make it hard for you to catch your breath, much less flourish.

Some of us are weary of death; we have said goodbye to many loved ones. Some of us are weary of the constant responsibilities of adulthood: tending to kids, bills, and the anxiety caused by our to-do lists. Some of us are weary of our inner self, relentlessly pushing to be better and better. Some of us are weary of the exclusion and discrimination we and our loved one's experience; we fight a sense of hopelessness that it will ever end. Some of us are weary of conflict—of seeing people undermine others and get their way, even if they are left with broken relationships. What are the sources of persistent suffering that deplete your energy?

Conversely, does reflecting on these areas in life provide perspective, hope, optimism, or joy? Indeed, paradoxically, awareness of suffering can also reveal sources of strength and hope. What are your sources of strength, hope, peace, love, and compassion? What does it mean to honor your greatest fears without letting them define you? How can you offer your clients compassion in a way that does not undermine their sources of meaning and purpose?

The art and science of mindfulness is the result of a growing interest in contemplative practices within the mental health profession. To answer some of these questions, many psychologists have begun to look beyond Western thinking and ideologies. They have begun to explore a variety of contemplative traditions, particularly Eastern spiritualities and philosophies, which offer an alternative perspective on modern life. Namely, that life *is* suffering and change.

WHY DID WE DECIDE TO WRITE THIS BOOK?

We want to begin by describing some of the organic circumstances that led us to write this book. Several years ago, two of this book's authors, D. D. and C. D., had a student in our department who introduced us to a group called Octagon (http://www.octagon.life.edu) that was interested in contemplative practices and their implications for larger systems (e.g., education, business, health). Members of the group also had connections with the team at Emory University that developed *compassion-based cognitive therapy*, an approach that integrates theory and practices and is inspired by Tibetan Buddhism (Ozawa-de Silva & Dodson-Lavelle, 2011). While trying to work out the details of how to make contemplative practices available in various settings, Octagon was grappling with practical questions and gaps in the professional literature on mindfulness. So, this community deserves credit for sparking the professional curiosity that led to this book.

The general tone of the group was positive: They viewed the mindfulness movement as an opportunity to make a difference. The group believed that contemplative traditions had something important to offer a variety of systems (e.g., health, education, business) that had seemingly taken on a life of their own. Many of these systems no longer existed to serve people; people existed to serve them or whoever was at the top of the hierarchical scheme. The group believed the interest in mindfulness provided an opportunity to partner in making these systems more humane. The mainstreaming of mindfulness interventions meant that many core systems—often governed by strict social norms related to secularization—had a growing receptiveness to meditation as long as the framing did not violate secularization norms related to proselytizing a religion.

At the same time, the group also raised concerns. First, they were concerned about positivity bias within the mindfulness literature. Through personal communications, they were aware of conversations among professionals about potential barriers or problems with implementing mindfulness interventions, but these problems seemed muted in the professional literature. Furthermore, many people in this group had undergone extensive meditation training within various Buddhist traditions. They were concerned that practitioners using mindfulness might not be aware of the common problems that arise when people engage long-term meditation practices. For example, starting to meditate can make stress worse before it gets better because people may gain awareness of previously unconscious feelings, especially people with a trauma background (Rapgay & Bystrisky, 2009).

Second, the group was also concerned about cultural diffusion of mindfulness. Members of Octagon had trained within Buddhist traditions. They were also aware of mindfulness-based approaches being used in psychotherapy or other venues. They noticed a growing gap between the two: those groups that joined the so-called mindfulness movement and sought to explore its potential usefulness and those who made explicit arguments about the need to differentiate from Buddhism and draw explicitly on other contemplative traditions within other religions (e.g., Knabb & Frederick, 2017; Knabb & Vazquez, 2018). If not for the shared name, anthropologists in a few hundred years might have little hope of matching what is happening in therapy with the ancient practices from which they were derived.

To give a sampling of potential reasons for cultural diffusion, *therapeutic mindfulness* (the term we use in this book to refer to mindfulness within psychotherapy) has a different goal. The goal of therapeutic mindfulness is primarily symptom reduction. Within Buddhism, however, mindfulness is part of a much broader spiritual perspective and worldview that seems to promote enlightenment and spiritual awakening. People seek to see the world as it is, with less delusion and distortion, which happens as people attempt to avoid trying to control suffering (Kang & Whittingham, 2010; Rapgay & Bystrisky, 2009).

Therapeutic mindfulness detaches mindfulness from community life; it is an individualistic expression. Within Buddhist traditions, mindfulness is part of a broader culture that provides people with the support and meaning-systems to deal with challenges that arise in meditation. Practicing alone removes a major source of support. Therapeutic mindfulness has the potential to oversimplify a sophisticated spiritual tradition into à la carte activities: People pick and choose parts of various traditions that can fit into segments of a fragmented and overburdened schedule (and life).

Third, the group alluded to cultural difficulties some clients may have with mindfulness. For example, the people who ran meditation groups in the greater Atlanta area noted that many clients dropped out early on. Their sense was that some clients dropped out because meditation wasn't a good fit with their cultural identities (e.g., religious or spiritual background as well as the intersection of religion or spirituality and other identities, particularly race and ethnicity). They weren't entirely sure, however, and despite a bourgeoning literature on mindfulness, they were not seeing much scientific literature on cultural problems and difficulties.

Taken together, Octagon seemed to have questions that would be of interest to mental health professionals wanting to use mindfulness in their clinical work. We were especially curious how therapists devoted to multicultural values would engage some of these larger systemic challenges, such as adapting mindfulness to different groups while also attending to concerns about cultural appropriation. In short, how could therapists—regardless of commitment to using mindfulness—meet the rising interest in meditation in the general public in an ethical, culturally humble way?

WHAT IS THE MAIN POINT?

Our goal in this book is to extend ideas on cultural humility—and the multicultural orientation framework (MCO; Owen, 2013; Owen, Tao, Leach, & Rodolfa, 2011)—to consider these emerging questions about how to contextualize mindfulness to different clients and settings, especially clients from different cultural backgrounds. This contextualization relates to feminist understandings of self-reflexivity and intersubjectivity (van Stapele, 2014). These processes encourage self-reflection, self-analysis, and self-contextualization as a platform for understanding our interpretations of our interpersonal interactions; inherent power differentials are also named in these interactions (e.g., van Stapele, 2014). At the heart of this framework is the virtue of cultural humility.

Cultural humility is the virtue language of the MCO framework, and it is infused throughout the other aspects of the model. A variety of scholars converged on the intuition that humility language provides an important complement to the competencies language used to incorporate multicultural values into the training standards of many helping professions (see Foronda, Baptiste, Reinholdt, & Ousman, 2016). Intrapersonally, humility involves having an accurate view of one's strengths and limitations; interpersonally, it involves an other-oriented stance (as opposed to self-centered) expressed through a lack of interpersonal superiority. Scholars have studied humility in contexts that make it difficult to practice—situations that evoke egoism and defensiveness. Given that belonging to a group comes with commitment- and loyalty-related biases, cultural differences can strain the practice of humility (Davis et al., 2018). Accordingly, Hook, Davis, Owen, Worthington, and Utsey (2013) defined cultural humility as "the ability to maintain an interpersonal stance that is other-oriented (or open to the other) in relation to aspects of cultural identity that are most important to the client" (p. 354).

In practical terms, cultural humility involves a way of being more than doing (Hook et al., 2017), openness to the other, inclusiveness, and a willingness to put these values into action—not just in session but across all aspects of life. It also involves refining your ability to listen carefully and compassionately and accept feedback of all kinds without defensiveness. As we have shared the MCO framework more widely, people resonate with the use of humility language as a complement to competence language, which can focus people on how they are doing (rather than their cultural way of being in session). Cultural humility encourages a stance of openness and receptiveness that is other oriented rather than self-preoccupied. People seem to get this concept and appreciate the balance that humility language offers.

The most common reactions and questions tend to be practical in nature: What does it look like to express cultural humility? How can I make this more a part of my practice of therapy and lifestyle? Thus, the authors of this book realized that it is important to keep fleshing out what applying the MCO framework looks like in real life. Therefore, as a team of authors, we decided to look for some important places to apply it.

The mindfulness movement in psychology seemed like a timely and challenging area to apply the MCO framework next. It is timely because of massive growth in research and the popularity of mindfulness. As we elaborate in Chapter 2, over the past half-century, the use of meditation in psychology has evolved from being a relatively fringe practice to being one of the more popular approaches in psychotherapy (Norcross, Pfund, & Prochaska, 2013). Where prior attempts to promote meditation were met with cultural resistance (Harrington & Dunne, 2015), mindfulness-based interventions offer a way of presenting meditation that has not only gained entry into, but has been well-received by, several major systems (e.g., health care, education, business). Mindfulness is now a billion-dollar industry, and various segments of society are seeking to compete for a share of the market (Clarke, Black, Stussman, Barnes, & Nahin, 2015). Psychology is a small cog in a much larger industry, and all are situated (in the United States) within a dominant society that perpetuates systems of oppression, discrimination, and racism. As counseling psychologists interested in culture and identity, it is fascinating to entertain the "Why now?" question. It seems likely that a confluence of factors has set the stage for the popularity of the current mindfulness moment (e.g., smartphones, growing self-help industry, positive psychology movement, growing individualism, increasing suspicion of institutions such as religion; C. J. Miller, Elder, & Scavone, 2017).

Mindfulness is a daunting challenge for thinking about the application of the MCO framework because of the nature of emerging cultural critiques. For a time, mindfulness seemed immune from typical lenses multicultural psychology scholars tend to apply to critique therapy approaches. Perhaps people considered mindfulness a fad that would eventually run its course. However, mindfulness now holds a prominent position in a variety of cultural structures and institutions. A striking example is that the U.S. federal government has invested hundreds of millions of dollars in the development and dissemination of mindfulness-based interventions (Hickey, 2010). The investment has paid off, at least in terms of making mindfulness more accessible. Now anyone with an Apple watch or smartphone likely has a mindfulness app installed by default, meaning you actually have to take action to turn off the app if you decide you don't want regular reminders to attend to your breathing.

Regardless of the reasons for the initial delay in criticism, the cultural critiques are strong now—and some are scathing (e.g., Hickey, 2010; Monteiro, Compson, & Musten, 2017; Sperry & Stoupas, 2017; Van Dam et al., 2018). We elaborate on these critiques in Chapter 3, but they range from (a) concerns about appropriation to (b) concerns about the need to adapt mindfulness to oppressed and marginalized groups of society to (c) arguments about the need to draw explicitly from the client's religious tradition to frame contemplative approaches. Our field's response to these critiques may change mindfulness in surprising ways, but regardless of what the future holds, all signs suggest that mindfulness is here to stay. So, for socially conscious therapists—for those attempting to work out the MCO framework in all aspects of their work and lives—it is time to clarify values and consider important questions. These questions provide an opportunity to apply and test the ideas within the MCO framework.

We are particularly interested in the dynamics that occur between groups and social systems. Mindfulness is a social evolutionary success story. The framing of mindfulness interventions is flexible so that they are able to align with secular norms and accommodate people from a variety of cultural backgrounds. Mindfulness interventions fit in with a growing agenda to offer a more scientific alternative to guiding the good life rather than simply relying on authority structures of religious traditions (Dahlsgaard, Peterson, & Seligman, 2005). The mindfulness movement also follows the pattern of successful positive psychology research programs: Basic research documents benefits to health, mental health, and relationships, and intervention research follows closely behind. We might view mindfulness as one of the most successful fruits of positive psychology. After becoming well-established in several powerful contexts (e.g., hospitals; treatment of depression, personality disorders, bipolar disorders) and exhibiting some treatment success in clinical trials, mindfulness-based approaches have captured the hearts of a generation of therapists (and their clients).

Given the proliferation of mindfulness interventions, we explore in this book the next set of practical questions for therapists committed to a multicultural orientation and who want to work these values out in their potential use of mindfulness in therapy. For example, how should we balance concerns about values regarding avoidance of appropriation with the need to adapt therapies to clients from marginalized groups? How should therapists view their collective influence on people of faith as well as nonbelievers? When, if ever, is it appropriate to intentionally conceal the Buddhist roots of mindfulness for clients who may have a negative reaction to religion and spirituality (C. G. Brown, 2017; Purser, 2015)? Altogether, our focus is especially on addressing a gap in the professional literature on how to contextualize the use of mindfulness to cultural diversity.

WHO IS THE INTENDED AUDIENCE?

Our last book (Hook et al., 2017) focused on a way of thinking about how to integrate multicultural principles into the process of psychotherapy. We offered humility language to complement competence language. On the surface, many of the movements within psychology send a hopeful and positive message about humanity and their potential for growth, but some have pointed out that it may be more difficult than we think to escape cultural narratives regarding the flawed nature of our humanity (Bingaman, 2011).

Psychotherapy is one part of a massive set of industries designed to help people continually work to improve themselves. For many, including therapists in training, an implicit message churns beneath this activity (and reactivity): that we are inherently flawed. Indeed, in our process of training to become therapists, the language of cultural competence implies that someone presumably evaluates skills related to serving clients with marginalized identities. When that person determines a discrepancy between ideal skills and actual practice, they render a judgment. Or even if no such evaluator exists, the implication is that a standard must be achieved, and if that standard is not met, clients suffer because of our failures to succeed. Put simply, competence language antagonizes perfectionistic tendencies, which evoke concerns about performance relative to a standard.

It is important to acknowledge, however, that competence language has served a crucial purpose in the multicultural movement. We wholeheartedly affirm the values and mission of the trailblazers who catalyzed the multicultural movement in psychology and related fields (e.g., D. W. Sue et al., 1998). Moreover, competence language has helped align theory, research, and practice through its goal of infusing multicultural values into training practices. However, as we elaborate in Chapter 4, we developed the MCO framework to apply multicultural values to the context of training therapists about how to engage cultural dynamics in psychotherapy.

From research on expertise and factors that contribute to better therapy outcomes (Tracey, Wampold, Lichtenberg, & Goodyear, 2014), we have some hints about what this process might involve—for example, a commitment to a lifelong pursuit of taking on new challenges, putting ourselves at the crossroads of better feedback, and continually seeking to grow. This challenge is greater when we sit with clients who not only have the pain of life but have this pain amplified by systemic exclusion and marginalization. Many of our clients come to us with little reason to expect responsiveness because they live in family and social systems that are unresponsive to their pain. We agreed with the cacophony of other voices encouraging alternative language related to multiculturalism that would encourage trainees to attend to their moment-to-moment inner world in a way that would, over time, lead to growth in their ability to offer a high-quality presence (e.g., Geller & Greenberg, 2002).

Therefore, the current book picks up the ethos and line of logic of the prior book and extends them to an important opportunity and challenge regarding how therapists express their multicultural values. The mindfulness movement is an important test for the multicultural community, and we are glad to see more voices engaging these conversations. This book is for therapists who want to work out multicultural values in their use of mindfulness. We hope it will help therapists who want to use mindfulness in their therapy but feel ambivalent because of the debates and cultural critiques (e.g., appropriation of mindfulness practice; ethical quandaries, such as training soldiers with mindfulness; fears that mindfulness may blame the victim or somehow imply that people should accept marginalization). As therapists, we practice our profession within a culture that finds it difficult to stay connected with pain. This book is for therapists who want to cultivate spaces in which people can let their guard down and find healing. Given the intense demand for various forms of escape or numbing, it should come as no surprise that psychologists have begun to listen and draw from spiritual traditions, such as mindfulness, that diagnose this modern malady and offer a potential remedy.

A CRUCIAL CAVEAT

At the outset, it is important for us to not overclaim our knowledge and experience. Our expertise is not in mindfulness: We did not develop any of the major approaches, we are not advocates of any particular approach (and we are unable to attempt to recontextualize mindfulness within a Buddhist tradition, as some have called for), and we will not attempt to advocate for any particular therapeutic or Buddhist tradition of mindfulness.

What brings our set of authors together is an intention to explore how cultural identities influence the relationships that develop in therapy and how therapists can show responsiveness to the client's identities to improve therapy outcomes. We approach our task with the assumption that most therapists using mindfulness are integrating it as a technique within their broader theoretical framework. We also assume attempts to carefully regulate the use of mindfulness will likely fail. For example, a variety of self-help interventions have been developed; the trend is to make mindfulness more accessible and easier to disseminate. So, what training and skills will be required for therapists to engage the growing interest in mindfulness in the broader population?

In addition to a caveat on our professional vantage point, we want to be explicit about the audiences we kept in mind as we wrote the book. We view mindfulness as a practice heavily influenced by Buddhism, which we consider one of the five major religions of the world. We are aware of the notion that many people hold that Buddhism is more of a philosophy than a religion (the perspective makes the most sense when Judeo–Christian religions are viewed as normative); but, for the purposes of this book, we consider it a set of religious traditions. We also hold that many clients are religious or spiritual; many are not Buddhist; and many, when they engage in mindfulness, experiences changes in their religion or spirituality (for a review, see Stratton, 2015). Therefore, we explicitly focus on spiritual diversity in all of the cases throughout this book.

In light of intersectional theories, we were curious about how religious or spiritual identity might interact with other identities (e.g., race, ethnicity, social class, gender). The mindfulness-based interventions were negotiated within markets that comprised predominately White women who were highly educated and living in urban areas; yet, many of the prominent leaders within the mindfulness movements are White men (Hickey, 2010). We were curious about how a lack of diversity within leaders might have shaped current practices. We tried to develop a way of thinking that could span these various groups and their diverging concerns and interests.

Therefore, we sought to dovetail this commitment to attending to spiritual diversity with a commitment to attending to intersectionality. So, all of the cases in this book consider either a marginalized religious or spiritual identity or Christians who hold at least one or several marginalized identities. For example, we kept in mind American Buddhists, Asian American clients (who may have reactions to the evolution of mindfulness ideas as they interact with an increasingly individualistic culture), African American and Latinx groups that may be theologically conservative about engaging other faith traditions, and marginalized religious or spiritual groups in the United States (e.g., Muslims, Jews, atheists).

A WORD FROM EACH OF THE AUTHORS

We hope one of the advantages of our writing team is that we each hold different identities that allowed us—collectively—to keep a range of perspectives in mind as we were writing and revising this project. In terms of professional expertise, authors D. D. and J. N. H. specialize in positive psychology and the integration of spirituality into counseling. Authors C. D. and J. O. are multiracial and have invested in recent work about the implications of intersectionality theories. To prepare for the book, we conducted interviews with a variety of people who integrate mindfulness into various aspects of their work. These conversation partners were an integral part of our writing team, especially as we developed case studies to illustrate ideas. In the following paragraphs, we each say a little about our interest in mindfulness and how it relates to our professional experience and expertise. We hope this information will give you, as the reader, a better sense of where we are coming from.

Author D. D.

My interest in mindfulness comes out of a general interest in spirituality and its intersection with other identities. Before I even knew I wanted to be a psychologist, I joined my mom in a master's program that focused on spiritually sensitive counseling. She had entered the program in preparation for a second career. Soon after, though, she was diagnosed with ovarian cancer. I wanted to spend time with her and thought counseling skills would potentially be helpful for serving within my local church or community. I did a specialization focused on spiritual formation within various Christian traditions. What I learned most during my time there was a more open and curious perspective of other religious and spiritual traditions. Some things are better "caught than taught," and some of my professors modeled a curiosity and engagement with other faiths that has served me well, not just with religious or spiritual identity but cultural identities in general.

In my doctoral training at Virginia Commonwealth University, I distanced myself from some of these initial interests. Instead, I focused on positive psychology, especially the virtues of humility, forgiveness, and gratitude. For a variety of reasons, I was hesitant (and ambivalent) about being too focused on religion or spirituality. I did not want to get pigeonholed within my clinical training. Also, I was processing ambivalence and grief toward my own religious and spiritual tradition, as well as religion and spirituality in general, after my mom died. Her life seemed cut short by cancer, and as I reflected on her life, I wanted to learn how to avoid passing on the perspectives on gender roles that limited some of her sense of choices earlier in her life—and that were at the heart of some of her identity struggles during her 30s.

At the same time, there is something core to my work as a psychologist (and probably as a human) that relates back to some of those early interests in how religious and spiritual identity can influence people's development. As a person of faith, I know that my religious and spiritual identity is infused into all of my other identities—for better and worse. In our profession—and society more broadly—we sometimes struggle to talk about religious or spiritual identity. Strong secularization norms help keep the peace—and distance. We have lost some of the skills to relax these norms and cultivate spaces of intimacy with each other about matters of ultimate importance. I am interested in more than just religion and spirituality; I'm interested in how therapists relate themselves to existential questions—to the givens of life—such as facing death, feelings of meaninglessness, responsibility to determine values, and inevitable loneliness (Yalom, 1980). Cultural differences in existential worldviews seem particularly difficult to bridge. These areas are particularly painful and daunting. They have the potential to make us feel very small and powerless. Yet, part of me wants to understand more about how to help people build on their strengths while also learning to address painful aspects of their religious or spiritual or existential identity.

I also need to acknowledge one other person. Terrence Jordan, a doctoral student at the time, introduced me to theorizing on intersectionality in his dissertation work on racial trauma. His dissertation was inspired by societal events that led to the Black Lives Matter movement. His courage to engage that project inspired some of the ideas that eventually motivated this book project. Intersectionality theory gave a language to something I sensed but didn't have words for: It delved into the complexity of belonging to different identities and groups and how that affects people's process of seeking integrity and becoming who they hope to be.

Author C. D.

I have always been a ruminator. I can think about a topic for ages. Sometimes ruminating can be helpful, such as when I think through how to approach a particular problem I'm facing. Other times, I can sit in places of high anxiety and self-critical thoughts. The same energy that helps me to think of a way through to an answer for a complicated challenge can betray me and fuel hours-long or even days-long consideration of an argument I wish I had handled differently. Until graduate school, where I discovered mindfulness meditation, I struggled with how to quiet my more persistent, less helpful, version of rumination.

In my second year as a doctoral student, I had the privilege of being assigned to a supervisor who used mindfulness in her personal and professional life. She was a student of Pema Chödrön and had been participating in Tibetan Buddhist practice. I remember when she recommended Chödrön's book *When Things Fall Apart: Heart Advice for Difficult Times* and showed me her own very worn copy. Her name was Roberta Seldman, and she passed away in 2018. Roberta was an amazing supervisor in every way I can imagine, but what struck me most about her was her vitality. She was so present! It was something that I could feel. She was not afraid to be in all of her emotions at once and accepting of them. She modeled for me how to sit with authenticity and not ego. I felt seen by her in a whole new way, and it was an awakening for me as a therapist.

I could probably write pages upon pages about all of the things I learned from Roberta, but here I highlight two primary points. First, she started me on a path of self-compassion. She was the first person to point out to me that I had, up to that point, been defining myself by achievements. She reminded me that I had been neglecting or had been actively subduing whole other aspects of myself that actually yearned for expression: my artistic side, my joyful self, my softer self. Second, she created a space that invited vulnerability and pain as part of the full human experience. She helped me to embrace my vulnerabilities along with my strengths. Neither was better or worse; both just were. These lessons put me on a different path as a therapist but also as a person.

In my fourth year of doctoral study, I participated in a mindfulness meditation group in which I learned the basics of mindfulness practice and various meditation practices. This practice deepened and grew the lessons that Roberta had planted within me years earlier. In particular, through the challenges I faced in trying to participate in daily and prolonged practice, I was forced to face my self-critical voice in a different way and the lengths to which my mind would go to distract me from being in the present moment. I also learned that, for me, self-compassion was going to have to be an intentional activity. Importantly, I discovered that, as much as I considered myself to be compassionate toward others, my abilities in that area were limited by my own self-critical lens. One of the greatest lessons I learned was that you can only be as compassionate to others as you are to yourself; those practices do not occur in isolation. An extension of this awareness was that I became more accepting of my vulnerable feelings and even embraced them (Roberta's second lesson). To experience them all is to live fully within my present experience.

So, I don't practice mindfulness these days as much as I would like. Sometimes, my only mindful moment in a given day is when I sit, reflect, and recognize how many thoughts are pulling me away from being present—but I continue to try. It's a work in progress and one that is more about a way of being than a goal—just like the MCO. For me, this book on integrating mindfulness into therapy practice seemed like such a logical extension of our prior one. Like mindfulness practice itself, cultural humility is so much about compassion, presence, and being okay with the ambiguous. My hope with this book is that in helping therapists and therapists-in-training to integrate mindfulness practice with cultural humility, they are able to grow in both. This one's for you, Roberta!

Author J. N. H.

My interest in mindfulness and mindfulness-based interventions is connected to my interest in acceptance and commitment therapy. When I was beginning my training in graduate school, I was initially drawn to cognitive behavior therapy. I liked the structure of the therapeutic approach, and I also appreciated the focus on making concrete changes. I found cognitive behavior therapy to be quite helpful in the lives of my clients as well as my own life as I tried to work through my own issues and become a more emotionally healthy person.

One of my struggles, both in the lives of my clients and in my own life, was that some things weren't quite so easy to change. This was especially true about some of my own internal struggles with anxiety both in my personal life and relationships. Even though I "knew" in my head that a thought was unreasonable, for example, I had difficulty getting rid of the unpleasant thoughts and emotions. And I found some areas of my life that I just couldn't change (e.g., a loved one's dying, the behavior of a coworker or partner) or "improve." Some aspects of my life weren't turning out as I wanted them to, and there wasn't anything I could do to change them.

These were the places where acceptance and mindfulness were game changers for me. I recognized that even if I couldn't "get rid of" an anxious thought, I could accept the anxious thought and move forward in my life anyway. For example, I had to do so when I decided to get married. No amount of therapy was going to make my anxiety about marriage completely disappear. I had to accept feeling a certain amount of anxiety and moving forward anyway. Mindfulness and acceptance helped me do that. Mindfulness helped me to accept the things I could not change so I could live a more peaceful and full life. I'm excited about the possibility about helping therapists integrate mindfulness into their work in a culturally humble way.

Author J. O.

Growing up, I was an energetic kid with lots of passions and, at times, without much control of those emotions and passions. Yet, two main influences became more readily influential in my life: my mother and martial arts. Indeed, my interest in mindfulness came when I was exposed to martial art traditions. The class would spend time focusing on aligning the mind–body connection to promote healing and a sense of clarity. I learned how to meditate and ground myself during stressful situations. I learned how to focus on the energy in my body, channel sources of stress and distraction, and how to translate these lessons across my life. Around the same time, I noticed that one of the best role models for mindfulness had been with me all along—my mother. Her sense of calm, peace, and patience was amazing. I didn't fully realize it as a child, but she frequently practiced mindfulness. It wasn't until later in life that I fully appreciated her influence.

Throughout my life, I have found a sense of calm and peace when I have been able to use the principles of mindfulness. This sense of perspective also has transformed the ways in which I learn new skills in a therapeutic context. I have found a better sense of my own reactions in sessions and a way to work through complex reactions. In many ways, this approach also has helped me understand my own development as cultural person and professional. I can now sit with the complexity of my own identities as well as how others understand me. Unlike some of colleagues, I did not directly use mindfulness with patients—at least on a consistent basis. Rather, I would channel the spirit into my life as a professional to stay balanced and centered.

Over time, truly reflecting on my core values, feelings, and beliefs has helped inform the MCO framework. The heart of the MCO is a greater connection to others around us and the ability to cherish those interactions for the richness of cultural understanding that they can bring. For me, this book is an extension of the process that led to the MCO: reflecting, slowing down, and being true to one's self. I hope you enjoy the book and find nuggets of wisdom to inspire your practice.

OVERVIEW OF THE BOOK

The book has two major parts. In Part I (Chapters 1–5), we establish the conceptual foundation of the book. In Chapter 2, we illustrate how daunting it would be if cultural competence about mindfulness was primarily about "knowing enough." From an MCO perspective, our knowledge helps us in a particular way: It prepares us to approach new situations with a sense of cultural humility so that we don't make as many costly assumptions.

In Chapter 3, we set up the primary tension of the book. The multicultural critiques of mindfulness come along two fronts: (a) concerns about responsiveness to marginalized groups (especially concerns about various religious or spiritual identities), which calls for contextualization; and (b) concerns about appropriation of Buddhist traditions, which calls for appropriate respect of these traditions and the many cultures that currently represent them in the world.

In Chapter 4, we describe the MCO framework and apply it to the two concerns raised in Chapter 3 and also describe how principles of mindfulness align with the skills required to express the MCO framework in therapy. We have you complete self-assessments that show how the MCO concepts complement the traditional multicultural competencies approach.

In Chapter 5, we draw on theories of expertise as well as work on factors that promote a strong therapy alliance to describe the key aspects of self-awareness related to implementing mindfulness in a culturally humble manner. Given our assumptions about mindfulness as a practice derived from contemplative religious and spiritual cultures, the focus of this chapter is especially on how to develop cultural comfort for religious and spiritual or existential issues.

Part II (Chapters 6–9) focuses on what it looks like in therapy to apply the MCO framework to mindfulness. In Chapter 6, we focus on assessing the client's religious or spiritual identity and forming a strong relationship. In Chapter 7, we consider how to take this awareness of the client's intersectional identities to negotiate a plan that may include using mindfulness. Cultural humility calls for an awareness of power (rather than denial or minimization) and a willingness to ally with the clients' goals and ways of wanting to pursue those goals. In Chapter 8, we consider the cultural context of the individual client. Specifically, we consider how to coordinate care with a religious or spiritual authority figure or community in regard to implementing mindfulness interventions. Many of our clients belong to religious or spiritual traditions, and some communities harbor reservations about the growing cultural interest in therapeutic mindfulness. In Chapter 9, we present a group supervision session. The clients, therapists, and supervisor are based on the interviews we conducted with practitioners who use mindfulness in their therapy practice. It is our hope in this chapter to illustrate challenges presented in the book through real-world applications.

CONCLUSION

Spoiler alert: We do not think the questions we plan to raise are simple or easy to "solve." Sometimes our work in this book has raised more questions than answers. But we do believe the journey is a worthwhile one—and we are honored to be part of a community that cares about such issues. Our approach to writing this book was not to try to overly simplify complex and thorny matters. We know we cannot tie a pretty bow on the concerns swirling around the use of mindfulness in our profession. Rather, our goal is to use the MCO framework to encourage therapists to reflect and hold their approach to using mindfulness to greater scrutiny. We want to promote a community that is getting better at "not knowing" and is responding appropriately to its cultural limits.

We believe it matters if psychologists (a) get better at exploring their limitations and biases, (b) engage other groups by building cooperation with the exemplars rather than perpetuating hostility by engaging stereotypes (Volf, 1996), and (c) learn to ask questions that can bridge across disciplines and identities. Where we could, we have tried to draw on direct evidence, but, in many cases, the literature was conspicuously silent, so we tapped our social and professional networks and did the best we could to generate reasonable lines of thought. We present cases rooted in real-life experiences, although all case examples in this book are fictionalized. We have tried to distill the core issues. We hope that what we say in this book will be helpful for your work as a therapist. But even more important than what we say will be what you, as the reader, decide to say and do next. So, let's begin again.

2

What We Need to "Know" About Mindfulness

In traditional multicultural competence models, knowledge is one of the crucial components (D. W. Sue, Arredondo, & McDavis, 1992). In this chapter, we try to give a sense of the sheer scope of knowledge that would be required to develop cultural expertise in using mindfulness as a therapist. The reason we begin here is because the first stage of growing in knowledge and expertise is to know how much one has to learn. Indeed, most people start the learning process with an inflated view of their skills (Kruger & Dunning, 1999), and this overconfidence only begins to match reality as people gain experience.

Accordingly, an entire book—much less one chapter—would never suffice to provide everything you need to know to effectively adjust your use of mindfulness to the diversity of identities you will encounter as a therapist. In addition, imagine what that chapter would have to entail! Think of all the identities of therapists reading this book, as well as an equally diverse set of potential clients. So much is known, and it would take years to fully master the relevant bodies of knowledge on gender, race or ethnicity, spirituality, ability, sexuality, and socioeconomic status as well as how these factors influence one another. Even with this knowledge, what we currently understand might not be enough to make a difference in therapy outcomes with some marginalized groups. As this chapter indicates, many of the most important questions about using mindfulness in therapy have yet to be answered.

Becoming a know-it-all of mindfulness is impossible. Perhaps a more realistic goal of this chapter, then, is to help develop awareness of the scope of

http://dx.doi.org/10.1037/0000156-002
Mindfulness-Based Practices in Therapy: A Cultural Humility Approach, by D. Davis, C. DeBlaere, J. N. Hook, and J. Owen

knowledge that would be relevant to our topic: using mindfulness in a culturally sensitive and humble way. Thus, as authors, we are interested in mindfulness and wondering what we can glean from the various conversations happening in our field about this practice and discipline as well as how it was adapted for a pluralistic and Western audience.

With this focus in mind, we first describe what mindfulness is, including a brief overview of the diversity of traditions that may have influenced the modern uses of mindfulness in therapy. Second, we briefly note evidence about when and how practicing mindfulness may be helpful. Third, we give a brief overview of the most influential mindfulness-based interventions (MBIs). Fourth, we describe some of the key strengths and limitations of theory and research on when to use mindfulness interventions in therapy. Our hope is that by the end of the chapter, the basic knowledge we have shared will set the stage for the remainder of the book. Indeed, some of the ideas we explore later in the book assume a degree of familiarity with therapeutic forms of mindfulness.

Activity 2.1: Write a Preliminary Definition. Before we continue, take three minutes to write down your own definition of *mindfulness.* What is your current understanding of the cultural history of mindfulness and how it came to its growing prominence in psychotherapy?

WHAT IS *MINDFULNESS*?

Casting a Wide Frame of Mindfulness

Much ink has been spilled in recent years on understanding what mindfulness is. This question has many possible answers, and one's answer is more of a story about how our profession came on mindfulness in its present form. The arc of that story depends on where one starts and who is included in the progression.

Many mindfulness traditions in psychotherapy trace their ideas of mindfulness loosely to contemplative traditions within Buddhism. Before we delve further into variants of this narrative, note that alternative perspectives describe mindfulness as common to many world religions and indigenous spiritualities (e.g., Plante, 2010). This is an easy enough story to tell given that modern forms of mindfulness were influenced by a variety of indigenous cultures as Buddhist ideas spread from India to China, Japan, other parts of Asia, and to the rest of the world (Kang & Whittingham, 2010). Thus, one way to consider the history of mindfulness is to cast a wide-open frame. We might consider all human societies that may have cultivated meditational practices similar to have focused attention (e.g., mantras) or open monitoring of awareness. As psychotherapists, we could then consider a diversity of expressions as these practices unfold within the context of different cultural values, goals, and narratives.

Activity 2.2: Describe Your Initial Impressions of Mindfulness. Take a moment to examine your assumptions about the history of mindfulness. If a client asked you for your understanding of where mindfulness came from, what would you say?

Contextualizing Mindfulness Within Buddhist Traditions

Another way we could seek to understand mindfulness is to examine the various influences of therapeutic mindfulness within Buddhist cultures. Mindfulness has a particular meaning within the core beliefs and practices of Buddhism, such as the Four Noble Truths or the Eightfold Path. The *Four Noble Truths* describe the problem of suffering and how to end suffering. Suffering is seen as inevitable and a consequence of attachment to the various aspects of life. The *Eightfold Path* offers principles to free oneself from attachment and, therefore, suffering. These principles are commonly grouped into three sections: wisdom (right understanding and intention), morality (right speech, action, and livelihood), and concentration (right effort, mindfulness, and concentration). Therefore, people are understood as being on a path toward liberation from the cycle of reactivity, so the practice of mindfulness is imbued with spiritual meaning and significance. Likewise, within Buddhist traditions, these spiritual goals are pursued within community, and these communities share stories and spiritual models.

Even if we limited this exploration to the traditions that fall under the diaspora of Buddhist cultures, we would still need to consider a vast array of traditions and perspectives that have evolved over time. In their article, Kang and Whittingham (2010) provided a helpful overview of the dialogue between Buddhism and the use of mindfulness within psychotherapy. They offered a pointed review of the three most influential schools of Buddhism and where those schools are prominent (i.e., Theraveda: Thailand, Sri Lanka, Cambodia, and Myanmar [formerly Burma]; Mahayana: China, Japan, Mongolia, Nepal, and Tibet; and Vajrayana: Tibetan Buddhism in North India). Their article also contextualized mindfulness within the foundational teachings of Buddhism, including the Four Noble Truths and the Eightfold Path. These teachings are akin to a conceptualization and treatment plan for the human condition. They focus our attention on the nature of suffering and how our reflexive attempts to limit suffering are based on false premises (e.g., we can evade suffering, things are as they seem in terms of our flow of experience) that lead us astray. The authors sampled from Buddhist texts that developed over time the ways in which different traditions have redirected the concept of mindfulness toward their particular priorities.

Activity 2.3: Consider Your Knowledge of Buddhist Cultures. What is your current level of knowledge about Buddhism? The following set of questions is intended to assess more intensive forms of knowledge about Buddhism. How familiar are you with some of the foundational ideas within Buddhism, such as the Four Noble Truths or the Eightfold Path? How many hours have you spent in meditation? Are you aware of the sacred texts within the three most prominent schools of Buddhism? Have you read them? Can you engage in critical scholarship about their interpretation? Have you ever been trained by an expert within a Buddhist tradition? Are you able to read them in their primary language? Have you ever lived in a country in which a significant proportion of the population identified as Buddhist? How long did you live there? Have you ever spent significant amounts of time (at least 6 weeks) in any countries in which a significant proportion of the population identified as Buddhist?

Note whatever feelings you have right now. For the time being, just note them without trying to fix, judge, explain, or quiet them. For now, it is enough to acknowledge that at least some of these areas of knowledge may be beyond your current experience. These are expansive bodies of knowledge, and they probably require a commitment—in some form—to living out the principles in real life. Taken together, it is important to remember that therapeutic mindfulness, as expressed in MBIs, has evolved in complex ways, and the proliferation of mindfulness in popular culture has increased the importance of distinguishing the various ways of understanding mindfulness.

Negotiating Definitions of *Therapeutic Mindfulness* Within Psychology

Definitions of *therapeutic mindfulness* within psychology typically do not give proper attention to major aspects of Buddhist religion and history. Many modern approaches begin, or at some point relate to and differentiate from, the work by Jon Kabat-Zinn, the founder of mindfulness-based stress reduction (MBSR; Kabat-Zinn, 1982). Although MBSR was not the first attempt to integrate Eastern spirituality into physical or mental health systems (Harrington & Dunne, 2015), it is certainly the most prominent success story of the MBI movement. Mindfulness-based stress reduction, which we describe later in the chapter, was designed for a pluralistic health setting. Kabat-Zinn framed mindfulness in a way that would align with professional and ethical standards to respect the client's cultural worldview. For popular audiences, he described mindfulness in approachable terms that might be accessible to a variety of cultural backgrounds: "the awareness that arises from paying attention, on purpose, in the present moment, and non-judgmentally" (Kabat-Zinn, 2011, p. 291).

Definitions are a key place where knowledge is negotiated. As basic and applied research on mindfulness grew, definitions of mindfulness multiplied, researchers and clinicians adapted definitions to their goals and context, and interdisciplinary groups also attempted to consolidate and align definitions (for a review, see Quaglia, Brown, Lindsay, Creswell, & Goodman, 2015). For example, an influential attempt to forge an interdisciplinary definition focused on two parts: (a) focusing attention on experiences in the present moment;

and (b) adopting an attitude of openness, curiosity, and acceptance (Bishop et al., 2004). Undoubtedly, these debates about definitions will continue. This is a normal process within culture: negotiating language over time. Therefore, people interested in mindfulness are consistently renegotiating the definitions, and the values, goals, and interests of groups influences the evolving understandings.

Navigating Sources of Knowledge

Given these vast domains of knowledge, it is important to develop a strategy for cultivating interest and curiosity rather than get bogged down by feeling intimidated or discouraged about the scope of knowledge. To name a few sources, knowledge may come from personal experiences, expert viewpoints, research on mindfulness, or religious or spiritual ways of knowing. All sources of knowledge are important to attend to, and we caution against relying on a single source. The reflective process of understanding the self and others truly relies on a mindfulness frame of mind: suspending judgment, honoring others' perspectives, and understanding the strengths and limitations of all ways of knowing. Although this advice is a good framework, we also want to provide a few potential handholds as we start to engage these conversations.

Consider Cultural Motives and Perspectives

First, keep in mind that as masterful and knowledgeable as some mindfulness leaders are, we are all cultural beings embedded within various cultural communities. Remembering this fact can help us consider potential motives of authors or speakers. For example, some may want to use mindfulness within secular therapy settings (e.g., MBI developers). Others may want to conserve traditional accounts of mindfulness by contrasting therapeutic mindfulness with mindfulness as it is described in traditional texts (e.g., Dreyfus, 2011). Others may want to understand how mindfulness works through conducting basic science experiments or ruling out alternate explanations for benefits. We have something to learn from all of these voices.

Get Concrete About What Is Being Measured

Second, it may help to acquaint yourself with some of the items used to measure mindfulness to give you a more concrete sense of the types of experiences being scientifically studied. Many of the studies on experiences of mindfulness involve people who do not engage in mindfulness meditation. It may also help to read recent review papers to acquaint yourself with measurement issues (e.g., Van Dam et al., 2018), such as questions about whether people can accurately report their own level of mindfulness. One study, for example, found that heavy drinkers viewed themselves as more mindful than meditators with a lot of experience (Leigh, Bowen, & Marlatt, 2005). Another study showed evidence that how people rate items on mindfulness measures changes as people move from little experience to more extensive experience with meditation (Krägeloh, Bergomi, Siegert, & Medvedev, 2018). Some studies have suggested that mindfulness is more of an art than science and subsequently cannot be easily measured. Although we agree that measurement of mindfulness is inherently reductionistic, we see great value in attempts to incrementally improve measures. As a source of information, empirical approaches may prove meaningful for some individuals (and maybe not others). Ultimately, we hope that folks will consider a way to track their progress, presence, and sense of self throughout their mindfulness journey.

Activity 2.4: Take a Measure of Mindfulness. At first, and without sufficient grounding in personal experience, discussions of mindfulness can seem abstract. If you haven't done so already, we strongly encourage you to take common measures of mindfulness to give yourself a sense of how mindfulness is being operationalized. In Exhibit 2.1, we have included items for one of the commonly used mindfulness measures, the Mindful Attention Awareness Scale (MAAS; K. W. Brown & Ryan, 2003), which distills mindfulness down to a single factor: attentiveness/awareness. Take a moment now to complete the MAAS.

As you took the MAAS, what were your reactions to the items? What items did you wish would have been included? In this and other common measures of mindfulness you may have taken, were there other ways of expressing your experiences that the measures did not capture? Have you had experiences with meditation? Did you notice any ways in which your own experience or cultural background seemed to influence your reactions to the items? Take a moment to amplify any curiosity you may have. What are the big questions you have about mindfulness now? Where do you perceive gaps in your understanding or knowledge of mindfulness?

If you are interested, it might be worth taking two other measures: the Five Facet Mindfulness Questionnaire (Baer, Smith, Hopkins, Krietemeyer, & Toney, 2006), which covers a much larger conceptual range, including items measuring nonreactivity, observing, awareness, describing, and nonjudging (see https://ggsc.berkeley.edu/images/uploads/Five_Facet_Mindfulness_Questionnaire.pdf), and the Kentucky Inventory of Mindfulness Skills (Baer, Smith, & Allen, 2004), which was developed specifically for assessing clients with mental health concerns (see http://www.ruthbaer.com/academics/KIMS.pdf).

BENEFITS OF THERAPEUTIC MINDFULNESS

A second knowledge base relevant to the use of mindfulness in therapy is research on its benefits. As a practitioner, it probably feels daunting to make sense of the innumerable articles and books coming out on the topic of mindfulness. The four authors of the present book are researchers by

EXHIBIT 2.1

The Mindful Attention Awareness Scale

Instructions: Below is a collection of statements about your everyday experience. Using the 1–6 scale below, please indicate how frequently or infrequently you currently have each experience. Please answer according to what really reflects your experience rather than what you think your experience should be. Please treat each item separately from every other item.

1 = *Almost always*
2 = *Very frequently*
3 = *Somewhat frequently*
4 = *Somewhat infrequently*
5 = *Very infrequently*
6 = *Almost never*

1. I could be experiencing some emotion and not be conscious of it until sometime later.
2. I break or spill things because of carelessness, not paying attention, or thinking of something else.
3. I find it difficult to stay focused on what's happening in the present.
4. I tend to walk quickly to get where I'm going without paying attention to what I experience along the way.
5. I tend not to notice feelings of physical tension or discomfort until they really grab my attention.
6. I forget a person's name almost as soon as I've been told it for the first time.
7. It seems I am "running on automatic" without much awareness of what I'm doing.
8. I rush through activities without being really attentive to them.
9. I get so focused on the goal I want to achieve that I lose touch with what I'm doing right now to get there.
10. I do jobs or tasks automatically without being aware of what I'm doing.
11. I find myself listening to someone with one ear, doing something else at the same time.
12. I drive places on "automatic pilot" and then wonder why I went there.
13. I find myself preoccupied with the future or the past.
14. I find myself doing things without paying attention.
15. I snack without being aware that I'm eating.

Scoring: To score the scale, simply compute a mean (average) of the 15 items.

Note. Adapted from "The Benefits of Being Present: Mindfulness and Its Role in Psychological Well-Being," by K. W. Brown and R. M. Ryan, 2003, *Journal of Personality and Social Psychology, 84*, p. 826. Copyright 2003 by the American Psychological Association.

training, so part of our job is to conduct primary research. Even though we regularly engage in research and write systematic literature reviews, the literature on mindfulness is so expansive that it is difficult to track things closely or well. Even tracking the narrative reviews and meta-analyses requires exceptional skill. Consistent with the theme of this chapter, our hope is to consider ways of framing this task so that we can provide you with traction for engaging these bodies of knowledge.

A large set of studies falls under the umbrella of basic science. These studies explore potential short- and long-term benefits of mindfulness. For example, researchers have linked mindfulness to positive outcomes for physical health, mental health, relationships, recovery from stress, and neurological functioning (for reviews, see K. W. Brown, Creswell, & Ryan, 2015). Without question, the breadth of samples, methods, and research questions provides a robust base of scientific evidence that mindfulness can be helpful for promoting better physical and mental health. Research on mechanisms through which mindfulness has its benefits often falls under the umbrella of self-regulation (Hölzel et al., 2011). Thus, mindfulness appears to be linked with the capacity to regulate one's internal states, especially in the face of stressors, mental, and physical health issues. When people feel confident that they can slow down and pump the brakes on mental reactivity, it often leads to a growing sense of equanimity and contentment.

Another large set of studies falls under the umbrella of applied research—such as clinical trials on interventions that prominently feature mindfulness (Gotink et al., 2015). The promising results of these studies is one of the factors that therapeutic mindfulness approaches are so popular (we describe four prominent MBIs in the next section). Meta-analyses on the effectiveness of MBIs have found weak to moderate effect sizes of mindfulness on mental health outcomes (e.g., Goyal et al., 2014; Hofmann, Sawyer, Witt, & Oh, 2010; Quaglia, Braun, Freeman, McDaniel, & Brown, 2016; Strauss, Cavanagh, Oliver, & Pettman, 2014). Weak to moderate effect sizes were also found when researchers focused on specific interventions, such as MBSR or mindfulness-based cognitive therapy (MBCT; Alsubaie et al., 2017; Chiesa & Serretti, 2011; Gu, Strauss, Bond, & Cavanagh, 2015), acceptance and commitment therapy (ACT; A-Tjak et al., 2015; Öst, 2014), and dialectical behavior therapy (DBT; Panos, Jackson, Hasan, & Panos, 2014; Valentine, Bankoff, Poulin, Reidler, & Pantalone, 2015).

Activity 2.5: Navigate the Mindfulness Research Literature. If you are an academic, you may feel comfortable navigating large bodies of literature, but if you haven't completed a dissertation or haven't engaged a lot in psychological science since you completed your dissertation, then these skills may feel a little rusty. How comfortable do you feel navigating the empirical literature on the effectiveness of mindfulness? Take 10 minutes and see if you can find some of the most recent articles that engage these questions.

Here are a few hints. First, try using PsycINFO (if you have access; see https://www.apa.org/pubs/databases/psycinfo). Start by limiting your search to systematic literature reviews. Skim the abstracts and find the articles that are most relevant to your interests. Second, try using the program Publish or Perish (free to download at https://harzing.com/resources/publish-or-perish) from Harzing.com, which partners with Google Scholar. What is nice about this program is that it pulls the article information, year, and citation. For a large body of literature like work on mindfulness, it will give you a sense of which articles are getting cited by a lot of other professionals. After entering your search terms, try skimming the most cited five or 10 articles for each year. Do you want to explore ordering a few books? Consider perhaps keeping a running list of potential books to read. A good place to start might be the *Handbook of Mindfulness* (K. W. Brown et al., 2015), which will give you a sense of prominent names in the area. Are there any popular books on mindfulness you may want to read? Do you like listening to books on tape? Such resources can be a nice way to understand how popular authors are framing mindfulness.

OVERVIEW OF THE BIG FOUR MINDFULNESS INTERVENTIONS

A third body of knowledge relevant to using mindfulness is knowledge about the most prominent MBIs. We are generally writing this book to the growing number of therapists who are working from a primary theoretical orientation and want to incorporate mindfulness to help address the client's presenting problem. Although used with a variety of clinical syndromes, therapeutic mindfulness is most commonly used for symptoms related to anxiety, depression, emotional dysregulation, or all three. Some readers of this book may have formal training in an MBI, but we assume most of our readers are working from another primary orientation (e.g., cognitive behavior, psychodynamic, interpersonal, humanistic, systemic, integrated models) and interested in how it might make sense to integrate mindfulness techniques into their therapy approach.

It is beyond the scope of this book to provide a detailed summary of even one of the major MBIs. Book-length works are available if you are interested in reading more about any of these approaches. Each has its own recommended training process that varies in degree of oversight. Later in the book, we assume some familiarity with the primary MBIs and basic techniques, so in the following section, we give a brief overview of the four most prominent MBIs: (a) MBSR (Kabat-Zinn, 1982), (b) MBCT (Teasdale et al., 2000), (c) ACT (S.C. Hayes, Strosahl, & Wilson, 2012), and (d) DBT (Linehan, 1993). We describe the theoretical underpinnings and development of each approach, as well as key interventions.

Mindfulness-Based Stress Reduction

Theory

MBSR (Kabat-Zinn, 1982) was the first prominent MBI. Designed for clients living with chronic pain, it involves teaching clients to engage in intensive habits of meditation to deal with physical suffering in their lives. Later, it was also extended to other symptoms, including mental health concerns. The theoretical principles of MBSR align with stress and coping theory (Lazarus & Folkman, 1984). For example, what determines one's degree of stress is not just physical pain but also one's reaction to pain. Here, a foundational teaching within Buddhism aligns squarely with theorizing on stress. Stress intensifies pain. The more people resist their pain, the more it amplifies the subjective experience of suffering. As a result, MBSR interventions seek to help clients learn to view stressors as challenging rather than threatening, commit to a lifestyle change that involves immediately changing daily habits, and cultivate an open and receptive orientation to growing and learning (Santorelli, 2014). Adopting a more receptive and accepting stance toward pain helps reduce suffering, which is amplified by resistant appraisals.

Format and Key Techniques

MBSR groups tend to be conducted with between 15 and 40 participants, consistent with typical psychoeducational groups. Leaders conduct pregroup and individual interviews (2.5 hours) to ensure that members are appropriate for the group. The manual instructs group facilitators to exclude people with severe psychological symptoms (e.g., depression, anxiety, posttraumatic stress disorder, suicidality, psychosis, substance use), unless the instructor determines that the potential risks are small. Over the years, teams have used MBSR with other presenting problems; note, however, that the manual places the onus on the instructor to evaluate the potential risks for clients with psychopathology. In terms of the intervention, MBSR involves a dose of nearly 90 hours of assigned time, which includes around 30 hours of class time over eight sessions (2.5-hour meetings except for an all-day silent retreat for the sixth session) as well as 45 minutes of homework per day. The manual describes and provides a core set of practices that have been used or adapted in subsequent MBIs.

Eating a Raisin. One of the first introductions to mindfulness in MBSR is an activity in which patients learn to eat a raisin mindfully. The activity provides clients with a concrete illustration of the shift in awareness that MBSR seeks to promote. Clients seek greater conscious awareness of routine and automatic daily habits rather than let the usual reactive patterns play out uncontested. They begin to practice and refine the mental skills of holding the focus of attention and short-term memory. A similar practice could be applied to washing dishes or spending time listening to a partner (e.g., Hanley, Warner, Dehili, Canto, & Garland, 2015).

Performing a Body Scan. The body scan is a second staple of MBSR. Given the original focus on pain management, the body scan and yoga (described next) are viewed as particularly important for helping clients learn to engage their pain with less resistance and frustration because these feelings amplify the subjective experience of pain. The body scan activity involves a guided meditation. Clients progressively attend to different objects of attention (i.e., parts of their body). They practice the intrapsychic skills involved in holding and shifting attention to different parts of the body. The body scan is similar to progressive muscle relaxation (Feldman, Greeson, & Senville, 2010). However, instead of focusing on relaxing, clients practice attending to the present moment. Clients also practice an attitude of kindness toward their arising experience. They build on the skills learned in the body scan to flexibly engage their experience of pain. Instead of allowing the reactivity of the mind to take over, they learn to intentionally hold and shift their awareness and cultivate an attitude of acceptance rather than fight against their pain and feel helpless and more distressed.

Practicing Yoga. Gentle yoga activities also align well for clients with chronic pain, the original target population of MBSR. Like the body scan, clients learn to develop a more accepting and curious stance toward whatever is happening within the body. Many MBSR leaders view this practice as a core mechanism underlying the effectiveness of MBSR, although this claim has yet to be tested with dismantling designs (Santorelli, 2014).

Doing a Sitting Meditation. In terms of sheer time and mental energy, sitting meditation is the core practice of MBSR. In a typical meditation, clients begin by noticing the flow of their breath. When their attention strays, they gently return focus. These moments of returning to the breath are like mental reps (imagine lifting a 5-pound weight). These activities can be presented as aligning with contemplative practices from a variety of spiritual traditions that include a foundation of concentrative meditation (Plante, 2010). Focusing attention on the breath (or a word or other object) provides a way of slowing down and grounding the mind, which can help a person face more difficult internal experiences with greater confidence (Harrington & Dunne, 2015). Over time, and as clients practice these skills on a daily basis, they gradually gain greater mental awareness "muscles" associated with noticing that one's attention has shifted, refocus their attention, and quiet any judgment that arises as they gently correct their attention. Therefore, sitting meditation helps clients internalize a new way of being that stands in stark contrast to the over-controlled mental habits (e.g., suppression of emotion; avoidance of pain) of the typical person coping with chronic pain.

Doing a Walking Meditation. Walking meditation is a less formal meditational practice that provides an alternative to sitting meditation. This alternative may be especially helpful for clients who have trouble sitting for long periods (e.g., due to chronic pain or other troubles with concentrating for a long time). Similar to sitting meditation, this practice applies mindfulness skills (e.g., focusing attention, noticing when attention strays, letting go of self-critical thoughts and feelings) to the process of walking. As with the body scan, clients can turn their focus to various aspects of the bodily experience (e.g., altering the pace of their walking, curiously attending to aspects of the process of walking). Like other practices, clients learn to gently return focus when the mind invariably wanders. Walking meditation is an example of an informal practice that a person can complete almost anytime and anywhere.

Doing a Loving-Kindness Meditation. Up to this point, the MBSR practices described have focused on promoting awareness and kindness toward the present moment. During a daylong silent retreat, clients engage in practices of loving-kindness meditation (e.g., Fredrickson, Cohn, Coffey, Pek, & Finkel, 2008); namely, they learn to cultivate feelings of compassion toward various objects. They begin by meditating on an object or relationship for which it is easier to evoke compassion (e.g., thinking of a relationship with a parent, child, other family member). For example, the client may internally repeat phrases that will help cultivate compassion toward the object or relationship (e.g., "May you be happy and whole"). Clients attend to and amplify the feelings of compassion toward the object of attention. Just as they learned with the body scan, clients move their focus to different objects, expanding on each and extending compassion and benevolent wishes to each object. Clients attend to objects for which it may be harder for them to feel compassion (e.g., an enemy or competitor, all humanity). Through practice, it is possible to learn to extend compassion for even difficult objects (e.g., relationships involving physical distance, intergroup competition, interpersonal conflict).

Activity 2.6: Try a Mindfulness-Based Stress Reduction Activity. Go to this website (https://mbsrtraining.com/mindfulness-exercises-mbsr-practices) and pick one of the MBSR techniques to try yourself. Spend about 10 minutes engaged in the mindfulness technique and notice what comes up for you. Did engaging in the mindfulness technique feel natural or unnatural? What questions or concerns do you have about the mindfulness technique? What barriers might get in the way of your adopting this mindfulness technique into your everyday routine? Are any of these barriers related to aspects of your cultural identity?

Mindfulness-Based Cognitive Therapy

Theory

In terms of position in the marketplace, MBCT moved mindfulness from the hospital to psychotherapy. Whereas MBSR was designed for clients experiencing chronic pain, MBCT was designed for clients at risk for chronic depression (see Tirch, Silberstein, & Kolts, 2015). To extend mindfulness to psychotherapy in which the dominant theoretical paradigm is cognitive behavior therapy (CBT), the developers identified a potential weakness in cognitive behavior approaches, namely, relapse remained high for some clients. In addition, sometimes trying to change thoughts using traditional CBT methods seemed to reinforce the thoughts. At the same time, developers aligned MBCT with aspects of cognitive theory (e.g., interactive cognitive subsystems model; Barnard & Teasdale, 1991), which likely allowed the model to gain interest from people attracted to CBT but who perhaps encountered similar challenges.

Clients with a history of chronic depression have high relapse rates even after receiving gold standard treatments for depression. According to MBCT, people relapse because they experience negative moods that can trigger a downward spiral: specifically, temporary negative mood triggers schemas, rumination, and ineffective attempts to avoid the pain of depressive symptoms (e.g., experiential avoidance), which further worsen mood. Thus, MBCT interventions focus on changing how clients relate to their thoughts. Rather than viewing thoughts as objectively "true" (e.g., "I am not a very good person"), clients learn to decenter and experience their thoughts as passing experiences (e.g., "I am having the thought that I am not a very good person"). Similarly, clients learn a new strategy of engaging negative moods. Rather than trying to avoid negative moods and engaging in reactive thinking (e.g., "driving for miles on autopilot"), clients learn to recognize and interrupt early warning signs with ways of decentering from (i.e., not identifying so strongly with) negative thoughts and feelings.

Accordingly, the thrust of the research program on MBCT has been on documenting evidence that it can provide an alternative strategy to medication (Kuyken et al., 2016). MBCT quickly rose in prominence with an original clinical trial published in the *Journal of Consulting and Clinical Psychology* (Teasdale et al., 2000) followed by several other successful clinical trials (e.g., Godfrin & van Heeringen, 2010; Kuyken et al., 2008; Teasdale et al., 2002). These trials accelerated and solidified the scientific interest in mindfulness within the mental health disciplines (Kabat-Zinn, 2017).

Format and Key Techniques

The format of MBCT is similar to that of MBSR except that groups are smaller (up to 12 members), which is consistent with typical group sizes for therapy groups as opposed to psychoeducational groups. In the initial clinical trials, groups met for 2 hours for 8 weeks, but subsequent studies have used a 1-hour format (Tovote et al., 2013). Activities involve a combination of MBSR-like activities with traditional CBT techniques for treating depression. MBCT gives clients daily homework assignments designed to help them internalize the mind-set of the intervention. Taken together, MBCT contextualizes the focus of MBSR on chronic physical pain to the context of chronic psychological pain. It extends many of the activities (e.g., sitting meditation, informal meditation, body scan) from MBSR to the treatment of chronic depression. We do want to highlight an innovation of MBCT called the 3-minute breathing space because brief activities like this one are the kinds of techniques that many clinicians may consider suggesting, even if they are not teaching a more rigorous program on mindfulness meditation.

In the 3-minute breathing space activity, clients learn to think of an hourglass to remember the process. Sand in an hourglass begins in a wide space, moves into the narrow neck, and then moves again into another wide space. Based on this analogy, clients direct their attention from broad to narrow and then back to broad. During the first minute, clients engage in open monitoring and direct their attention to a range of internal experiences without trying to change them. In the second minute, clients narrow their focus and engage in concentrative meditation. They slow down and place their full attention on the movement and sensation of the breath. In the final minute, clients again broaden their focus and expand their awareness to the body as a whole (e.g., facial expression, posture, embodied emotions). This final movement helps to ground clients again in their senses and what is happening in their current environment. Thus, the 3-minute breathing space is one of the core strategies of empowering clients to interrupt the cycle that can lead to relapse. They learn that they can engage this simple practice anytime they feel a decline in mood and want to decenter from negative rumination patterns.

Acceptance and Commitment Therapy

Theory

ACT was developed as an extension of behavioral therapy (in particular, relational frame theory, applied behavioral analysis, and functional contextualism; Fletcher & Hayes, 2005; S. C. Hayes et al., 2012). The basic premise of the theory focuses on how language shapes and becomes intertwined with how people engage their environment. Language gives humans a major advantage for analytical thinking and problem-solving. They can imagine hypothetical situations and their likely consequences. Negative complications arise when people become too reliant on analytical thinking, which can decrease their responsiveness to what is happening in their environment. They can deplete psychological resources on hypothetical threats rather than invest in addressing actual threats present in real life. Thus, ACT defines psychopathology in terms of the psychological inflexibility that occurs when people rely too heavily on language (also including mental images—not just words). For example, golfers can get stuck in their head if they focus on each part of what they need to do. Optimal performance for a golfer often involves working to decrease reliance on conscious processing given the potential for negative self-talk or other rumination that can interfere with consistency. In a similar way, ACT teaches clients to get out of their heads and learn to increase their responsiveness to their actual environment.

Perhaps more than MBSR or MBCT, Steven Hayes, the originator of this approach, has drawn primarily from behavioral theory, although, at times, he has acknowledged convergence with principles of Buddhism (S. C. Hayes, 2002). A basic premise of ACT is that suffering is unavoidable and part of being human. Different from other MBIs, ACT does not use formal meditation protocols, but mindfulness is infused throughout. Training materials intentionally align mindfulness with a scientific, rather than religious, framework (e.g., considering when and why mindfulness practices may be useful).

Format and Key Techniques

Therapists tend to deliver ACT through individual therapy, although it is also available in other modalities (e.g., group or self-directed). A variety of ACT manuals are consistent with the approach and vary in length and treatment focus (S. Hayes, 2006). What these manuals have in common is a focus on promoting psychological flexibility. When providing ACT, therapists seek to understand the context of the client's life, gather information to understand the client's values, and explore factors that have hindered the client's ability to live in alignment with their values and goals.

The core organizing structure for interventions is based on six aspects of the psychological flexibility model: acceptance, cognitive delusion, being present, self as context, values, and committed action. The following are descriptions of these aspects and example techniques for each (Fletcher & Hayes, 2005).

Acceptance. Acceptance helps clients learn to come to terms with the futility of trying to avoid suffering. The paradox is that the more people try to avoid suffering, the more they may amplify it in themselves. Indeed, aversion to suffering may distract people from focusing their energy on pursuing goals in line with their values. *Acceptance* is defined as the "active and aware embrace of those private events occasioned by one's history without unnecessary attempts to change their frequency or form, especially when doing so would cause psychological harm" (S. Hayes, 2006, p. 7). The point of promoting acceptance is to clear the way for seeking integrity between one's actions and values. To promote greater acceptance, therapists might use exposure-based exercises (e.g., exposing clients to a fear stimulus, not allowing avoidance behaviors, supporting the client to tolerate distress until extinction occurs).

Cognitive Defusion. *Cognitive defusion* techniques involve working to "alter the undesirable functions of thoughts and other private events, rather than trying to alter their form, frequency, or situational sensitivity" (S. Hayes, 2006, p. 8). Often, clients give their thoughts a lot of power because they believe that their thoughts "cause" their problems. ACT therapists direct their clients to do things that diminish the typical negative associations people have with thoughts. For example, the therapist might have a client learn to practice adding the phrase, "I am having the thought that . . ." to ongoing experiences so that the client gains a more objective stance.

Another example is the "Milk, Milk, Milk" exercise, which therapists can use to illustrate the process of cognitive defusion. Clients say the world *milk* and describe whatever comes to mind. The therapist notes that although nothing other than the sound of the word *milk* is in the room, the client experiences a range of internal stimuli related to prior experiences and associations with the word *milk*. Next, the client conducts an experiment by repeating the word *milk* for 1 minute. When the client finishes, the therapist processes the experience and highlights how repeating the word can sometimes bring the client into greater contact with the sound of the word milk while also diminishing the other associations. Once clients understand the abstract principle of defusion, they can generalize the skill to other words that may cause them distress.

Present Moment. ACT therapists also seek to help clients maintain attention on their environment—internal and external—while minimizing judgment, which comes from comparing their current experiences with implicit ideals. When clients remain in contact with the present moment, they have reactions more closely tied to their current situation. As such, instead of trying to avoid discomfort, they can act more flexibly and in greater alignment with their values. Growth in this domain requires clients to learn to use language in more circumscribed ways—more for noting and describing, less for predicting, judging, and trying to control the future. Clients also learn the concept of *self-as-process,* which refers to the ability to see one's ongoing and dynamic stream of thoughts and feelings without identifying too strongly with them or trying to judge or change them. An important way to decrease reliance on problem-solving modes of thinking is to simply note and observe one's current experience. For example, therapists might ask clients to pay attention to each sense at a time. An example of another technique is to ask clients to practice their "sunset mode of mind": Therapists encourage clients to recall their mental stance while thoroughly enjoying a sunset. Clients then extend that frame of mind to the present moment by recalling what it is like to appreciate and savor the beautiful aspects of their experience.

Self-as-Context. Therapists can also help clients become less attached to rigid views of understanding themselves. According to ACT, these rigid self-views occur through repeated use of certain language (i.e., I–you, now–then, or here–there). People apply self-language arbitrarily (i.e., they draw boundaries "here" when they could just as easily draw them "there"). An example technique involves encouraging clients to access a future, wiser version of themselves. Clients begin by noticing their breath and becoming aware of the present moment. They then consider all the discussions that might happen in the upcoming session and carry over the same acceptance and awareness from the mindfulness induction. Next, the therapist encourages clients to imagine themselves years later as a wiser person who can see themselves in full awareness of all their emotions and desires. The therapist then asks clients to consider what advice their future self might give to their current self regarding their anticipated concerns for the upcoming counseling session. Thus, self-as-context interventions aim to free up people's ways of viewing and relating to themselves.

Values. Instead of letting aversion to suffering rule one's decisions, clients in ACT learn to clarify their values and use them to make daily decisions. The goal is to help clients learn to base behaviors on values rather letting distress (and attempts to avoid distress) drive decisions. Through acting in line with their values, clients learn to increase their sense of integrity. *Values* are defined as "chosen qualities of purposive action that can never be obtained as an object but can be instantiated moment by moment" (S. C. Hayes, Luoma, Bond, Masuda, & Lillis, 2006, p. 8). Clients clarify their values across various domains, such as family, career, health, and spirituality. Clients cannot achieve their values, but they can set value-congruent goals, which can then be sought after and achieved.

Therefore, a primary goal of ACT is to help clients increase responsiveness to their values and decrease how often emergent motives (e.g., avoidance of suffering, social compliance, cognitive defusion) eclipse valued goals. An example activity includes the exercise "What Do You Want Your Life to Stand For?" In this exercise, clients imagine themselves attending their own funeral. They envision listening to the eulogies given by their closest friends and family. They say what they hope each person will remember about them. Clients relate their imagined eulogies to their values in life. Another example is the bull's-eye intervention. Clients place an *X* on a bull's-eye based on the degree to which their current life situation expresses their ideal values. The closer the *X* is to the center, the more aligned the person perceives his or her life to be with his or her values. This bull's-eye activity gives concrete expression to the client's sense of integrity. It helps promote motivation to bring choices into alignment with values.

Committed Action. Once clients clarify their values, the next movement of ACT is to help them develop patterns of behavior that align with those values. Accordingly, clients form goals, consider alignment of those goals with core values, and determine value-congruent actions. Then, the therapist and client can note and celebrate when the client takes small steps toward those goals. This aspect of the ACT model can incorporate most behavioral techniques (e.g., exposure, learning new skills, shaping, goal setting). As people encounter challenges in achieving their goals, they will likely need to cycle back through other aspects of the model. In this way, the parts of the flexibility model work in unison.

Dialectical Behavior Therapy

Theory

DBT was designed for treating clients with symptoms of borderline personality disorder (Linehan, 1993). Like MBSR, clinical trials have explored DBT for other symptoms as well. DBT is a cognitive-based, collaborative psychotherapy. In DBT, therapists seek to strengthen clients' ability to regulate their distressing emotions.

DBT includes four modules: mindfulness, interpersonal effectiveness, emotion regulation, and distress tolerance. In the mindfulness module, therapists work with clients to function within a wise mind, which balances strengths and weaknesses of the reasonable mind (i.e., analytical, rational, and logical) with the emotion mind (i.e., emotions drive behavior). This module includes "what" skills of learning to observe and describe experience and participate in mindfulness as well as "how" skills of cultivating an accepting stance toward one's experience. The interpersonal effectiveness module helps people learn to say no or ask for support or help. The emotion regulation module helps clients learn skills to identify emotions, attend to sensitivity and intensity, and understand how these emotions can help them make better decisions. The distress tolerance module teaches clients practical skills (e.g., radical acceptance of reality as it is) to deal with crisis situations rather than engage in self-destructive behaviors (e.g., self-harm, substance use).

Format and Key Techniques

The standard treatment involves a time-intensive regimen that includes individual psychotherapy, daily coaching, case management, a focus on structuring the environment, and a consultation team to help support the therapist's growth. People also meet in groups for around 120–150 minutes per week over the course of 24 weeks. Therapists prioritize addressing life-threatening behaviors, therapy-interfering behaviors, quality of life behaviors, and skill acquisition, respectively. Accordingly, stages of treatment include increasing behavioral control (Stage 1); moving from quiet desperation to emotional experiencing (Stage 2); learning to pursue a life worth living through the definition of life goals, increasing self-respect, and finding peace and happiness (Stage 3); and finding deeper meaning through spiritual existence (Stage 4). Because many settings do not have the resources to adhere to the full DBT protocol, some initial work has offered evidence for using the skills components as a stand-alone treatment (e.g., Valentine et al., 2015).

"What" Skills. Given the focus of this book, we concentrate on and describe the mindfulness module (and its six skills) in greater detail. The first three skills (i.e., observe, describe, and participate) are known as "what" skills and focus on what actions are needed to practice mindfulness. DBT therapists guide the client through one skill at a time, allowing the skills to build on each other as the client grows in the capacity to be mindful.

- *Observe.* For the observe skills, clients learn to attend to present experiences without trying to avoid, change, or label them. Clients practice recognizing bodily sensations, emotions, and thoughts along with external experiences in the environment. Instead of fixating on the thoughts or sensations that arise, they let experiences emerge and fall away. To practice observing skills, clients might engage in activities such as imagining the mind as the sky and that each thought, bodily sensation, or emotion is a cloud passing by. As clients practice observing their inner experience, they begin to pay attention to evidence that all experiences are transient, which can reduce the intensity of experience. As a result, clients experience greater mental flexibility as they become less controlled by unexamined and unconscious attempts to avoid negative feelings (e.g., fear, sadness).
- *Describe.* For the describe skills, clients learn to put words to their ongoing experiences. They verbally label thoughts, emotions, and sensations. Rather than getting immersed in their experience, they learn to take a more objective and distanced perspective through noting each passing experience.

For example, a person who thinks "I have really messed this presentation up" may be tempted to process the thought and accompanying emotions as proof that she is a failure. To practice the describe skills, the client may intentionally think something like "I am having a thought right now" or "I feel shame." One way to make this process more concrete might be to visualize observed experiences as moving down a conveyor belt. The goal is to sort each experience into thoughts, emotions, or bodily sensations. Practicing the describe skills helps clients increase their self-awareness as they learn to adopt a less attached or fused relationship with emergent experiences.

- *Participate.* For the participate skill, clients practice being wholly present. Within therapy training, we sometimes refer to this ability as *immediacy*—focusing one's attention on the here and now—in contrast to letting the mind engage in typical wandering and reactivity (i.e., imagining the future or ruminating on the past). Clients learn to optimize attentiveness to the present moment. By reducing attentiveness to memories or daydreaming about the future—both often laced with fear or anxiety—clients can increase their engagement with what is happening in their current environment. To practice this skill, therapists might have clients go on a walk while seeking full attention to the experience. As clients practice this skill, it becomes more habitual to remain actively engaged in attending to the here and now rather than get caught up thinking about the past or future.

"How" Skills. Once clients have practiced what to do to be mindful, they move to the "how" skills—nonjudgmentally, one-mindfully, and effectively—that focus on how clients engage in awareness of the present moment. These skills are used in conjunction with the "what" skills to promote a mindful experience that can engender equanimity and the ability to handle difficult feelings.

- *Nonjudgmentally.* For this skill, clients learn to regulate their tendencies to evaluate and judge their experiences in the moment. Rather than going along with the tendency to view thoughts as good or bad, clients learn to discern thoughts as just thoughts and to distinguish objective facts from their tendency to reflexively form opinions and attitudes. They learn to note, rather than judge, the content (i.e., who, what, where, when). For example, rather than focusing on an opinion (e.g., "I should not be angry right now"), the client steps back and focuses on the objective (e.g., "I am feeling anger right now"). Of course, sometimes clients do have judgmental thoughts. They note this too—"I am criticizing myself right now"—rather than get caught up in self-criticism. Another activity that can help promote this skill is asking clients to try to pay attention to times when they get fixed in self-critical thoughts. Rather than accepting these thoughts as fact, they develop the ability to simply note them, let them go, and work toward a more objective stance toward the current moment.

- *One-mindfully.* The one-mindfully skill involves learning to focus on doing one thing at a time instead of multitasking. Many clients waste emotional energy tracking various daily tasks all at once. For this skill, clients work on practicing mindfulness in how they approach each of the things they are doing. They work on giving their full attention to each and every task. Again, it is normal to have lapses in attention, but as soon as clients notice a distracting thought emerge, they train their minds to note the distraction and then return their attention to the focal task. To practice this skill, it may help clients to pick a simple task, such as drinking a cup of tea—something they could easily complete mindlessly. However, rather than letting their mind run ahead to other concerns or distractions, clients can practice giving the activity their full and undivided attention.
- *Effectively.* The effectively skills involve clients' evaluating whether their behaviors work well. They pragmatically assess their choices based on whether they are likely to make their desired ends more or less likely. Often, emergent goals (e.g., winning an argument, saving face after embarrassment) can engage people in reactive and unproductive behaviors. Thus, the effectively skills require clients to differentiate between what feels right or fair and what is most suitable to the current situation. To develop these skills, clients might recall times when they were caught trying to prove a point. Remembering their goals at the time (e.g., to receive an apology from their partner), they can consider how their behavior (e.g., yelling at a partner) might have undercut the potential for achieving their goal. Through reflection and gathering insight, clients can develop new and creative ways to pursue their goals (e.g., telling a partner how it felt when a call was not returned).

Activity 2.7: Take Stock. Let's press the pause button and take stock of where we are. We just presented you with a lot of information. And the reality is that this information only scratches the surface. Mastering any one of these formal approaches would require a tremendous commitment of time, energy, and willingness to engage an extended training process. Furthermore, new approaches are being developed each year.

Now that you have learned more about these four approaches, which one did you like the most? Which could you see potentially integrating more into your therapy approach? Based on your current caseload, which clients do you think might be most receptive to mindfulness? Which clients do you think would find mindfulness especially helpful; or which clients might struggle, for various reasons, with integrating mindfulness skills and habits into their daily routines?

Also, we would like you to begin thinking about how you would describe mindfulness to your clients. Have you started to try anything like mindfulness in your own life? Many of these approaches strongly recommend having extensive practice on your own before you begin to try to assist clients develop similar practices. If you have started a practice, what is your own sense of how it can be helpful? What are some of your personal reasons for seeking to maintain a consistent mindfulness practice?

LIMITATIONS IN SCIENTIFIC KNOWLEDGE ABOUT THERAPEUTIC MINDFULNESS

So far in this chapter, we have touched on several expansive bodies of knowledge that will help you prepare to use mindfulness with clients from a range of identities and presenting problems. Learning more about how mindfulness has evolved across time and cultural traditions can give you more flexibility for exploring how to contextualize mindfulness to your clients' identities. Furthermore, having a broader sense of various Buddhist cultures may allow more creative ways of connecting with clients who have little familiarity with Buddhism but may have similar principles within their own cultural background. These bodies of knowledge alone are vast, and we have yet to consider the client's specific identities (e.g., gender, race, ethnicity, nationality, religion or spirituality, ability status, sexual orientation, socioeconomic status). Indeed, the intersection of each of these identities with mindfulness yields an even more expansive body of knowledge that might be helpful for increasing your discernment of how to approach the use of mindfulness in therapy.

In this section, we also acknowledge that even with all that is collectively known—and assuming you have had a lifetime to devote to learning from others—vast areas of knowledge still remain unexamined. Thus, before we consider cultural questions that have emerged regarding how to use mindfulness—the focus of Chapter 3—we want you to have a general sense of the state of research on the efficacy and effectiveness of mindfulness interventions.

Research on Efficacy and Effectiveness

Clinical trial research prioritizes evidence that an intervention works compared with a comparison group (e.g., clients who do not receive treatment or receive an alternative treatment); the focus is on efficacy. As the research base on efficacy becomes more developed, it is also important to explore evidence of effectiveness—that is, evidence that approaches work well as used in various field settings (e.g., community settings: private practice, hospitals, Veterans Affairs hospitals). Evidence that interventions work compared with comparison groups prioritizes internal validity; evidence of effectiveness prioritizes external validity. For example, the National Institutes of Health has a five-stage model for classifying intervention research: intervention generation (Stage 1), evaluation in research clinic (Stage 2), evaluation in community clinic (Stage 3), evaluation of effectiveness in typical practice (Stage 4), and implementation and dissemination (Stage 5; Dimidjian & Segal,

2015). Currently, almost all of the research on mindfulness has focused on the first two stages (Dimidjian & Segal, 2015). Little work has focused on what tends to happen in the field: therapists using mindfulness alongside a primary theoretical orientation. Thus, we consider key warnings that should inform decisions to use mindfulness as an adjunctive technique.

Instructor Qualifications

Clearly, it would be inappropriate to claim to offer an MBI without going through proper training channels. However, many therapists use mindfulness activities in conjunction with their primary therapy orientation. Less clear is the level of training that is advisable for a therapist to obtain before using mindfulness as an adjunctive technique. For example, training standards for MBSR and MBCT emphasize the need for instructors to develop their own personal meditation practice (e.g., Williams, Fennell, Barnhofer, Crane, & Silverton, 2015). This suggestion makes intuitive sense. Clients might generally trust an approach more to the degree that they see their counselor as well versed in the approach. Nonetheless, research evidence is currently lacking to demonstrate that therapists need advanced training for clients to benefit from mindfulness (Hanley, Abell, Osborn, Roehrig, & Canto, 2016).

The availability of online interventions certainly challenges the view that therapists should only offer mindfulness after they have received rigorous training and experience (for a review, see Cavanagh, Strauss, Forder, & Jones, 2014). More advanced forms of meditation may require the aid of experienced spiritual practitioners, but given that clients seem to benefit from teaching themselves basic techniques in therapeutic mindfulness seems to contradict attempts to place a high bar on counselor experience with mindfulness. So—for better or worse—unless a major change occurs in professional regulation of therapeutic mindfulness, we expect that therapists will be able to justify the use of some mindfulness activities with minimal training.

We encourage therapists to consider their ethical responsibilities seriously when conducting any form of treatment, including mindfulness. Consistent with other training guidelines, we suggest that therapists engage in didactic lessons; experiential lessons (preferably supervised); and continued lifelong education and feedback to enhance their knowledge, skills, and awareness. How much didactic or experiential exposure, or both, is necessary to perform effectively will likely differ from practitioner to practitioner, so we encourage you to seek consultation.

Weak Evidence of Specificity

Another limitation in current evidence for therapeutic mindfulness is that MBIs have limited evidence of specificity. *Specificity* refers to evidence that the treatment works better than other well-established treatments, such as CBT. The strictest version of the critique might argue that it is unwise to use an alternative approach, such as mindfulness, unless there is good evidence that it works at least as well as tried-and-true approaches. Of course, this critique may be an unrealistically high standard. It would be difficult to distinguish DBT or ACT from cognitive behavior approaches because the therapies have much in common. For an intervention such as MBSR, dismantling studies would be helpful to determine which parts of the intervention account for its effects. The sheer amount of time involved in many MBIs raises the possibility of a dose effect. It is possible that just being in a group and having something that people do for a significant amount of time may account for the benefits—not mindfulness specifically (e.g., Kirsch, Wampold, & Kelley, 2016). For example, in other positive psychology work, time spent doing anything on a daily basis has similar effects on increasing psychological well-being (e.g., Sin & Lyubomirsky, 2009). Given the sheer amount of assigned meditation time, another alternative explanation is that the intervention requires large amounts of sacrifice, which introduces competing mechanisms that may explain the positive effects of MBIs (e.g., cognitive dissonance, placebo effects; Wampold, Frost, & Yulish, 2016). For our purposes, it is worth being aware that some within the scientific community have called for more stringent tests of the role of mindfulness within MBIs.

Potential Moderators

Given the massive investment of federal funding in mindfulness interventions, there is a conspicuous gap in the literature, namely, little research on client factors that may moderate treatment outcomes (e.g., gender, race, ethnicity, education, religion or spirituality; *cf.* Tovote et al., 2017). A recent systematic review of 117 articles found that only 29% of samples were male, and the vast majority of studies did not report how gender influenced effect sizes of the intervention (Bodenlos, Strang, Gray-Bauer, Faherty, & Ashdown, 2017). Given the growing influence of mindfulness within psychotherapy, leaders have begun to call for research on how well (Dimidjian & Segal, 2015) and with what presenting concerns (e.g., DeRubeis et al., 2014; Does the mechanism for reducing anxiety differ from depression?) therapeutic mindfulness works.

Currently, little research has examined client factors that amplify or undermine the potency of MBIs (e.g., Ma & Teasdale, 2004; Segal et al., 2010; Teasdale et al., 2000). We also need research on when other treatments (e.g., CBT) tend to outperform MBIs (e.g., Craigie, Rees, Marsh, & Nathan, 2008). For example, more research is needed on the traits or symptoms that may amplify (e.g., psychological mindedness) or weaken (e.g., neuroticism, perfectionism) people's odds of benefiting from the use of mindfulness. Thus, despite large bodies of research on the benefits and effectiveness of therapeutic mindfulness, we have much to learn about how and when clients may have difficulties with mindfulness (e.g., men, religious minorities, clients with attention-deficit/hyperactivity disorder symptoms).

Contraindication

Research on adverse effects is another area of underdevelopment within scholarship on mindfulness (Van Dam et al., 2018). Common concerns that arise in the applied literature include trauma, psychosis, and conservative religiosity (Lindahl, Kaplan, Winget, & Britton, 2014; Stratton, 2015). For guidance, therapists might consult available practitioner-friendly reviews of potential contraindications (Dobkin, Irving, & Amar, 2012; Hanley et al., 2016; Lustyk, Chawla, Nolan, & Marlatt, 2009). Whereas adverse effects tend to be rare, people who regularly engage in meditation have reported moderate and sometimes severe neurological, psychological, physical, social, or spiritual reactions from that practice (Hanley et al., 2016). An important problem is that most clinical trials of mindfulness have not assessed adverse reactions, so we have limited research to inform clinical decisions (e.g., Britton, Shahar, Szepsenwol, & Jacobs, 2012; for reviews, see Dobkin et al., 2012; Hanley et al., 2016; Lustyk et al., 2009).

Opportunity Costs

Another major unknown includes how therapists should think about the opportunity costs of having clients work on mindfulness. Mindfulness is not a panacea. Mindfulness seems less proximally related to some treatment goals (e.g., making a career decision). Even if mindfulness is consistent with your theoretical orientation and case conceptualization, it is one of many possible interventions for treatment. Research supports its use for some symptoms more than others (e.g., Kearney, McDermott, Malte, Martinez, & Simpson, 2012). So, given that some mindfulness approaches require a heavy time commitment (e.g., 30–45 minutes a day), it is important to carefully weigh the use of mindfulness against other potential interventions. Currently, we have little direct evidence to guide such decisions about using mindfulness as a technique in outpatient therapy and outside the parameters of a clinical trial.

Activity 2.8: Assess Limits in Your Own Knowledge. In our reading of the literature, we highlighted a few areas of knowledge that remain drastically underdeveloped. Many of these areas contribute to what people refer to as the *science-practice gap.* The methods and approach to science sometimes lag behind the complexity of day-to-day life within community settings. With the emphasis on cultural humility, we see a changing perspective on how knowledge may be related to working well with cultural diversity. The issue may not be how much one knows, but, rather, one's general orientation toward learning. Rather than shrinking back in fear, cultural humility involves embracing one's limits in knowledge with a voracious hunger and curiosity. So, with this idea in mind, as you were reading through the chapter, what questions did you have? Are there any gaps in your knowledge that you want to learn more about?

CONCLUSION

Taken together, this chapter documents the expansive scope of knowledge relevant to mastering the use of therapeutic mindfulness. Mindfulness comes to us through at least a 3,000-year history of traditions within Buddhism. In a different telling of the story, we might even highlight the many indigenous communities, known and unknown, that have contributed to the modern-day mindfulness movement within psychology.

Many therapists using mindfulness are not using a manualized approach, but it is good to know the origins of these approaches. So, we provided an overview of the four major MBIs to give you a general sense of what would be required to specialize in one or more of these formal approaches. We also described areas of knowledge that remain concealed by scientific mystery. In the next chapter, we begin to explore cultural considerations for using mindfulness in therapy.

3

Balancing Two Multicultural Concerns Related to Mindfulness

The previous chapter provided a sense of the scope of knowledge required to develop expertise in using mindfulness; namely, it might help to learn about the cultural diversity that contributed to therapeutic mindfulness, learn how mindfulness can be helpful, get training in specific approaches, and attend to the gaps in scientific knowledge. In the current chapter, we explore issues related to culture and diversity with regard to using mindfulness in therapy.

In terms of dissemination, therapeutic mindfulness has been wildly successful. It has influenced almost every major system in the Western world: health care, mental health, education, business, military, government, technology industries, self-help, and religion (Purser & Loy, 2013). Nowadays, anyone with a smartphone or watch can receive constant reminders to exercise, check e-mail, take a break, or engage in 2 minutes of meditation practice (Trub & Starks, 2017).

Many therapists have joined in this general enthusiasm for secular and therapeutic mindfulness interventions. One study of 2,607 therapists on a psychotherapy network found that 78% of therapists used mindfulness as an adjunctive technique, and 41% reported mindfulness as a primary theoretical orientation (Cook, Biyanova, Elhai, Schnurr, & Coyne, 2010). Even in trauma therapy—which many view as a riskier context for using mindfulness (Khusid & Vythilingam, 2016)—a recent study found that 68% of therapists incorporated mindfulness into their treatments (Waelde, Thompson, Robinson, & Iwanicki, 2016).

---

http://dx.doi.org/10.1037/0000156-003
Mindfulness-Based Practices in Therapy: A Cultural Humility Approach, by D. Davis, C. DeBlaere, J. N. Hook, and J. Owen

For all we can tell, mindfulness is here to stay. The most powerful structures within psychotherapy support its use. The federal government is investing hundreds of millions of dollars to integrate mindfulness into various physical health and mental health interventions (Hickey, 2010). The premier journal in applied psychology (i.e., *Journal of Consulting and Clinical Psychology*) has published more than 59 papers on mindfulness over the past 2 decades (PsycINFO search on May 29, 2017). The *Mindfulness* journal has become a high-impact outlet that releases six issues each year specifically dedicated to theory, research, and practice on mindfulness. Moreover, in a study of expert psychotherapists asked to anticipate trends in psychotherapy over the next decade, mindfulness-related therapy systems were rated as one of the approaches most likely to gain prominence (Norcross, Pfund, & Prochaska, 2013).

Perhaps because of the apparent permanence of mindfulness within psychotherapy, critiques of therapeutic mindfulness have intensified in scope and tone. The main purpose of this chapter is to describe and characterize a developing multicultural tension regarding the use of mindfulness in therapy. To make mindfulness appropriate for the largest number of clients, experts sought to distill parts of various Buddhist traditions for a pluralistic audience of potential clients—clients from many cultures and dealing with many kinds of physical or mental suffering (Purser, 2015). The strategy "succeeded," but as therapeutic mindfulness went from the margins to the mainstream of modern psychotherapy, many (e.g., Buddhist practitioners, scholars) sought to differentiate therapeutic mindfulness from traditional mindfulness practices. Accordingly, in recent years, people have subjected therapeutic mindfulness to a range of cultural critiques.

The diversity of perspectives on how to understand and integrate mindfulness into therapy raises fundamental questions about whether it is sufficient to simply avoid imposing values (secularization narrative) on a client, or whether the therapist has an obligation to learn about the client's cultural worldview and align mindfulness approaches with the client's perspective. Our primary goal for this chapter is to frame this discussion as a conflict between two multicultural values: (a) avoiding the appropriation of cultural practices from Buddhist communities and (b) adapting mindfulness to the cultural or existential worldview of the client. We explore key cultural critiques that have arisen in recent years, as well as initial responses.

Activity 3.1: Read an Example of Concerns About Mindfulness. For this activity, read the article "Beyond McMindfulness" (Purser & Loy, 2013; https://www.huffingtonpost.com/ron-purser/beyond-mcmindfulness_b_3519289.html). Imagine you were one of the Buddhists in the United States who practiced mindfulness before it became trendy. How might you feel that the damage may already have been done? Mindfulness is now a billion-dollar industry that expands well beyond the borders of physical and mental health care. The legal system has already been presented with a few opportunities to get involved and define cultural parameters. These cases have made it fairly clear the law will give only limited protections against appropriation of mindfulness. Conservative forces within Buddhism (i.e., religious traditions engaging modern trends) can differentiate from the movement, but it seems likely that there are many options for understanding mindfulness designed to appeal to non-Buddhist individuals. Given this reality, what would you hope for? What would you say to therapists considering the use of mindfulness? What might you ask of them?

TWO CULTURAL CONCERNS

Concern 1: Lack of Responsiveness to Specific Groups

The first concern aligns squarely with the multicultural movement in psychology, which noted the lack of responsiveness of psychology (and allied mental health professions) to the needs of marginalized groups. Indeed, research documented that people of color (as well as other marginalized groups) were not being served well by the mental health profession. The problem is pervasive and systemic and based on the fact that people of color are not appropriately represented within any of the processes that led to the development of psychotherapy theory, research, or practice (Betancourt, Green, Carrillo, & Ananeh-Firempong, 2003). Multicultural theory has consistently sought to scrutinize the potential influence of systemic limitations in the field. In various ways, this literature has sought to increase therapists' attentiveness to how the client's cultural background and confluence of identities might require flexibility in treatment.

When therapists fail to honor cultural diversity, doing so can undermine trust—both with the individual client and with various minority communities that have little historical reason to expect the profession to show appropriate responsiveness to their needs and interests. A common value of the various traditions within multiculturalism is the need for therapists to cultivate a sense of cultural humility. More specifically, cultural humility is necessary to recognize and own that we, as therapists, have cultural gaps in awareness that may lead to (sometimes severe) limitations in our understanding of the client's cultural worldview and perspective. Moreover, assumptions embedded within a therapy approach may not fit well with the client's cultural background.

Within the multicultural movement, one research tradition involved attempts to culturally adapt interventions to various racial or ethnic groups. In a recent meta-analysis of 99 studies, Soto, Smith, Griner, Rodriguez, and Bernal (2018) used Bernal, Bonilla, and Bellido's (1995) ecological model to code adaption strategies and provided persuasive evidence for the value of different types of adaption (e.g., language, translation of language, goal alignment with cultural values, use of metaphors, treatment methods). Although the research approach was crude (i.e., making adaptions based on generalizations about a group), these moderators improved the effectiveness of interventions. So, although the cultural adaption tradition only partially addresses the need to contextualize interventions to the client's culture (with a focus on adaption to a group but omission of variability within a group), it still demonstrates clear signs that cultural responsiveness can improve therapy outcomes.

From the perspective of cultural adaption, if one is going to use mindfulness in therapy, it may be important to communicate the principles of mindfulness to clients without imposing the values of the Western Buddhist tradition (as it has intermingled with various other Western systems). One might also consider ways (e.g., the ecological model; Bernal et al., 1995) for adapting mindfulness to seek greater alignment with the cultures of marginalized groups, which has the potential to increase the acceptability and efficacy of mindfulness. As such, secularizing mindfulness—that is, distilling principles from Buddhism for a pluralistic audience—might be construed as a good and important first step. Developers had to identify a compromise between drawing on and acknowledging inspiration from Buddhist traditions while also aligning with secularization norms within Western health care systems. Striking this balance involved an extended process of applied scientists' exploring how to potentially integrate mindfulness into physical and mental health care (Harrington & Dunne, 2015).

From the cultural adaption tradition, these first steps do not go nearly far enough. Indeed, all the broader systemic critiques seem to apply. Racial and ethnic minorities continue to be underrepresented in the process of developing theory, designing treatment approaches, and delivering care for mindfulness interventions. Moreover, according to national surveys, some groups (e.g., White women, those of higher educational status) tend to engage mindfulness or related practices more frequently than do others (Olano et al., 2015). Furthermore, although the big four mindfulness interventions—mindfulness-based stress reduction (MBSR; Kabat-Zinn, 1982), acceptance and commitment therapy (A-Tjak et al., 2015; Öst, 2014), mindfulness-based cognitive therapy (Alsubaie et al., 2017; Chiesa & Serretti, 2011; Gu, Strauss, Bond, & Cavanagh, 2015), and dialectical behavior therapy (Panos, Jackson, Hasan, & Panos, 2014; Valentine, Bankoff, Poulin, Reidler, & Pantalone, 2015)—have focused on diversification to various symptom clusters, little research has sought to adapt interventions to racial or ethnic minorities (DeLuca, Kelman, & Waelde, 2018). For example, only 24 clinical trials focused on samples comprising predominately racial or ethnic minorities (i.e., at least 75%). Of those trials, only three adapted the approach to the racial or ethnic minority group, and none of the studies in the review focused on men of color. Furthermore, only 25% of the 24 trials focused on adult samples. Clearly, anyone viewing the mindfulness movement through the lens of the cultural adaption tradition will find much room for improvement.

A related difficulty is the struggle to adapt mindfulness interventions for clients who have a variety of religious or spiritual backgrounds (Walsh &

Shapiro, 2006). Because mindfulness has Buddhist roots and is viewed by many clients as a spiritual intervention, introducing mindfulness can be difficult for clients who have a range of religious or spiritual identities. For example, clients who identify as a different religion (e.g., conservative Christian) might feel wary about incorporating a spiritual practice from a different religion. Similarly, clients who identify as atheist or agnostic might feel uncomfortable about engaging in any kind of religious or spiritual practice. Therefore, as it relates to the current book, the intersection of religion or spirituality with other marginalized identities is an important consideration for potential adaption.

Activity 3.2: Consider a Case. Let's try a quick test. Imagine you have a client who is an African American woman. She's willing to try out mindfulness, but she wants it adapted to her religion. You can dedicate only 30 minutes to exploring possible options for bibliotherapy or guided meditations she could use. See what you can find online, assuming three possible religious identities (i.e., Christian, Muslim, or Jewish). Did you notice any difference in accessibility of religiously adapted materials on mindfulness?

Concern 2: Cultural Appropriation

The second concern about mindfulness and cultural diversity involves cultural appropriation (for an overview, see Table 3.1). For the purpose of this chapter, we define *cultural appropriation* as a form of cultural diffusion (i.e., a process in which cultural traditions change across contexts and time) in which dominant cultures adopt or integrate the cultural traditions of a marginalized group without acknowledgment or a show of appropriate respect (e.g., Hoshmand, 2005; Schneider, 2003; Wilson, 2014). The general theme of these critiques is that psychotherapy has extracted mindfulness out of its cultural tradition, is using mindfulness for a different purpose than was originally intended, and is showing little respect for the traditions that refined and conserved the practice within parts of Buddhism. If left unchecked, these forces of diffusion could render mindfulness unrecognizable and perhaps use mindfulness for goals that fundamentally conflict with core values of Buddhism (e.g., nonviolence).

For the reader interested in engaging these discussions more deeply, we recommend two articles that provide an introduction to what we see as the more difficult critiques of therapeutic mindfulness. C. G. Brown (2017) argued that therapeutic mindfulness approaches draw heavily on the ethical foundations within Buddhism and that not naming this foundation more explicitly is misleading and represents a lack of transparency. Furthermore, Purser (2015) elaborated on concerns about attempting to camouflage Buddhist ideas within mindfulness as a strategy for cultural influence and dissemination.

Activity 3.3: Consider the Implications of Filling in the Gaps With One's Own Worldview. Before you read further, consider this question. Many therapists are not

TABLE 3.1. Critiques Based on Concerns About Appropriation

Concern	Critique
Poor alignment with Buddhist teachings	Buddhist practitioners might evaluate the degree of congruence between therapeutic mindfulness and their cultural tradition, including views of current leadership, interpretation of canonical texts, and views within the community.
Stealth Buddhism	Psychologists might intentionally conceal the Buddhist roots of mindfulness to avoid concerns about the ties to Buddhism.
Excesses of capitalism	Psychologists could collude with goals of systems rather than meet the interests of clients.
Scientism	Psychologists could prioritize ideology associated with science as culturally superior to perspectives that do not give science primary authority.
Colonialism	Psychologists could collude with a history of engaging marginalized communities and only granting participation if members agree to normative views (e.g., secularization, scientism) that function to put subgroups into subservient roles.
Insufficient informed consent	Psychologists might fail to give appropriate informed consent, especially the obligation to describe potential adverse effects or to not overestimate benefits.
Lack of intellectual integrity	Psychologists might fail to acknowledge the sources of ideas for therapeutic mindfulness (similar to plagiarism).
Stereotyping of Asian cultures	Psychologists might glorify elements of Asian cultures while simultaneously presenting themselves in a special and patriarchal role of rescuing Buddhist ideas from indigenous superstitions.
Patriarchal engagement	Psychologists could target marginalized groups thereby reinforcing implicit stereotypes about marginalized groups.
Ignoring spiritual identity	Psychologists could ignore the salience of religious or spiritual identity for clients from marginalized groups.
Coercive practices	Psychologists might fail to respect the autonomy of groups that do not have the opportunity to provide consent (e.g., required trainings for employees).

Buddhist and will have limited exposure to its various traditions. Thus, they will likely draw on their own cultural traditions to fill in the gaps of how they explain Buddhism to their clients. What are the potential problems of therapists' filling in the gaps with their own cultural worldview?

The concern is that once mindfulness is extracted from its cultural roots, albeit in the name of cultural adaption, it is all the more vulnerable to cultural diffusion (Purser, 2015). Think of a game of telephone in which a line of people passes a message from one person to the next, but by the end of the line, the message is seriously distorted. In kind, a series of people—none embedded within a Buddhist tradition—tells each other about "mindfulness," and the result is that the original message, without any of the cultural context to conserve its meaning, has little chance of staying true to its original intent.

Activity 3.4: Try a Game of Telephone. These discussions have the potential to stay in the abstract. Let's make it concrete. Find a group of at least four people. The first person—say it's you—describes (quietly) the person's own practice of mindfulness. (Or if you do not practice mindfulness, pick a habit that is most foundational to your daily routine. Tell the person next to you about your daily or weekly discipline.) Explain why you engage in the discipline, how to build good habits, and what might be gained. The second person's job is to adapt the practice to suit his or her own life. What might optimize its meaning and usefulness? Imagine it works perfectly and becomes an important part of your life, and then tell the next person about your innovated discipline. Each person turns to the next person and does the same thing. Have the last person share his or her practice out loud with the entire group—not just the next person. What happened? What were the aspects of the practice that seemed to suffer the greatest change and distortion? What, if anything, was conserved across the group? Why do you think that part was able to be conserved? If nothing was conserved, consider why that was the case.

To some who are affiliated with Buddhism in the United States (around 1%; Pew Research Center, n.d.), the field of therapeutic mindfulness is already way off course, and the general arc is set for even further distortion. A part of their cultural heritage has caught the interest of mainstream U.S. American culture and has been integrated, in refracted form, into the process of mental health care delivery—but by therapists with little awareness of (and perhaps little respect for) the cultural history and traditions that led to the practice. The contextualization was done in the name of "secularization," but as many have highlighted, secularization tends to favor privileged groups and is often used as a force of assimilation to obfuscate differences that might interfere with the collective goals of the dominant group (C. G. Brown, 2017).

Activity 3.5: What Do You Think? This activity offers you a chance to share your perspective. Author D. D. shared something he has been thinking about, and we invite you to engage these ideas. Ideally, if you are taking a course, this is a conversation you might have with a colleague or a small group. Read the following comments from author D. D. and then write down a few notes. Then, see if you can find a few people to talk with about your own ideas.

AUTHOR D. D.: Different Buddhist cultures are more or less amenable to engaging a global culture and the Western interest in Buddhism. For example, a fascinating part of the MBSR folklore is when founder Jon Kabat-Zinn (1982) met with His Holiness the Dalai Lama (a Buddhist spiritual leader) to hopefully receive his blessing over the formation of the mindfulness program (Hickey, 2010). I wonder if the members of the MBSR team breathed a sigh of relief when the prominent spiritual leader did not veto their efforts to bring mindfulness into the scientific community. But it is an interesting power dynamic. What if MBSR was not authorized? Or what if traditions that are more concerned about Western influence had been consulted? Might they have been less likely to extend a blessing? For me, this authorization process raises questions about who gets to absolve us of appropriation. For example, what should we do if, 50 years from now, another prominent spiritual leader adopts a different position? I am curious about how we decide to weight different perspectives in our engagement of mindfulness. It seems like there is a tendency to prefer voices that align with what we already want to do. But, with the virtue of cultural humility in mind, it seems unwise to ignore the other strong voices that warn that using mindfulness for its medical usefulness has potential risks as it gets increasingly separated from the ethical and spiritual goals (e.g., spiritual maturity, promotion of prosocial motives and behaviors) that were meant to frame the practices.

So how might the concern about appropriation manifest in therapy? A therapist could potentially commit offenses of appropriation by mimicking an aspect of the client's cultural background without permission or discussion. For example, consider using mindfulness with an international student from Thailand. Just assigning a mindfulness intervention without any conversation or exploration of the client's cultural background might result in a relational rupture. The client might already have an extensive meditation practice—or maybe not. Spirituality may or may not play a major role in the client's life. Regardless, there is clearly a potential to come across as ignorant or insensitive to the client's cultural background. As such, offenses of cultural appropriation could be seen as a form of microaggression. They involve a form of discrimination that clients may experience daily that are likely to have contested meaning (e.g., people from the dominant culture tend to minimize, justify, or dismiss the offensiveness of the behavior).

How much of a concern is appropriation? Is this a real issue? Perhaps one reason to take another look is that our profession's use of mindfulness is not a stand-alone practice; rather, it is part of a broader pattern of engaging the interests of marginalized groups. If our profession develops a reputation for consistently appropriating mindfulness with minimal attempts to honor its cultural roots, then the inattention may send a regrettable message. Clients who identify as Buddhist might hear the message loud and clear. In addition, any other groups that have experienced types of inconsiderate behavior might get the hint. This idea is somewhat speculative, but as critiques of appropriation are more widely circulated, what if some clients come to view sensitivity to this issue as a signal of broader cultural responsiveness and trustworthiness?

Given the systemic nature of cultural issues, we contend that concerns about appropriation are important to explore carefully. Particularly for therapists committed to multicultural values, how can we show responsiveness to a group of people who are giving strong warnings about the misapplication of mindfulness outside of its original context? What, if anything, should we change about our approach to using mindfulness with our clients?

AMPLIFIED ETHICAL TENSIONS

The concerns about the appropriation of Buddhism have triggered discussions about the ethics of mindfulness. Given that some research has documented that mindfulness-based interventions cause changes in spirituality (Stratton, 2015), mindfulness has caught the attention of people who specialize in the integration of spiritually oriented interventions into therapy.

Concerns About Cultural Appropriation

A recent example comes from Sperry and Stoupas (2017), who highlighted four questions related to using mindfulness with clients who are religious or spiritual. The first question is: Under what circumstances is it appropriate to adopt a practice from another culture for one's own purposes? For example, the United Nations developed a proscriptive against cultural appropriation of practices from indigenous communities: "cultural, intellectual, religious and spiritual property" should not be taken without a group's "free, prior and informed consent or in violation of their laws, traditions and customs" (United Nations General Assembly, 2007). Who has the right to draw on a spiritual tradition and adapt its beliefs and practices for therapeutic use? For example, some deem Kabat-Zinn (who developed MBSR; Kabat-Zinn, 1982) as a spiritual insider from a community that has a positive stance toward translating the dharma into secular language so that seeds of the religion are planted within broader society. Regardless of how these questions are worked out in real life, most psychotherapists are probably insufficiently embedded within Buddhist structures to have the authority to adapt mindfulness for their own purposes.

The second question is: Under what circumstances, if ever, would it be appropriate for therapists to intentionally conceal the religious or spiritual underpinnings of mindfulness? This is what some have called the "stealth Buddhism" critique. We know that some clients will have reservations about mindfulness if it is presented as being too closely aligned with Eastern spiritual traditions. If it increases the potential market of clients willing to try mindfulness, when is it appropriate for clinicians to purposefully conceal the roots of mindfulness? Perhaps the therapist possesses a secular worldview. Perhaps the therapist aligns with narratives that view mindfulness as a universal capacity that, through science, was rescued from its indigenous superstitions and religious dogma. The therapist may not be intentionally misleading clients but may still represent critiques associated with colonialism and patriarchy (see Table 3.1). Discussions about appropriation have gained prominence, thus leading to stronger calls for therapists to have transparent conversations to ensure appropriate informed consent (Stratton, 2015).

Activity 3.6: What Do You Think About Purposefully Concealing Cultural Roots of Mindfulness? The question of transparency about the religious or spiritual roots of Buddhism seems important to consider for yourself. What do you think? Is it okay to conceal the Buddhist roots of mindfulness if you know that doing so might upset the client? Does it make it easier for you to justify concealment if your own way of thinking about mindfulness has already detached mindfulness from its historical, philosophical, and spiritual roots?

The third question is: Under what conditions is it appropriate to change the goal of mindfulness? For example, instead of focusing on an entire system of moving toward spiritual maturity and enlightenment, therapeutic mindfulness approaches tend to use mindfulness for other goals or problems within the professional culture (e.g., reduction of stress, prevention of future depressive episodes). One visceral example sometimes used is that of snipers who have been trained to use mindfulness-based techniques to calm themselves before taking a shot (Monteiro, Musten, & Compson, 2015). Mindful sniping clearly violates the value of nonviolence held by many Buddhist traditions. Other possibilities for unethical use of mindfulness might include corporations' using mindfulness because it reduces what they have to pay employees or results in employees' being less likely to file lawsuits related to sexual harassment or racial inequality. Does the intention or goal of mindfulness matter (e.g., Lovett, 2015)?

The fourth question is: How does the potential for some clients to view mindfulness as a spiritual intervention potentially raise issues related to scope of practice? Namely, mindfulness could be framed to the client as a spiritual intervention, a psychological intervention, or a psychospiritual intervention. Although it may ease concerns about appropriation, the more therapists frame mindfulness as a spiritual or psychospiritual intervention, the greater the potential risk that therapists are operating outside their scope of practice. It also raises the possibility that clients will imbue them with spiritual authority, even if this was not a therapist's intent.

Activity 3.7: React to Concerns About Possible Abuses of Mindfulness. We want to make you aware of attempts to justify the use of mindfulness within psychology. In one example, Baer and Nagy (2017) defended the stance that the general profession has its own values and cannot adopt Buddhist values to govern mindfulness interventions. Rather, as a profession, we have adopted a soft universalism (or a pragmatic value-neutrality). It is not possible to be completely neutral, but we can acknowledge differences and defer to the clients' values in most cases. Rare exceptions might involve values with exceptionally broad consensus (e.g., preventing harm of another person). Then there are covert exceptions. For example, a therapist may decide to confront views of his client in the name of social justice. The therapist is justified based on theory, but this approach may not align with the principle of not imposing values. These cases involve calculated risks. To the extent that the therapist feels protected by professional norms, he can take risks to challenge clients to change their values without fear of repercussions. In some cases, therapists may exert covert pressure without the client's knowledge. This happens when the therapist's values are infused into the entire approach (e.g., at the heart of some multicultural critiques of the entire enterprise of psychotherapy is that a European institution is embedded within other power structures within Western society). What are your initial thoughts on the best way to think about how to ensure that mindfulness is used in an ethically appropriate manner? How would you handle situations in which teaching a client mindfulness might somehow enhance the client's ability to harm other people?

Reactions to Concerns About Appropriation

There is a certain irony in the responses to cultural appropriation. Clearly, concerns about cultural adaptation exert a centripetal force on the expression of mindfulness, but attempts to call mindfulness back to its roots cause greater diffusion. Which roots? There are a lot of options because Buddhism has many variants, given that it moved from India to China, Japan, and other parts of Asia, and then across the globe. Thus, we see varied new mindfulness approaches being developed with the goal of returning to Buddhist roots. Other various new mindfulness approaches seek greater contextualization to marginalized cultural groups (or privileged groups, in many cases). Regardless of the motive for innovation, these reactions continue to contribute to diversification of options for therapeutic mindfulness. In this section, we give a brief sampling of these reactions.

Activity 3.8: What Would the Buddha Think? Imagine that Siddhartha Gautama (the Buddha) woke up today and went to a training in therapeutic mindfulness (e.g., MBSR, mindfulness-based cognitive therapy, dialectical behavior therapy, acceptance and commitment therapy). What aspects of the teaching might seem most strikingly different? What parts might have survived over time and might seem familiar? This may be a good question to keep asking yourself as you learn more about mindfulness and the cultural traditions that brought it to us today in its current form. See if you can even visually imagine the process. For example, you might think of a river with various tributaries. What are the tributaries that you may currently be overlooking in your current perspective of therapeutic mindfulness? What other groups or structures likely influenced the negotiation of how the mindfulness movement was expressed in the United States?

First, there is a response that involves explicit integration of Buddhism. These developers engage authoritative sources within Buddhism to add explicit Buddhist content to their interventions. They seek to conserve and remain true to the original intent of mindfulness within whatever tradition or set of traditions are considered authoritative. Within the literature, these are sometimes referred to as *second-generation mindfulness interventions* (Van Gordon, Shonin, & Griffiths, 2015). The rationale for these interventions has sometimes focused on moral issues (e.g., preventing uses of mindfulness for training snipers or oppressive business systems) or effectiveness (e.g., interventions work better if they align with wisdom refined over many generations within the tradition; see Monteiro et al., 2015). Indeed, 3-minute mindfulness activities are a far cry from the time-honored traditions that have survived many millennia and cultures (Lomas, Etcoff, Van Gordon, & Shonin, 2017).

Second, there is a response that involves implicit integration of Buddhism. These individuals are committed to Buddhism and simultaneously would like to have a seat at the table within psychology. A growing number of psychologists have been influenced by Buddhism (Vieten et al., 2013). At certain times, Kabat-Zinn (1982) seems to frame his work this way. He has described his thinking as infused with his own identity and beliefs. Many psychologists view their spirituality as infused in their work. This response provides an opportunity for ongoing dialogue between Buddhists and people of other faiths to discuss common principles of engaging spirituality while also respecting the faith perspectives of clients and others within one's professional community.

Third, there is a response that involves explicit integration of mindfulness with other faith perspectives. Again, the argument is focused on morality (e.g., a desire to avoid offending clients who may feel disrespected by integration of Buddhist practices into therapy; Stratton, 2015) and effectiveness (e.g., clients will have better outcomes if mindfulness is adapted to their existential worldview). This idea aligns with theory that *sanctification*—viewing an aspect of life through a religious or spiritual lens—amplifies the potency of beliefs or practices (Pargament & Mahoney, 2005). For example, an early study that compared spiritually focused mindfulness with a secular form of mindfulness found that the spiritually oriented condition had stronger effects. More recently, Plante (2010) published an edited volume that describes contemplative traditions within a variety of religious or spiritual backgrounds as well as intentionally ecumenical approaches.

Fourth, there is a response that involves defending the values of the therapist community. We have professional ethical codes, negotiated over many years, within a diverse and pluralistic community. From this view, we can rest assured that psychotherapy is not a nihilistic system that would exploit mindfulness for its own utilitarian ends (in contrast to perhaps the military or corporations). As such, the calls for recontextualization within Buddhist values can be relaxed within the context of psychotherapy (e.g., Baer & Nagy, 2017). In a similar vein, some have appealed to "universal values," such as love or compassion, or have suggested that we can trust the values negotiated by the profession or the values of clients (C. G. Brown, 2017).

Fifth, there are also intersectionality responses in which people are beginning to consider how effective use of mindfulness may require attending to all of the client's salient identities. For example, Christian African Americans may require treatment adaptation that not only aligns with trusted authority structures within the Black church but also explicitly addresses the potential for internalized racism. Mindfulness is not a "blame the victim" approach that puts the burden on clients to come to terms with suffering without also considering their right to pursue justice. Specific adaptation may be required to ensure that mindfulness is not simply an emotion-focused strategy of accepting the status quo and "getting used to" racism (Proulx et al., 2018). Others have noted the paradox that the diffusion of mindfulness is so strong that even though many Asian cultures have strong Buddhist roots, the therapeutic mindfulness approaches in the West may now conflict with the values of some Asian cultures (Hall, Hong, Zane, & Meyer, 2011).

HOW TO MOVE FORWARD

As approaches to using mindfulness proliferate, we view these options as competing for clients, talented researchers (to seek empirical support for the approach), and clinicians who use these approaches in their practices. Put simply, prominent approaches vie for alignment with client preferences, scientific credibility, and gifted therapists. Systemic (e.g., feminist, multicultural) theories predict that the winners of this competition will reflect the power structures within a society. As authors, we are torn about the tension between the need to put the client first and the need to remain (at the very least) aware that the systemic results of "putting the client first" may result in collusion with dynamics that are appropriating an important practice within many Buddhist traditions.

In Chapter 4, we describe the multicultural orientation (MCO) framework as a potential way of holding these cultural concerns about mindfulness in tension. By drawing on the MCO framework, we hope to give therapists a way of beginning to think about the process of psychotherapy that could potentially inform how we engage various options for using mindfulness in our clinical work. For example, when it is okay to use secular forms of mindfulness, and when and how is it important to adapt one's approach to the client's perspective and cultural background? At the same time, we want to honor the various leaders within the Buddhist tradition. It would be self-serving to only listen to gracious voices, such as the Dalai Lama who has given some degree of blessing toward Western interest in mindfulness. We also want to heed the prophetic declarations of those who are concerned about potential misuses and abuses of mindfulness. We are curious if it is possible to hold these values in tension with one another. Can we suitably honor these warnings while also engaging in innovations that will continue to diversify how mindfulness is translated and expressed by different groups?

Before we lay out our ideas based on the MCO framework, we want to end this chapter by posing a few thoughts to frame our subsequent discussion. We are alert to the fact that many Buddhists within the West experience a cultural threat due to the rapid interest in a specific part of their religion or worldview. If the federal government is going to invest hundreds of millions of dollars on empirical research, we see a case to be made for investing in the ability of people from various Buddhist communities to document the variety of reactions they may experience to the mindfulness movement. Drift is happening in many ways, and it seems just and fair to allow communities to name these differences. We see this as a shared investment in honoring rather than collapsing and subsuming differences. For example, for a devout Buddhist, a secular practice may lack ethical framing, community support, community accountability, spiritual goals, and the potential for the integration of wisdom based on the authoritative writings within the tradition. As scholars who are invested in promoting greater responsiveness to spiritual diversity, we hope our professional community can somehow find resources to develop interventions that will appeal to committed Buddhists and come alongside the challenges facing these communities in the West.

Activity 3.9: Consider a Mindfulness Example in Real Life. Again, we want to make sure these ideas connect with current real-world situations. Read the article "Mindfulness-Based Programs and the American Public School System: Recommendations for Best Practices to Ensure Secularity" by Jennings (2016) about the ethical issues regarding use of mindfulness in school. After reading this article, consider the following situation. Imagine you are a school psychologist charged with implementing a mindfulness intervention for students in the fifth grade. How would you engage the minority of parents who have expressed concerns that mindfulness might be introducing religious or spiritual teachings into the schools? If you are not Christian but are living in a predominately Christian area, how would you feel about going to the Parent–Teacher Association and hearing other parents talk about how excited they are because their child will have an opportunity and reminder to pray to Jesus while at school? Would you generally view the inclusion of greater training in spiritual diversity as a positive thing? Or would you tend to prefer stricter boundaries around religious or spiritual content within public education? Would your attitudes differ at all based on the age of the children? How would you react to mindfulness in schools potentially making it easier for people to "share their faith" with others around them?

Here are some thoughts we had about the example. First, it is reasonable to assume that students will tend to integrate what they learn about mindfulness with their own cultural worldview, which, for some students, will involve a strong religious or spiritual lens (Stratton, 2015; Worthington, 1988). For example, in work examining religious accommodation of forgiveness interventions, researchers have found that many participants in the so called "secular" interventions infused the ideas with spiritual meaning (Rye et al., 2005). So, based on what we know about spiritual identity, it is an absolute certainty that some clients will infuse mindfulness with religious or spiritual meaning. So, if we want to promote mindfulness in schools, we have to be prepared to have discussions about spiritual diversity and to hold those spaces with honor and respect and with an awareness of power imbalances (in terms of composition) within the local community.

Second, and related to this point, we see no simple way to "make mindfulness secular." We understand the spirit behind trying to delineate symbols that are clearly religious (e.g., ringing a bell to begin meditation) and those that are deemed appropriately secular. But, a more nuanced view of culture seems to make this a bit of a fool's errand. Just the word *mindfulness* may hold spiritual meaning for some people. Once students have associated mindfulness with aspects of their own religious or spiritual tradition (or of someone else's, after potentially painful experiences of feeling marginalized), it would seem difficult to "force" secularism on the theme.

Therefore, we tend to think our society has a lot of work to do to address cultural diversity, and it may be good to acknowledge how much we have to learn—even within our early educational structures. This awareness may set the stage for new and helpful conversations about what it means to develop interpersonal and emotional skills to engage cultural differences. What do you think? Is mindfulness an inherently religious or spiritual activity? What norms do you think should be in place for pluralistic spaces, such as education?

Third, we encourage you to engage in a general thought experiment: How do you see mindfulness drifting over time? How might the changes occur differently in the United States versus other countries? Imagine the game of telephone mentioned earlier in which people try to share the same message, but the message becomes increasingly distorted from speaker to speaker over time. What seems to help ground the message sufficiently to convey its meaning? What do you imagine it would take for the Buddhist community in the West to "succeed" at "recontextualizing" mindfulness (e.g., Lomas et al., 2017)? Do you think it is possible to do so even if that form of mindfulness does not become as successful as other options that cater to the general public? We suspect that your answers to these questions will inform your thinking about how to integrate mindfulness into your work as therapists.

Fourth, perhaps we can all agree to acknowledge that the psychotherapeutic goal of mindfulness departs substantially from mindfulness within various Buddhist cultures. Indeed, mindfulness-based interventions only touch on beginning skills compared with traditional Buddhism and the prescribed path toward spiritual maturity. To present the starkest of contrasts, there is a different depth to something that requires lifelong devotion (i.e., traditions that involve years of practice within a community and under rigorous instruction) and a cognitive behavior tool that can be learned in 3 minutes. Indeed, many Buddhist traditions have extensive regimens designed to train people to have greater freedom from patterns and reactive ways of thinking—thinking constrained by fear of pain and death. So, consider a few questions. How interested would you be in seeing some psychologists explore how to integrate more advanced ideas of spiritual maturity into their approach as therapists? What limits should be placed on such exploration and inquiry? As a general attitude, do you think it would be generally fruitful for therapists from other traditions (e.g., Islam, Hinduism) to explore a similar integration of psychology and their faith traditions?

Fifth, unless you are a mindfulness expert, we strongly encourage you to undertake a little background reading. At least skim some of the recent and ongoing debates regarding definitions and measures of mindfulness. Listen to a course on the history of Buddhism (e.g., Eckel, 2010). Consider attending a retreat that is open to people wanting to learn more about Buddhism. Even a little exploration can help avoid problems of overconfidence and underestimation of one's limitations in knowledge. We hope all therapists will take steps to avoid errors of taking a myopic view—only looking at conversations over the past 30 years and neglecting to learn about a nearly 3,000-year process of evolution within Buddhist thought and culture. Even a little familiarity with the breadth of both cultural and scientific work on mindfulness can temper our assumptions.

CONCLUSION

From the perspective of cultural humility, we see these conversations of critiques as the beginning of a dialogue—not an end. In its array of diversity, mindfulness is likely here to stay. Research on and dissemination of mindfulness interventions are continuing to proliferate, and there is little reason to expect professional organizations or the federal government to step in and stop the process given their current level of financial investment.

We are pleased to see that after a period of relative calm, the multicultural community has begun to speak up about the important cultural concerns and critiques of mindfulness (e.g., Hall et al., 2011; Masuda, 2014). The concerns seem overdue given the prominence of White (and mostly male) leaders over indigenous people in disseminating mindfulness (Hickey, 2010). Too little of the massive federal investment in mindfulness has gone to considering and investing in the needs of marginalized groups (DeLuca et al., 2018). Thus, the professional community has an important responsibility to amplify the voices of marginalized people.

From an MCO approach, we are especially concerned with potential cultural ruptures as well as processes that would engender greater trust across a range of clients with marginalized identities. We framed the multicultural issues arising from the mindfulness movement as a tension between a value of seeking to avoid cultural appropriation and a desire to align mindfulness with the client's cultural background and existential worldview. We had you engage some of your initial ideas and assumptions about how to balance these values. In the next chapter, we provide an overview of the MCO framework and apply its principles to this issue of using mindfulness with clients from marginalized groups.

4

Understanding a Multicultural Orientation Perspective of Mindfulness

In Chapter 3, we described two key cultural concerns about using mindfulness in therapy. As a result of the multicultural movement, mental health professionals have made a collective commitment to attend to cultural diversity and how it may require contextualization of approaches for clients. What is unique in the case of mindfulness is a second concern: the possibility that adapting mindfulness may contribute to a larger systemic problem in how psychology is using mindfulness for its own purposes. Some people have sought responsiveness from psychologists regarding how we approach practices inspired by indigenous cultures, including, in this case, spiritual practices. For people wanting to use mindfulness in their clinical work, it may seem difficult to simultaneously attend to these conflicts and hold them in tension.

The purpose of the present chapter is to consider these potentially conflicting critiques from the perspective of the multicultural orientation (MCO) framework (Owen, Tao, Leach, & Rodolfa, 2011; for a review, see Davis et al., 2018). As we elaborate, we see a natural fit between the core tenants of MCO and common principles of therapeutic mindfulness approaches. First, we review factors that motivated the MCO development, define and illustrate key concepts, and demonstrate how these concepts overlap with mindfulness-based practices. Second, we describe research evidence supporting the MCO framework and evaluate the developing literature on integrating mindfulness into psychotherapy from the lens of the MCO framework. Third, given the focus of this book on spiritual diversity and use of mindfulness with clients

http://dx.doi.org/10.1037/0000156-004
Mindfulness-Based Practices in Therapy: A Cultural Humility Approach, by D. Davis, C. DeBlaere, J. N. Hook, and J. Owen

from marginalized groups, we end the chapter by contrasting a self-assessment based on the competencies tradition with a measure of cultural comfort for working with spiritual issues in therapy.

DEVELOPMENT OF THE MULTICULTURAL ORIENTATION FRAMEWORK

The MCO framework is a descendant of the multicultural competencies (MCCs) tradition and was developed to integrate multicultural theory into research on psychotherapy. The MCC tradition exerted tremendous influence on the discipline of psychology and allied disciplines (e.g., Constantine & Sue, 2005). Scholars presented converging evidence documenting disparities in the care provided to racial and ethnic minorities (e.g., Drinane, Owen, & Tao, 2018; Imel et al., 2011; D. W. Sue, Arredondo, & McDavis, 1992) and, later, other marginalized groups (Drinane, Winderman, Roberts, Frierson Freeman, & Wang, 2019; D. W. Sue, 2017). The tireless work of groundbreaking scholars allowed advances in our knowledge of identity development, the impact of prejudice and discrimination, and the various ways that culture can play an important role in the counseling process.

Nonetheless, as the scientific community took stock after nearly 50 years, we realized that an important gap remained in terms of initial goals of the multicultural competence literature (S. Sue, Zane, Nagayama Hall, & Berger, 2009). One of the most important gaps was the need to establish stronger evidence linking MCCs (particularly as a therapist effect) to better therapy outcomes. Many theories had been proposed, but none had demonstrated strong evidence linking therapist MCCs to better outcomes in therapy. This conclusion was based on limitations in two lines of work based on two different strategies (S. Sue et al., 2009).

Cultural Adaptation Strategy

One strategy for establishing the importance of cultural competence was to adapt existing treatments to discrete cultural groups. In this approach, the researcher first makes a case (theoretical or empirical) that a treatment is less effective or inappropriate for certain groups (e.g., cognitive behavior therapy [CBT] for African American clients). On the basis of this rationale, the therapist adapts the treatment to potentially actualize the potential for improving outcomes by tailoring the treatment to the group. Although a crude strategy that overlooks heterogeneity within groups, the approach has demonstrated better effectiveness in some cases, especially when researchers carefully consider a cultural group's needs, work to reduce barriers, and seek to capitalize on strengths (see Huey, Tilley, Jones, & Smith, 2014; Soto, Smith, Griner, Rodriguez, & Bernal, 2018).

Despite average benefits, the approach does not attend to issues of intersectionality and multiple marginalized identities, and some individuals respond poorly to explicit adaptions that are executed rigidly and without careful alignment to what is happening in the process of therapy (Huey et al., 2014). In addition, Huey et al. (2014) noted that more overt adaptations were associated with worse outcomes as compared with more implicit adaptations. The other limitation is pragmatic: It simply isn't feasible for therapists to learn adapted approaches to CBT for the range of ethnic identities, much less the intersections of several identities (e.g., CBT for depression for African Americans, CBT for anxiety with gay Asian men, mindfulness for older Latinx adults who are coping with loss).

Therapist-Focused Multicultural Competencies

The second approach has been to try to train therapists to become more culturally competent. This theoretical rationale played a prominent role in integrating multicultural values and approaches into the training of psychologists and counselors. However, despite these efforts, the impact of MCCs on client outcomes has been mixed (see Tao, Owen, Pace, & Imel, 2015). When clients see their therapists as higher in MCCs, they also report better therapy outcomes (on the order of 5%–7% of the variance of therapy outcomes). The problem is that the few studies that have sought to estimate MCC as a therapist effect (i.e., aggregated across client ratings) have found weak convergence of client ratings. That is, an implied assumption in therapists' MCCs is that some therapists are more culturally competent than others, and this cultural competence is an attribute that is somewhat consistent across clients. However, current research findings have provided no support for this assumption. Rather, it appears that cultural competence appears to be a dyadic process that is cocreated in a various and different ways across clients of the same therapist (Owen, Leach, et al., 2011). Given the low reliability of client ratings, MCCs as a therapist effect had little chance of accounting for better therapy outcomes (Owen, Leach, et al., 2011). These findings clarified earlier work documenting that clients' and therapists' perspectives of MCC showed little convergence (e.g., Fuertes & Brobst, 2002; Fuertes et al., 2006).

Based on the existing strategy, there are two major concerns. First, when rating the same therapists, clients do not seem to agree with one another (Owen, Leach, et al., 2011) or the therapist about the level of MCCs (Fuertes et al., 2006). Second, we currently know little about the kinds of behaviors or skills that can influence how a client sees his or her therapist's degree of MCCs (Owen, 2013). Multicultural competencies appear to function more like a relational construct (e.g., alliance) that rises or falls based on qualities of the therapist and the client and their interaction with each other.[1]

[1]For the interested reader, there are several other empirical challenges, including measurement concerns (see Drinane, Owen, Adelson, & Rodolfa, 2016) and overreliance on cross-sectional studies (see Tao et al., 2015).

Four Trends Informing the Multicultural Orientation Framework

These findings were daunting and required an abrupt shift in strategies for assessing therapist effects associated with MCCs. Therefore, Owen, Tao, et al. (2011) developed the MCO framework to address persistent challenges in establishing the link between MCCs and therapy outcomes (for a review, see Davis et al., 2018). To make the approach accessible, they intentionally focused on processes that could apply to any therapy approach or orientation. The MCO framework describes a way of being (i.e., cultural humility), a way of identifying key moments (i.e., cultural opportunities), and a way of understanding one's emotional reactions in session (i.e., cultural comfort) throughout the unfolding process of psychotherapy.

The following is an overview of the four trends that informed the development of the MCO framework (Davis et al., 2018). First, the research we just summarized led us to conclude that a new strategy would be needed. We began to explore areas for potential theoretical convergence between theories of multiculturalism and theories of psychotherapy process. We were particularly interested in concrete theories about how therapists might orient themselves toward clients from marginalized groups in a way that would enhance therapy outcomes. In this process, it was essential that MCO ideas could be easily integrated into the larger literature on psychotherapy change processes so that the approach could be easily adopted within theoretical approaches. We recognize that this approach also means an attempt to infuse cultural processes into systems (i.e., cultures) of psychotherapy that have a long history within a particular ethos, belief systems, and values—for better and for worse.

Second, the MCO framework aligns with theory and research on empirically supported psychotherapy relationships (e.g., empathy, working alliance, real relationship; Norcross & Lambert, 2018). The MCO framework provides therapists a way of being in session that is not dogmatic but rather seeks alignment with general principles of effective psychotherapy (e.g., flexibility, genuineness, openness, focus; Norcross & Lambert, 2018). In addition, we encourage therapists to attend to sociocultural–political factors that influence clients and therapists in their daily lives (e.g., Ivey, D'Andrea, Ivey, & Simek-Morgan, 2007). That is, we want to encourage therapists to consider systemic influences in their daily lives, to be more conscious of their role within these systems, and to be internally motivated to make changes. Accordingly, the MCO framework describes how processes of therapy interact with cultural dynamics in the relationship between the therapist and the client as well as others (and systems).

Third, the MCO framework uses orientation rather than competence language. We see the MCO tradition as an extension of similar values within a different context. Rightly so, the MCC movement prioritized the goal of causing structural changes in a profession that was poorly serving the needs of marginalized groups. In contrast, the MCO framework focuses on a specific problem: the lack of integration of multicultural theory into research and practice on psychotherapy. Orientation language is familiar to psychotherapists. Just like therapists are encouraged to commit to a theoretical orientation(s), which involves a community and professional culture with training structures (e.g., conceptualization, theory of change, interpretation of the process of therapy), they can also develop a similar professional identity and approach to attending to cultural diversity. In practice, competence language sometimes translates into attempts to articulate minimal standards for the purpose of gatekeeping. As many multicultural theories clearly assert (Foronda, Baptiste, Reinholdt, & Ousman, 2016; Tervalon & Murray-García, 1998), developing maturity to address cultural diversity requires a lifelong commitment and the growing ability to engage culturally difficult and ambiguous situations.

As we considered the implications of theories of intersectionality (e.g., Cole, 2009), it seemed implausible to keep pushing the traditional approach to studying MCCs one identity at a time. Intersectionality theory views identity as a dynamic and interlocking interaction of one's life experiences, development, and sense of belonging to and differentiation from various social groups within a matrix of power and dominance (Cole, 2009; Crenshaw, 1989). It highlights how a person (e.g., an atheist Asian American female) might experience multiple levels of marginalization. The confluence of exclusion may lead to a unique type of stress and adversity. Intersectionality theory also provides an account of why researchers in the multicultural community have had a difficult time capturing what aspects of culture are influencing the therapy process. Moreover, the saliency of any given identity might vary based on the unique cultural interaction between the client and therapist.

Historically, MCC approaches tended to focus on singular identities without attending to how most people's experiences reflect a unique intersection of their various salient identities in context. An intersectional perspective made it easier to see how many of the prior measures lacked content validity. For example, consider a measure of working with African American clients. We might not see it as having adequately sampled the appropriate domains if it did not include content focused on gender (i.e., many women experience sexism) or religion (i.e., many people have strong commitments to a religious or spiritual worldview; Boyd-Franklin, 2010; Constantine, Lewis, Conner, & Sanchez, 2000). Thus, the intersectional perspective was the theory that led us to assume that while maintaining similar values, an entirely different and pragmatic approach might be required to advance research that could provide practical and actionable implications for the work of doing therapy that integrates cultural issues.

MULTICULTURAL ORIENTATION FRAMEWORK AND MINDFULNESS

The early formulation of the MCO framework described three constructs (Owen, 2013), including a way of being (i.e., cultural humility), noticing and attending to culturally important moments (i.e., cultural opportunities), and noticing cultural reactions within the self (i.e., cultural comfort). These are the three pillars of the framework, although future work could potentially articulate additional constructs that might fall within these three domains.

In the following section, we describe each of these constructs and highlight how they dovetail with theorizing on therapeutic presence (Geller & Greenberg, 2012; Geller & Porges, 2014). Drawing on polyvagal theory (Porges, 2011), they suggest that what allows clients to form a strong therapy alliance is being with a therapist who has refined his or her ability to attend to the range of his or her own feelings and experiences. According to polyvagal theory, clients unconsciously intuit psychological safety often through reading nonverbal cues of a situation. When clients experience indicators of psychological safety—through facial expressions, gestures, and prosodic vocalization—they experience less defensiveness. Thus, therapists' attunement cultivates a sense of psychological safety in clients, which helps promote conditions in which psychological healing is possible. Clients can let down their guard and engage in the difficult work of therapy. This theorizing also aligns with a variety of theoretical orientations that focus on the quality of the therapist's attunement to the process of therapy (Geller & Greenberg, 2012).

Cultural Humility

Cultural humility is a foundational value of the MCO framework. It grounds the therapist's entire way of being with a sense of integrity and other relationship-oriented characteristics described within humanistic therapy approaches. Cultural humility is a subdomain of humility that refers to how people seek to understand their own and other's cultural experiences. Specifically, *cultural humility* is defined as "the ability to maintain an interpersonal stance that is other-oriented (or open to the other) in relation to aspects of cultural identity that are most important to the client" (Hook, Davis, Owen, Worthington, & Utsey, 2013, p. 354).

For several reasons, the training of therapists may interfere with the promotion of a nonjudgmental, open, curious stance. Indeed, current training practices assume beliefs about the nature of psychopathology (e.g., assumptions based on the *Diagnostic and Statistical Manual of Mental Disorders* [fifth ed.; American Psychiatric Association, 2013]), psychological health (e.g., lack of course work on positive ways of being), and relational functioning (e.g., how individuals should interact with one another). One of the major impetuses for the multicultural movement was that the perspectives of marginalized groups were not at the table when developing foundational theories and approaches. Accordingly, many perspectives are not fully accounted for in the understanding of distress, health, and healing. Therefore, given a long history of exclusion of marginalized voices within psychology, clients have legitimate reasons to wonder about the responsiveness they will encounter when attending therapy.

The core aspects of cultural humility align naturally with mindfulness, especially regarding values of openness to others, curiosity, unconditional positive regard, and a lack of judgment (Geller & Greenberg, 2012). Therapy often evokes cultural dynamics that can undermine collaboration, such as therapists' assuming an expert role or judging the client's actions, thoughts, and feelings. In addition, therapists may hold cultural beliefs rooted in psychotherapy theories (e.g., quest for radical independence) that can evoke a defensive response in their clients. These defensive processes may develop into patterns that can damage the therapy relationship. Cultural humility is a quality that can protect a relationship from the wear and tear of such dynamics, and therapists can draw on mindfulness-related skills to express cultural humility in sessions. For example, they can slow down their reactive chain of thoughts to invite conversations about the client's cultural beliefs and values. If fully integrated, cultural humility should activate a reminder that therapists are fallible, imperfect, and make assumptions on limited information. Meditation practices can provide therapists with training in sitting with whatever feelings arise in the moment and facing them without defensiveness or reactivity but, instead, adopting a present-centered, curious, and reflective stance (Geller & Greenberg, 2012).

Cultural Opportunities

Cultural opportunities are the second pillar of the MCO framework. *Cultural opportunities* are "markers that occur in therapy in which the client's cultural beliefs, values, or other aspects of the client's cultural identity could be explored" (Owen et al., 2016, p. 31). These markers can originate from clients' statements (e.g., a client who states that religion or spirituality is an important aspect of his or her identity) or from the therapists' approach to therapy (e.g., asking a client about the client's salient cultural beliefs). Regardless, when therapists encounter an opportunity to engage a cultural issue, they should have the flexibility and courage to express interest and learn more about that aspect of the client's life.

Once again, we see that the abilities trained over time through mindfulness practices can support therapists in the context of engaging their own or the client's cultural beliefs and values. Consider the case example in the box that follows.

Case Example: Debbie

Debbie, a 45-year-old, White, cisgender, able-bodied, middle–upper socioeconomic, female therapist, has been using a present-centered breathing exercise with her client Claire, a 29-year-old, Chinese American, cisgender, able-bodied, middle-class, female client, to help both of them become more focused and attuned at the beginning of the session. After completing this activity at the beginning of the third session, Claire has a negative reaction. Debbie notices a grimace on Claire's face and asks her what happened. In response, Claire describes feeling shame about her divorce, which got worse as she was engaging in the meditation. Until recently, she had successfully avoided many of her feelings, but in the stillness of the moment, she felt a sharp flash of pain as a variety of feelings flooded her awareness. Moreover, Claire finally discloses that she has not really been doing the assigned sitting meditations at home. Similar things had happened, so she just stopped and never said anything.

After these important disclosures, Debbie invites Claire to explore the feelings that came up for her. Claire is willing. She elaborates on the meaning of the divorce in her family. They experienced the end of the relationship as a deep insult to the family's honor. Although Claire has never talked with her father about what happened, she anticipated his rejection, which seemed unbearable to her. She said that often ruminating about his rejection led to a precipitous chain of thoughts and feelings that left her feeling utterly hopeless and alone and thinking about killing herself.

Now, Debbie has an important decision to make. She could focus on the symptoms, especially the suicidal ideation. Alternatively, she could also continue to explore the novel disclosure regarding family values about divorce. In prior sessions, Claire had certainly connected the divorce to the onset of her depressive symptoms, but this was the first time that she had alluded to strong cultural values in her family that were amplifying her feelings of shame, distress, and alienation. This time, Debbie decides to explore the new and emotionally active content associated with the cultural meaning of divorce for Claire because it seems especially connected to her values, cultural identities, and possibility of eventually envisioning a way forward.

This example provides a window into how common cultural opportunities can be in therapy. Part of what allowed Debbie the flexibility to attend to the cultural content in front of her was her long-term meditation practices. Earlier in her training, she might have gotten pulled off center by the scary content related to suicidal ideation. She would have worried about pleasing her supervisor or "getting things right," and this would have made it hard for her to take a risk. Instead, this time, she was patient, which gave her a sense of freedom and receptiveness to the moment. She was able to trust herself and attune herself to the client, including some of Claire's nonverbal reactions that made it clear to Debbie that the cultural content was especially salient.

This case example illustrates how a culturally humble approach helped the therapist join with the client. She followed the content that was most emotionally active with an openness to explore how the client's cultural identities were connected to her pain. This decision required courage, trust for the process, and confidence that there would be time to revisit the assessment of suicide risk later in the session. A less culturally oriented therapist might have let the internal anxiety drive the remainder of the session, which might not have given the client as much of a chance to integrate some of the deeply distressing feelings associated with the divorce.

Cultural Comfort

Cultural comfort is the third pillar in the MCO framework and involves expressing a sense of ease, openness, calm, or relaxation when engaging cultural topics or dynamics in psychotherapy (Owen et al., 2017). Importantly, just like courage is not the absence of fear, cultural comfort involves the ability to tolerate the natural aversion one feels when facing potentially uncomfortable cultural situations. As such, for therapists with refined cultural comfort, they can regulate their emotions to remain flexible, responsive, and engaged during cultural situations that tend to evoke egotism and defensiveness in most people. Another important point is that it is all right if one notices feelings of strong cultural discomfort. It is unrealistic (and entirely unhelpful) to hold oneself to unrealistic standards of being an android—completely flat emotionally. These major shifts in cultural comfort provide us with an internal cue that something important may be happening within the process of therapy (akin to countertransference reactions). Wise therapists learn to use such cues to devote all their available energy to attending to the moment and sorting through how their own experience may be influenced by what is happening in session.

Therapists who develop mindfulness-related habits get comfortable with a range of disconcerting feelings or shifts in feeling tone without being pulled into a cycle of reactivity. For example, in the session segment with Debbie, what if she had refrained from asking questions that might have led to her own or the client's discomfort? This choice might have begun or perpetuated a pattern of avoiding the conversations that could help the client heal and grow. Instead, from her own experiences in meditation, Debbie had learned to stay with her emotional reactions and let them rise and fall without having to take drastic measures to get rid of them. Her own patience to accept and follow the full course of her own emotions helped her gently, but confidently, lead the client into a similar experience. Furthermore, what really helped Debbie proceed when she might have otherwise turned back was her ability to quickly recognize judgmental thoughts. When she started to criticize herself, she saw these introjects for what they were and returned to a place of inner kindness, which also kept her emotional tone positive and engaged for her client.

Initial Research Supporting the Multicultural Orientation Framework

Initial research on the MCO framework has yielded promising results with psychotherapy data on more than 5,000 clients (and counting), and measures have been developed for the three constructs within the MCO framework (for a review, see Davis et al., 2018; Kivlighan, Adams, Drinane, Tao, & Owen, 2019). In addition, the MCO model has demonstrated links to key therapy processes and outcomes (for a review, see Davis et al., 2018). For instance, in a sample of clients at a university counseling center, cultural comfort not only predicted perceptions of improvement but also premature termination (Owen et al., 2017). Clients' perceptions of their therapists' cultural humility have been shown to predict positive therapy outcomes across studies, which further reinforces the foundational aspect of this element of the MCO framework (Davis et al., 2018). In addition, clients' perceptions of cultural opportunities were a significant predictor of positive therapy outcomes in multiple studies (Owen et al., 2015, 2016).

Multicultural orientation constructs have also been linked to relational processes of psychotherapy. More specifically, several studies found that people report a stronger therapy alliance to the degree that they view their therapist as culturally humble (e.g., Hook et al., 2013). Alternatively, clients who experience cultural offenses (or microaggressions) in therapy tend to view their therapist as less culturally humble (Hook et al., 2016). Recently, one study found that cultural offenses (or microaggressions) were more negatively related to viewing one's therapist as culturally humble when women of color had a White therapist relative to a therapist who was a person of color (DeBlaere et al., 2018). Furthermore, when cultural offenses were experimentally manipulated in the lab, prospective clients exposed to a microaggression tended to rate their therapist as lower on MCO constructs (i.e., cultural humility, opportunities, and comfort; Owen et al., 2018).

To this point, most work has focused on the client's perspective, so future work might benefit from multimethod approaches that integrate therapist perspectives with client ratings (and perhaps observer ratings). It is also possible that, aside from the three pillars, other related constructs might be integrated into the theoretical approach. For example, a recent paper focused on the degree to which clients felt they had to conceal important aspects of their identity (which represents an integration of cultural comfort and missed cultural opportunities; Drinane et al., 2018). Altogether, the MCO framework is one of only a few process-based approaches for psychotherapy that is culturally focused and empirically supported.

MULTICULTURAL COMPETENCIES AND MULTICULTURAL ORIENTATION AS COMPLEMENTARY WAYS TO GROW

The focus of this book is using mindfulness with clients from marginalized groups while also attending to the potential intersection of spiritual identity. For you to get a sense of how MCC and MCO approaches complement each other, we want you to participate in self-assessment to set the stage for the rest of the book (i.e., engaging in a lifelong process of growing in cultural comfort [see Chapter 5] and then integrating MCO into the phases of therapy).

Self-Assessment of Religious or Spiritual Competencies

Before we consider what cultural comfort might look like in the area of religion or spirituality, we first want to give you a sense of what self-assessment might look like from a traditional MCCs perspective. Vieten et al. (2013) generated an initial set of competencies with a team of mental health professionals who specialize in working with religious and spiritual issues. They piloted items with a sample of 184 mental health professionals and then worked with their team to reduce the initial pool of items to the 16 listed in Exhibit 4.1.

EXHIBIT 4.1

Proposed Religious and Spiritual Competencies for Psychologists

Attitudes

1. Psychologists demonstrate empathy, respect, and appreciation for clients from diverse spiritual, religious, or secular backgrounds and affiliations.
2. Psychologists view spirituality and religion as an important aspect of human diversity along with factors such as race, ethnicity, sexual orientation, socioeconomic status, disability, gender, and age.
3. Psychologists are aware of how their own spiritual or religious background and beliefs may influence their clinical practice and their attitudes, perceptions, and assumptions about the nature of psychological processes.

Knowledge

4. Psychologists know that many diverse forms of spirituality or religion exist and explore spiritual or religious beliefs, communities, and practices that are important to their clients.
5. Psychologists can describe how spirituality and religion can be viewed as overlapping yet distinct constructs.
6. Psychologists understand that clients may have experiences that are consistent with their spirituality or religion yet may be difficult to differentiate from psychological symptoms.
7. Psychologists recognize that spiritual or religious beliefs, practices, and experiences develop and change over the life span.
8. Psychologists are aware of internal and external spiritual or religious resources and practices that research indicates may support psychological well-being and recovery from psychological disorders.
9. Psychologists can identify spiritual and religious experiences, practices, and beliefs that may have the potential to negatively impact psychological health.
10. Psychologists can identify legal and ethical issues related to spirituality or religion that may surface when working with clients.

(*continues*)

EXHIBIT 4.1

Proposed Religious and Spiritual Competencies for Psychologists (*Continued*)

Skills

11. Psychologists are able to conduct empathetic and effective psychotherapy with clients form diverse spiritual or religious backgrounds, affiliations, and levels of involvement.
12. Psychologists inquire about spiritual or religious background, expedience, practices, attitudes, and beliefs as a standard part of understanding a client's history.
13. Psychologists help clients explore and access their spiritual or religious strengths and resources.
14. Psychologists can identify and address spiritual or religious problems in clinical practice and make referrals when necessary.
15. Psychologists stay abreast of research and professional developments regarding spirituality and religion specifically related to clinical practice and engage in ongoing assessment of their own spiritual and religious competence.
16. Psychologists recognize the limits of their qualifications and competence in the spiritual or religious domains, including any responses to clients' spirituality or religion that may interfere with clinical practice, so that they (a) seek consultation from and collaborate with other qualified clinicians or spiritual or religious sources (e.g., priests, pastors, rabbis, imam, spiritual teachers), (b) seek further training and education, or (c) refer appropriate clients to more qualified individuals and resources, or some combination of the three.

Note. Adapted from "Spiritual and Religious Competencies for Psychologists," by C. Vieten, S. Scammell, R. Pilato, I. Ammondson, K. I. Pargament, and D. Lukoff, 2013, *Psychology of Religion and Spirituality, 5*, pp. 135–138. Copyright 2013 by the American Psychological Association.

Activity 4.1: Complete the Measure of Religious or Spiritual Competencies. For this activity, using a scale ranging from 1 (*strongly disagree*) to 5 (*strongly agree*), rate each item in Exhibit 4.1 on your degree of confidence that you would be able to meet the standard while working with one of the clients you considered in the mindfulness exercise. As you rate the items, feel free to make notes about any thoughts that come to mind or feelings you experience. What clinical situations did you think of? Were your ideas vague or generally based on stereotypes? Or did you perhaps think of specific examples based on relationships you have formed in your life? In addition to these questions, questions in Exhibit 4.2 can help you explore how your own cultural identities may influence your work with clients who have a strong commitment to a religion or spirituality. You may want to write down or journal your responses. We also recommend discussing these questions with a trusted colleague or friend because it can be especially helpful to explore these ideas within your close relationships.

Self-Assessment of Cultural Comfort

Now that you have familiarized yourself with a recent and standard measure based on traditional MCCs, we want you to consider yourself from an MCO

EXHIBIT 4.2

Questions for Exploring Religious and Spiritual Competencies

We can all identify interactions in which we felt strong negative or positive attitudes toward another person because of our differing religious or spiritual identities or lack thereof. We can begin to explore some of the assumptions, biases, or identities that may have led to those reactions. With a discussion partner or within your journal, consider the following questions:

1. At what times do you feel less safe regarding religious or spiritual differences or discussions? What are some of the cultural ruptures related to religion or spirituality that you hope will never happen again in your life?
2. Can you think of clients you have seen who were from religious or spiritual cultures you knew little about?
3. Can you think of examples when having more implicit knowledge of your client's community as well as the variability within that client's community (e.g., within group differences) that might have helped strengthen the therapy relationship?
4. Which clients might have noticed that you were uncomfortable addressing religious or spiritual issues in session? How do you think they were able to discern your discomfort?
5. Can you remember any times when your clients seemed to react as though you did not fully understand how their religious or spiritual community might view the presenting problem?
6. Can you think of times early in your training or more recently when you failed to appreciate religion or spirituality as a source of strength? Or can you think of times when you were overly optimistic and did not fully acknowledge how negative religious or spiritual experiences were amplifying your client's distress?
7. Can you think of times when you have done things that fell short of aspirational standards of ethical practice (e.g., need for appropriate consent, boundaries of competence)?

perspective and assess your own cultural comfort for working with religious or spiritual diversity (Owen et al., 2017). According to Worthington (1988), people have zones of toleration for different religious or spiritual values based on three dimensions: the authority of religious or spiritual leaders, the authority of scriptures or sacred texts, and the degree to which one ought to conform to in-group social norms. Although originally focused on religious or spiritual culture, we want to extend the concept to consider other sources of cultural comfort and discomfort. Therapists vary in their cultural comfort for engaging diverse cultural identities based on their past experiences, loyalties, and commitments. They have sources of authority for evaluating ideas and develop patterns of thinking within training communities. As therapists get older, they may become part of different groups with different and conflicting norms for forming beliefs, moral judgments, and negotiating ways of being.

To explore potential areas of cultural comfort and discomfort, consider the case example in the box that follows.

Case Example: Geoff

The therapist, Geoff, is a 32-year-old White, cisgender, gay man who is completing an external rotation at a community mental health center. Geoff grew up going to church but stopped doing so in high school when he came out as gay and realized that his church was not affirming of his sexual identity. The client, Candice, is a 43-year-old African American, cisgender, heterosexual woman. Candice identifies as Christian and attends an African American church in her town. She is married and has three children. She is attending counseling for help with depression, anxiety, and family issues particularly focused on her oldest son whom she reports is being disobedient and disrespectful at home. Her son, aged 15, also recently was arrested for marijuana possession.

Geoff feels that he has made a good initial connection with Candice, although he feels some apprehension about the cultural differences between them (e.g., race, gender, religion and spirituality, sexual orientation). For example, Geoff gets the sense that Candice's religious or spiritual involvement is important to her because she reports attending services every week and being involved in the church community. However, because of his lack of experience, he is unsure about how to talk about religion or spirituality in the therapy room, or whether this topic would even be appropriate for conversation. He also recalls some of his own frustration with religion or spirituality growing up and how his moving away from religion or spirituality in high school was a point of conflict between his parents and him. Geoff wonders if Candice's son is experiencing something similar with his family, but he doesn't want his own experiences to get in the way of Candice's process. Geoff makes the decision to focus mainly on Candice's goals of symptom reduction and talk about religion or spirituality (and other aspects of culture) only if it seems clearly connected to the presenting problem. As a result, Geoff shies away from even thinking about using mindfulness with this client. He worries that using mindfulness may require delving into religious or spiritual themes, which might complicate the process of therapy.

What did you think of this case example? What was your reaction to how Geoff responded to Candice, particularly around issues related to her cultural background? How culturally comfortable do you believe Geoff is? How would you have responded if you were Geoff? What cultural opportunities were present or could be discussed?

Activity 4.2: Engage in Additional Practice. Read the following three brief client identity descriptions. We have intentionally varied the religious and spiritual identity of the client. Imagine what it would be like to sit with the client. Imagine having a conversation with the client about using mindfulness in therapy or as an adjunctive to therapy. Attend to sources of greater ease or discomfort. For each client, sit for 30 seconds and imagine being with this person. Then, using a scale ranging from 1 (*not at all comfortable*) to 10 (*completely comfortable*), rate the degree to which you would feel comfortable engaging the client, including having a conversation about the potential fit of using mindfulness within the session or as an adjunctive to therapy.

Case 1. A strongly religious client from a Pentecostal background from West Virginia

Case 2. A client from California who grew up strongly religious but, after deconversion, now identifies as spiritual but not religious and is exploring various Eastern spiritual perspectives

Case 3. A client who identifies as atheist and lives in Atlanta, Georgia

Activity 4.3: Think About Challenging Intersections. Now we want you to consider other potential intersecting identities. For example, when you thought about the three cases describe in Activity 4.2, what race, ethnicity, or gender did you imagine? Now, consider what systemic influences might be different if the client were a different race, ethnicity, or gender than you had originally imagined. We have created a grid to help with this thought exercise (see Exhibit 4.3). For each box, enter the potential cultural systemic influences that could impact your interactions with the client.

After doing some introspection, what configuration of identities did you imagine would be most challenging? What would concern you most about your ability to sit with the client and engage comfortably in discussions about religion or spirituality and the potential fit of mindfulness for your work with the client? Also, what configuration of identities did you imagine might be easiest? What about this configuration of identities and related experiences feels more comfortable for you to engage? What was a configuration you imagined as moderately difficult?

Activity 4.4: Complete the Cultural Comfort Scale. Now that you have explored situations that might benefit from consideration of potential intersecting identities, we want you to think of two clients: one with a moderately difficult

EXHIBIT 4.3

Intersectionality and Cultural Dynamics Grid

Case	Gender	Race or ethnicity	Sexual orientation	Ability status	Other identities
Case 1					
Case 2					
Case 3					

EXHIBIT 4.4

Cultural Comfort Subscale of the Multicultural Orientation Inventory

As described in Activity 4.4, please think of two cases: one that is moderately difficult and one that is very difficult culturally. Then, as you think about the last time you were with this client and had an opportunity to engage his or her most salient cultural identities, rate how you felt at the time using the following scale: 1 (*strongly disagree*), 2 (*mildly disagree*), 3, (*neutral*), 4 (*mildly agree*), 5 (*strongly agree*). Overall, how comfortable did you feel imagining yourself in this situation?

1. Comfortable
2. Awkward
3. Tense
4. Nervous
5. Confident
6. Uneasy
7. Relaxed
8. Calm
9. Edgy
10. Genuine

Note. To score these items, first reverse score items 2, 3, 4, 6, and 9 (e.g., if your score was a 5, it becomes a 1; a score of 2 becomes a 4, etc.). Adapted from "Construction and Validation of the Multicultural Orientation Inventory—Group Version," by D. M. Kivlighan III, M. C. Adams, J. M. Drinane, K. W. Tao, and J. Owen, 2019, *Journal of Counseling Psychology, 66*, pp. 54–55. Copyright 2019 by the American Psychological Association.

and one with a very difficult configuration of identities. Part of what may make these two cases seem difficult might be the context or things that have already happened in the relationship. Once you have thought of these two cases, fill out the measure provided in Exhibit 4.4. Then, based on the instructions (i.e., create a total score), score the measure for each client. These two scores can provide a baseline for your therapy work. It is possible that engaging in the exercises in this chapter may help increase your cultural comfort for these cases and can generalize to other aspects of your therapy work with religious or spiritual diversity. Our hope is that this preliminary exploration will help you develop greater confidence and flexibility to handle the various situations that may arise as you integrate mindfulness into your work.

AWARENESS OF LIMITATIONS AS A STARTING POINT

Cultural humility suggests that being aware of one's limitations is the starting point of growth and good work with cultural diversity. The kind of self-assessment you just did can be daunting if engaged honestly. Therapists and clients alike have complex histories and feelings related to culture and especially religion or spirituality. So, it is normal to feel intimidated by one's limits.

As daunting as this may feel, it is a good sign and the grounds for future growth if invested wisely. It is a good sign to have questions about your clients' cultural backgrounds. Although clients are a great source of information, it is not their responsibility to fully educate therapists. Accordingly, what avenues could you pursue to deepen your understanding of your clients' cultural values and beliefs?

Activity 4.5: Secure Support and Accountability. Growth in MCO requires persistence and support from others. Accordingly, we want you to identify at least two partners you can work with to clarify your goals and provide you with encouragement as you seek to grow in cultural comfort. First, find someone who knows you well, perhaps someone who shares important cultural identities. Sharing salient identities can allow for validation of your experiences, questions, and feelings. Second, find another person who can give you a different perspective, maybe someone who is several stages ahead of you in his or her life and career. Perhaps that person has cultural identities that will give you access to an unfamiliar perspective. (One caveat: Make sure to consider whether your request is appropriate to the current level of trust in the relationship because it would be problematic to tokenize someone from a marginalized group while responding to an activity in a book on cultural humility.)

Regardless of who you decide to connect with, it is important that you formally approach that person, describe your goals, and ask that person to commit to providing a supportive, encouraging, and reliable structure for supporting your goals. Coordinate a time to talk. Share with that person the activities you completed in this chapter and describe the cases you imagined. Also, tell that person about any similar situations you have experienced clinically or personally. Discuss the general baseline you established in terms of religious or spiritual competencies. Talk about the feelings that you experienced. This first step takes your intention to develop in your level of cultural comfort from an internal dialogue to actionable steps. You are establishing a commitment to grow in awareness of your strengths and limitations.

CONCLUSION

In this chapter, we reviewed factors that led to the MCO model and described its key components and initial research of the framework within psychotherapy. Then, we suggested that the MCO framework is a potential way to initiate an infusion of multicultural values into the mindfulness movement. The MCO framework urges therapists to commit to a process of engaging discomfort, promoting positive emotional engagement, and cultivating habits that broaden one's cultural span.

The process, elaborated on in the next chapter, is not for the faint of heart. Our hope is that you will do much more than just read this book and drift back into old habits. Each of us must put ourselves at the crossroads of good feedback, find stable sources of encouragement and replenishing, and develop habits of life so that we can be accountable to our goals. The rest of the book envisions what this might look like, but to prepare for the journey, we encouraged you to do self-assessment. We contrasted a traditional measure of MCC with an approach aligned with the MCO framework.

5

Increasing Cultural Comfort for Spiritual Diversity

In Chapter 4, we learned about the multicultural orientation (MCO) framework as a complement to traditional multicultural competency (MCC) models. Before we turn to the implications of the MCO framework for parts of the therapy process, it is important to understand and commit to the process required for therapists to grow in cultural comfort for addressing religious or spiritual identity and its intersection with other identities. Holding and maturing in our identities places complex and competing demands on people (Cole, 2009). This chapter aligns with what typically falls under the self-awareness component of MCC models. Consistent with the MCC tradition (D. W. Sue & Sue, 2016), we firmly uphold the need for therapists to commit to a lifelong process of personal growth and a willingness to engage difficult and sometimes painful feelings to increase their tolerance for moral ambiguity and diversity (Davis et al., 2018). Specifically, how do therapists refine their skill at forming cooperative and trusting relationships when cultural differences or similarities might make those connections especially difficult?

To answer this question, we draw on theory and research on how people develop expertise and apply those ideas to the goals of the MCC tradition (Tracey, Wampold, Lichtenberg, & Goodyear, 2014). The crux of this theory is a scientific elaboration on the idea that practice makes perfect. The principles of this theory were derived from research on areas in which ability level is easier to quantify, such as sports or chess. An important ingredient of expertise is the amount of time spent practicing, as popularized by Malcolm Gladwell

http://dx.doi.org/10.1037/0000156-005
Mindfulness-Based Practices in Therapy: A Cultural Humility Approach, by D. Davis, C. DeBlaere, J. N. Hook, and J. Owen

with the 10,000-hour rule (Gladwell, 2008). However, it is not just any random form of practice that leads to improvement but rather engagement in deliberate practice (Ericsson, Prietula, & Cokely, 2007).

DELIBERATE PRACTICE

Deliberate practice involves four elements (for a review in the context of psychotherapy, see Tracey et al., 2014). First, it involves a well-delineated task that can be objectively measured. Second, the trainee needs immediate feedback on his or her behavior. Third, the trainee must have the opportunity to repeat the task. Fourth, the trainee needs the opportunity to make gradual adjustments over time to learn and correct errors. These principles have received extensive empirical support in a wide variety of tasks (Ericsson et al., 2007). An important challenge is to apply these principles to more complex and ambiguous areas of practice, such as psychotherapy, in which progress is not as easy to operationalize.

Even when the strict conditions of deliberate practice cannot be achieved, training efforts can be improved by approximating the conditions of deliberate practice. Indeed, what appears to happen as a person increases in expertise is that the person becomes increasingly efficient at allocating his or her working memory. Experts learn to think and react differently. They integrate various sources of knowledge to refine their reactions to situations so that they can more quickly and effectively hone in on key aspects of a situation. Indeed, the way they perceive problems cuts to the heart of the issue, and they are able to avoid getting distracted by irrelevant factors. When experts have lots of time to practice receiving feedback, that process refines how they think as they approach complex and difficult problems. These new perspectives help them hone in on the crucial aspects of the decision, and, over time, they learn to become more consistent at making wise decisions in the moment.

Accordingly, a core assumption of this chapter is that to develop a type of cultural expertise for working with clients from marginalized groups, therapists will need to commit to a lifelong process of growth and expression of MCO values. After reading Chapter 2, we hope we have convinced you that the essence of such expertise cannot be just "knowing a lot." Some people who know a lot may not develop the wisdom to apply their knowledge, and people who know less can bridge major gaps to the degree that they make good use of their knowledge and appropriately understand their limitations.

The MCO framework suggests that what matters is not necessarily knowing a lot about different cultures—although knowledge often helps—but being able to sense cultural differences and adapt to them in a humble, flexible, and responsive way. In Chapter 3, we introduced mindfulness as one of a variety of disciplines that may help therapists cultivate a more robust and consistent ability to attend to their own thoughts, feelings, and behaviors in the moment. This groundedness can help improve connection with clients and is a prerequisite for clients' feeling a sense of relational safety, which is the foundation of forming a strong therapy alliance.

The task of cultivating therapeutic presence in the midst of potential cultural barriers is an important task for each relationship. Prior experience may help us avoid bad habits, but trust and a sense of cultural safety must be established for each client. Each relationship is new; some Buddhists refer to this idea as *keeping a beginner's mind* (Bishop et al., 2004). To keep improving as a therapist—rather than experiencing the stagnation that occurs on average (Tracey et al., 2014)—one needs to seek environments that facilitate deliberate practice in the arena of working with cultural identities.

Taken together, we view this process of growing in cultural maturity, comfort, and ability to span cultural differences as a long-term process requiring training of one's ability to attend to and integrate difficult feelings that may emerge as one experiences strong cultural dynamics in relationships. A variety of religious and spiritual traditions promote contemplative practices to help people learn to become more aware of and train their mind. We think mindfulness and related approaches and traditions have something important to teach us about how to prepare ourselves for the difficult work of attending to, learning about, and acquiring the ability to tolerate cultural discomfort within ourselves. Given that many psychotherapists are not necessarily engaged in a religious or spiritual tradition or may have had painful experiences associated with their prior engagement, it may take some work to engage in this process, but we believe it is well worth it.

In that vein, we have structured this chapter into two parts. First, we describe a two-step process of growth, which includes grounding oneself in sources of integrity and engaging in exploration in an effort to expand your ability to tolerate cultural diversity. These ideas are based on a model of how people develop spiritual maturity, although it was initially formulated by a sex therapist who was interested in how couples mature in the face of increasing anxiety that happens in intimate partnerships. Second, we encourage you to think of specific goals and habits that will help you develop greater cultural comfort, and we ask you to commit to a specific plan.

MULTICULTURAL ORIENTATION MATURITY THROUGH TWO ALTERNATING MOVEMENTS

Theories always have implicit assumptions about maturity and immaturity. The ideal of maturity within the MCO framework involves one's ability to consistently form collaborative and trusting relationships—even and especially in situations that tend to undermine trust between cultural groups. Examples of situations that test one's MCO maturity include holding different ideologies, having a history of conflict between groups, or having current competition for resources (e.g., psychological or physical). As the core virtue of the MCO, cultural humility has the potential to aid in this process and enhance one's cultural span. Having cultural span involves

> the ability to negotiate ideas fairly and form collaborative relationships with individuals or groups who are committed to ideologically different, and perhaps competing, perspectives. Span helps people manage conflict effectively in relationships, which usually involves seeking shared interests rather than resorting to less effective strategies such as avoidance, accommodation, or compromise. (Davis et al., 2018, p. 95)

Growing cultural span takes a long time and a lot of energy. Endurance requires an understanding and commitment to the process. Just like "every journey begins with a single step," growth proceeds through a repeated cycle of taking one step after another. Growing in cultural span similarly involves a repeated cycle involving two movements: (a) breaking out of the limits placed on us by avoidance and fear so that we can explore what causes stress and (b) fortifying our connection with core values and commitments in our life to sustain growth over time and maintain a sense of integrity.

Various theoretical traditions converge on describing a long-term process through which people grow in emotional and social maturity. For example, systems theories refer to differentiation as a maturity that comes from balancing needs for autonomy and connection (Bowen, 1976; Kerr & Bowen, 1988). Mature individuals can sit with the feelings of others without defensively overreacting either by avoiding the source of discomfort or seeking to control the emotional experience of the other person. Object relations theory—as well as attachment theory—describes similar dichotomies focused on emotion regulation and the ability to tolerate the anxiety of emotional intimacy (J. R. Greenberg & Mitchell, 1983; see the "Normal and Pathological Development" chapter in Kernberg, 1976).

Given the focus of this book on attending to the intersection of religious or spiritual identity with other identities, we use a theory of spiritual maturity and transformation (Sandage & Shults, 2007; Shults & Sandage, 2006) to describe the interplay between exploring while also remaining connected with sources of meaning and existential security. As a result of learning to tolerate this tension, therapists gradually expand their ability to accept cultural differences while they also maintain a commitment to strongly held personal values and a sense of integrity to those values.

Activity 5.1: Clarify Values. Because this process requires endurance, it is important to tap into your deepest sources of motivation. We use an activity called "What Do You Want Your Life to Stand For"—based loosely on the activity described in Chapter 2—that is sometimes used within acceptance and commitment therapy. Rather than orienting to life based on attempts to avoid or reduce fear, shame, anxiety, or sadness, clients learn to clarify their deepest values and make decisions by orienting and directing actions toward these core values.

Imagine being able to observe your own funeral one day and seeing the person closest to you give your eulogy speech. Then, imagine this person throughout the rest of that person's day, telling stories about you and honestly engaging her memories—positive and negative—about your life and what it is like to grieve your loss. This person might be a partner, parent, child, or other close friend. You might even consider the aggregate of your closest relationships. Consider these questions and write in stream-of-consciousness style without editing, censoring, analyzing, or critiquing your thoughts.

1. What do you hope that person will say? What do you hope that person will never say?
2. What do you hope that person will clearly see as your more valuable investments in life?
3. What qualities and values will that person notice were at the core of your character?
4. Who will that person clearly see that you cared about? What kind of influence will you have had in their lives?
5. What do you hope people will view as your most important contributions—personally, professionally, and spiritually?
6. What will that person view as your most fascinating interests or passions? What will that person view as inspiring about your life?
7. If that person know you well, what might he or she see as your substantial regrets?
8. What will that person view as your legacy? What parts of your life will live on?

OVERVIEW OF MODEL OF SPIRITUAL TRANSFORMATION

Now that you have revisited some of your core values, beliefs, and commitments, let's return to the model of developing spiritual or existential maturity. Many of our readers may not identify as spiritual, but this model could be applied to the full range of spiritual identification, including nonbelief or agnosticism. Thus, when we refer to *spiritual identity,* we are referring to core areas of identity shaped by existential questions about the origins of humanity, what happens after death, attempts to derive meaning or purpose in life, and the grounds on which judgments about what is right and wrong are substantiated (Yalom, 1980). To be inclusive of nonbelievers, we decided to refer to *existential identity* rather than just religious or spiritual identity.

According to this theory (see Figure 5.1), people naturally alternate through two modes throughout their lives: existential dwelling and seeking. *Periods of existential dwelling* (see Figure 5.1) are characterized by lower emotional

FIGURE 5.1. Balance of Spiritual Dwelling and Seeking

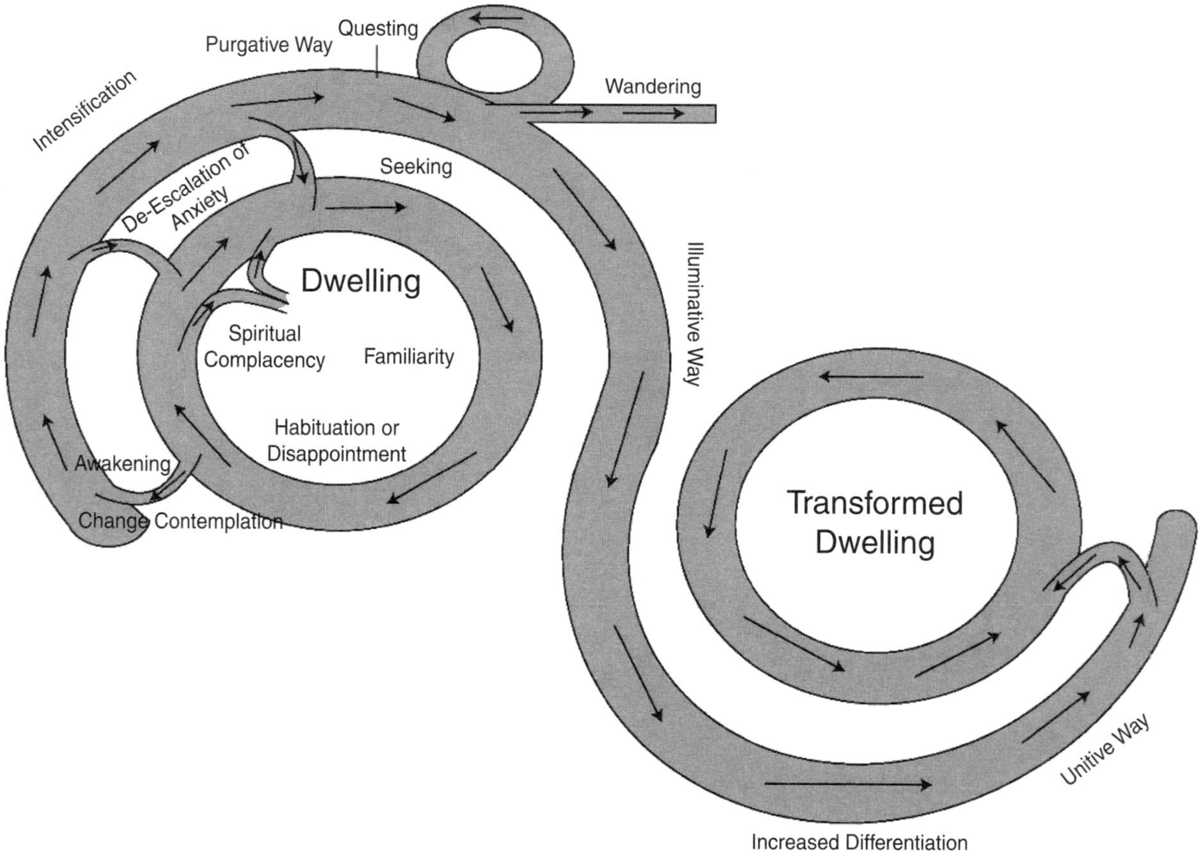

Adapted from *Forgiveness and Spirituality in Psychotherapy: A Relational Approach* (p. 55), by E. L. Worthington, Jr., and S. J. Sandage, 2016, Washington, DC: American Psychological Association. Copyright 2016 by the American Psychological Association.

arousal along with a sense of well-being and meaning in life. Although many people spend much of their lives in periods of existential dwelling, normative events of life (e.g., transition to parenthood, loss of a loved one, spiritual betrayals) can thrust people into a period of seeking. Indeed, this is similar to the encounter stage of many racial or ethnic and feminist identity models wherein people have experiences that propel them to face the existence of the status quo and begin a process of personal growth and exploration (Cross, 1991; Ossana, Helms, & Leonard, 1992).

In *periods of existential seeking* (see Figure 5.1), people may engage a process of searching for and exploring new ways of understanding the world (and possibly relating to the Sacred: God, nature, humanity, or whatever they consider the central object of their spiritual connection; Davis et al., 2016). For the purposes of this chapter, we want to especially draw on themes from this model related to self-regulation. Cultural differences can elicit powerful feelings. These feelings may represent transitions or stressors that initiate a growth cycle, and to use these opportunities well, we need to seek appropriate grounding and support. In attachment terms, we can draw on sources of relational security (e.g., a loving parent, partner, the Sacred) to soothe feelings of distress.

Growth Movement 1: Finding Sources of Dwelling

The first growth movement within this theory involves connecting with sources of existential dwelling. This theory suggests that increasing cultural comfort involves making it easier for people to draw on sources of existential comfort. Cultural differences can stir up existential anxiety. The presence of other people who understand the world differently makes us realize, perhaps unconsciously, that we may not know everything about how the world works. People who see the world differently remind us that we may have much less control over our lives than we would like to think. These threats to meaning can be particularly stressful (e.g., J. Greenberg, Pyszczynski, & Solomon, 1986).

Accordingly, growing in cultural comfort requires therapists to gain a deep sense of confidence in their ability to connect with sources of existential grounding. People experience confidence when they know that a sense of connection and grounding is only a moment away, which in turn allows for greater tolerance of feelings of disconnection and exclusion. They know these feelings will pass and will not cause permanent damage. From the models of how people develop mature forms of identity, we know that personal growth requires commitment and persistence (e.g., imagine the Tibetan monk who invests hours per day cultivating mental regimes that form the mind over long periods). To the chagrin of the self-help industry, a 5-minute shortcut to the good life simply does not exist. Existential maturity requires investment of thousands of hours—not a few minutes a day.

Growth Movement 2: Seeking Through Exploring

The second growth movement described within this theory involves intentional engagement of cultural discomfort. For therapists, it may be helpful to think of the idea of cultural transference and countertransference. *Cultural transference* and *countertransference* occur when clients and therapists react to each other's cultural identities based on their own cultural issues, internal conflicts, and history in prior close relationships (Foster, 1998; Racker, 1982). We know from experience (and research) that existential or spiritual topics can be a powerful source of countertransference (e.g., Griffith, 2006; Lannert, 1991). It might be worth a moment to consider why certain identities have such a powerful hold on the personality. Indeed, although some identities (e.g., being a student, being an athlete) may seem more circumscribed, others (e.g., gender, race, spirituality, sexual orientation)—particularly those that govern one's values and worldview—may come to influence how people see all aspects of their life (Worthington, 1988). Thus, people (i.e., therapists or clients) may not necessarily engage in a religious or spiritual community, but their existential worldview may still cause strong emotional reactions (e.g., concerns about the negative influence of organized religion or participation in nonreligious spiritual groups).

Groups that share a similar existential perspective can promote meaning systems that inform other aspects of people's identity (e.g., gender, race, sexuality), consolidate major life goals and prohibitions, and even give people a way of understanding good and evil, thus setting the boundaries that regulate shame (for a review, see McCullough & Willoughby, 2009). Thus, people understandably have strong reactions to existential or spiritual themes. They may have prior experiences involving powerful emotions that occurred during the context of an existential or spiritual experience (e.g., positive or negative spiritual experiences, perhaps painful experiences of conflict with people who identified as religious or spiritual). Therefore, given their connection to other identities and an ability to give an integrated sense of purpose, it should come as no surprise that existential themes can cause such powerful reactions.

The potency of such emotional reactions makes it essential that MCO therapists expand their cultural comfort for working with existential issues. A variety of therapy traditions converge on the idea that avoidance motivations restrain progress and growth. When people make a habit of shrinking back in fear, their ability to try new things and learn from those experiences also declines. They develop increasingly rigid patterns of reacting and lose flexibility. Because cultural countertransference raises such powerful feelings, if we as therapists do not intentionally work to expand our cultural comfort, our cultural span will likely diminish over time. As a result, our ability to form strong therapy alliances with diverse clients will similarly diminish. Consistent with the rationale for exposure therapy, the process of growing in cultural comfort requires leaning into areas of fear and discomfort.

We developed a twofold strategy for applying this theory of existential maturity to the MCO concept of cultural comfort. First, we want you to feel comfortable with how you handle the vast range of spiritual diversity, which means addressing your unavoidable limitations in knowledge and experience. Second, we hope you will intentionally invest in deepening your expertise in working with a particular cultural community that may benefit from greater attention given the current limitations within our profession. Although we focused on spirituality, these activities can be easily adapted to consider cultural comfort with other identities and their intersections with spiritual identity.

Activity 5.2: Examine Existential Memories. For this activity, we want to encourage you to examine some of your most vivid memories about spirituality or existential grounding. If you do not identify as spiritual, think of the times when you felt safest or at ease talking about existential themes (e.g., how you think about death, the potential for an afterlife, grappling with loss of loved ones, morality, finding meaning and purpose for your life). If you do identify as spiritual or religious, consider your strongest memories of feeling close to the Sacred (i.e., God, nature, humanity, the transcendent, whatever you consider at the heart of your spiritual practice). What was happening? Write down whatever comes to mind in a stream-of-consciousness manner.

After contemplating these experiences, we want you to complete a measure of spirituality (see Exhibit 5.1) defined based on the idea that spirituality involves people's sense of closeness or connection to the Sacred (Sources of Spirituality Scale; Davis et al., 2015). After you finish, consider how well the language fits your experience. It is important to acknowledge that aspects of this language may fit poorly for some readers even with attempts to avoid assuming a theistic spirituality. One of the challenges we face in addressing existential issues in therapy is using language that clients will find both inclusive and particular to their own experience. Even at the level of basic language, we may not necessarily know the verbiage that the client will find inclusive and culturally appropriate.

Activity 5.3: Explore Experiences of Existential Hurt. In your attempts to grow in cultural comfort, it may be helpful to explore hurtful experiences related to religious or spiritual identity. Close your eyes and let various memories come to mind. What happened? What were you feeling at the time? How does it feel now to remember what happened?

Then, complete the measure shown in Exhibit 5.2. The research team that created this measure included both religious believers and nonbelievers. They purposefully sought to include theistic and nontheistic content. The first subscale is the only one that assumes theistic belief, so these items are not given to people who do not endorse belief in a theistic being. The second subscale includes content focused on perceived action of evil forces in one's life. If you do not believe that evil beings are active in the world, then it is appropriate to just enter "Never" for Items 6 through 9.

EXHIBIT 5.1

Sources of Spirituality Scale

After you have spent some time doing the first part of Activity 5.2, pick one spiritual memory that was particularly vivid. Based on that experience, rate your agreement with the following items ranging from 1 (*strongly disagree*) to 5 (*strongly agree*).

1. I felt near to God (or the Sacred).
2. I felt close to God (or the Sacred).
3. I knew that God (or the Sacred) was with me.
4. I sensed God's (or the Sacred's) presence.
5. I had a sense of something infinite.
6. I felt a bond with an indescribable force of being.
7. I felt a sense of oneness with something I cannot describe with words.
8. I sensed something from another realm or dimension.
9. I felt entirely authentic.
10. I had a sense of integrity.
11. I felt completely genuine.
12. I had a sense of wholeness.
13. I felt close to nature.
14. I felt connected to nature.
15. I felt near to nature.
16. I felt connected to all of humanity.
17. I felt near to all of humanity.
18. I felt as if I were one with humanity.

Note. To score, sum Items 1–4 for score on theistic spirituality; sum Items 5–8 for score on transcendent spirituality; sum 9–12 for score on self-spirituality; sum Items 13–15 for score on nature spirituality; and sum Items 16–18 for score on human spirituality. Adapted from "Development of the Sources of Spirituality Scale," by D. E. Davis, K. Rice, J. N. Hook, D. R. Van Tongeren, C. DeBlaere, E. Choe, and E. L. Worthington, Jr., 2015, *Journal of Counseling Psychology*, *62*, p. 507. Copyright 2015 by the American Psychological Association.

Descriptions of Moral Feelings About Existential Issues

Now that you have spent time recalling some of the experiences that may intensify your reactions to existential themes, we want to move toward developing language to help you increase your cultural comfort for addressing existential themes as they arise in therapy. Indeed, transference and countertransference are not problems in and of themselves. They become a problem to the degree that they distort your sense of what is happening within your relationship with clients. This distortion can lead to a cycle of ruptures that undermine the effectiveness of the relationship. Some theories have posited that the work of therapy involves various forms of preventing or working through such potential ruptures (Friedlander, 2015; Kline et al., 2018; Safran & Kraus, 2014).

Often, our clients have different values than we do. When this happens, our ethical code guides us to not impose our values on clients, but it is sometimes unclear how this translates to actual therapy practice. First, perhaps we can agree on what it cannot mean. It does not suggest value neutrality, as such a thing does not really exist (Fowers, Anderson, Lefevor, & Lang,

EXHIBIT 5.2

Religious and Spiritual Struggles Scale

For the painful experience(s) you considered in Activity 5.2, to what extent have you struggled with each of the following? Rate each item using the following scale: 1 (*always*), 2 (*most of the time*), 3 (*about half the time*), 4 (*sometimes*), 5 (*never*).

1. Felt as though God (or the Sacred) had let me down
2. Felt angry at God (or the Sacred)
3. Felt as though God (or the Sacred) had abandoned me
4. Felt as though God (or the Sacred) was punishing me
5. Questioned God's (or the Sacred) love for me
6. Felt tormented by the devil or evil spirits
7. Worried that the problems I was facing were the work of the devil or evil spirits
8. Felt attacked by the devil or by evil spirits
9. Felt as though the devil (or an evil spirit) was trying to turn me away from what was good
10. Felt hurt, mistreated, or offended by religious or spiritual people
11. Felt rejected or misunderstood by religious or spiritual people
12. Felt as though others were looking down on me because of my religious or spiritual beliefs
13. Had conflicts with other people about religious or spiritual matters
14. Felt angry at organized religion
15. Wrestled with attempts to follow my moral principles
16. Worried that my actions were morally or spiritually wrong
17. Felt torn between what I wanted and what I knew was morally right
18. Felt guilty for not living up to my moral standards
19. Questioned whether life really matters
20. Felt as though my life had no deeper meaning
21. Questioned whether my life will really make any difference in the world
22. Had concerns about whether there is any ultimate purpose to life or existence
23. Struggled to figure out what I really believe about religion or spirituality
24. Felt confused about my religious or spiritual beliefs
25. Felt troubled by doubts or questions about religion or spirituality
26. Worried about whether my beliefs about religion or spirituality were correct

Note. To score, sum Items 1–5 for Divine subscale; sum Items 6–9 for Demonic subscale; sum Items 10–14 for the Interpersonal subscale; sum Items 15–18 for Moral subscale; sum Items 19–22 for Ultimate Meaning subscale; sum Items 23–26 for Doubt subscale. Adapted from "The Religious and Spiritual Struggles Scale: Development and Initial Validation," by J. J. Exline, K. I. Pargament, J. B. Grubbs, and A. M. Yali, 2014, *Psychology of Religion and Spirituality*, *6*, p. 213. Copyright 2014 by the American Psychological Association.

2015; Wendt, Gone, & Nagata, 2015), and even if it did, it would not be a good quality for a therapist. For example, neutrality in the face of clear offenses (e.g., domestic violence, sexual abuse) involves collusion with oppressive dynamics. As MCO therapists, we must hold certain values and strive to have a sense of integrity to those values. Indeed, how can we ever earn trust with our clients if we cannot trust ourselves? Not imposing our values on our clients also does not mean suppressing all moral reactions. When we see inhumane treatment of others, for instance, this warrants a moral response, and failure to experience those emotions is a sign of lack of compassion and empathy (two critical aspects of effective therapy). Rather, what we are learning to do as therapists is to manage value differences while regulating our emotions and seeking a sense of integrity. Doing so requires skills in alignment with Worthington's (1988) theory about therapists and clients having varying zones of toleration for handling cultural diversity. We elaborate on this theorizing in Figure 5.2.

There are three main categories of value differences, and we use different strategies for handling each. First, most people have a list of *moral imperatives* that they view as inherently wrong, and seeing these values violated leads to visceral reactions. Second, some issues involve *moral preferences* for which it is easier to extend latitude when differences exist, although it is certainly quite possible to moralize one's preferences. Some issues do not fall neatly into either category, and we might refer to these as *moral ambiguities*.

Strategies for Managing Differences in Preferences

This category is perhaps the simplest in terms of strategy. In our role as therapists, we should almost never get into major conflict with clients over different preferences. If a trainee frequently experiences stalemates of this kind, the person likely has personality traits (e.g., low agreeableness) that they will need to learn to regulate to promote more collaborative therapeutic relationships with clients.

Strategies for Managing Differences Related to Moral Imperatives

Sometimes we fundamentally disagree with a client about a deeply moral issue. Imagine a woman in a physically abusive relationship who does not believe she has sufficient justification to pursue a divorce because of religious

FIGURE 5.2. Practical Application of the Zone of Toleration Theory

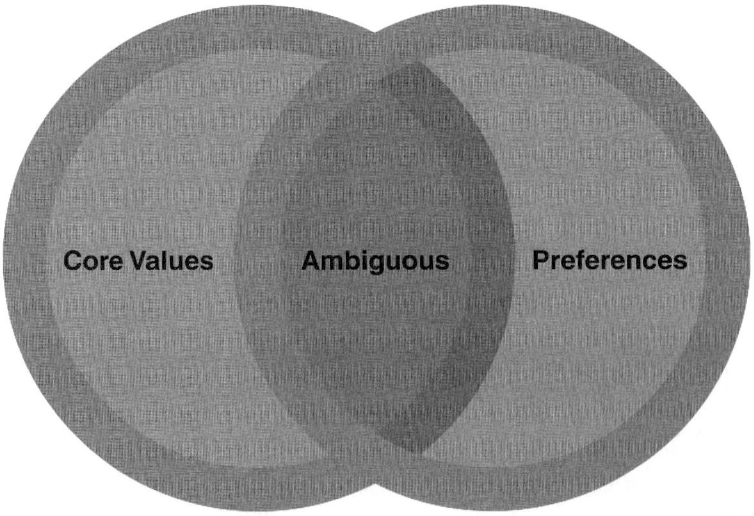

Data from Worthington, 1988.

convictions. The therapist disagrees. In some cases, our value of respecting the client's autonomy governs our strategy. We defer even if we do not agree with the client. This deference can sometimes cause feelings of a lack of integrity. In other cases, our profession has clearly agreed to prioritize a certain course of action even if we reach an impasse with the client. Examples include our duty to report an imminent threat to another person's life or instances of child or elder abuse.

As therapists, our priority for client autonomy and self-determination causes us, at least pragmatically and in our role as therapists, to keep our list of moral imperatives (i.e., circumstances in which we are compelled to override the client's autonomy) as short as possible. Our list of moral imperatives essentially involves ultimatums—and like ultimatums in any relationship, they must be used sparingly. If the other person does not submit to the ultimatum, then the relationship will be permanently altered. As such, moral ultimatums inherently limit the inclusiveness of a community. Moral imperatives require us to rupture trust with the client to maintain a sense of integrity within ourselves. Once people entertain extreme commitment to different values and different ways of supporting those values (e.g., different authoritative sources), there is little recourse to resolve differences. Nonetheless, sometimes we have to sacrifice our trust with the client to maintain integrity within ourselves and within our profession at large.

According to moral foundations theory, moral emotions function like a sixth sense. Similar to the ways in which our physical senses (e.g., vision, touch, hearing) assist us in navigating our physical world, moral emotions help each of us navigate our social world. Being a good citizen within a community often requires a degree of conformance to the core values of that community. Moral emotions help people anticipate changes in acceptance or exclusion (e.g., Leary & Baumeister, 2000). As such, people have an instant and visceral reaction when they sense that doing something may result in those closest to them viewing the action as morally wrong. People tend to withdraw acceptance and trust for relationships when someone violates a sacred value. Thus, our bodies—sensing the threat of exclusion—prepare to run, fight, hide, or freeze. Our minds prepare for the possibility of physical conflict. In preparation for potential violence, we may morally disengage from others. As therapists, we need to slow down these primitive fight-or-flight emotional reactions and remain connected to our compassionate and caring feelings towards the client.

Activity 5.4: Consider Moral Imperatives. Although having moral imperatives has positive qualities, it can also be problematic for therapists working to maintain an empathic stance. When we see that a moral imperative has been violated, this evokes moral judgments that if not handled wisely, can damage our relationship with clients. Thus, it is important to gain insight into our moral imperatives that may exist beyond our awareness. To develop this insight, we need to cultivate verbal fluency in talking about values.

An example of a taxonomy for talking about value differences is moral foundations theory (Graham, Haidt, & Nosek, 2009). This theory describes five moral foundations or value clusters that underlie how people make judgments about right and wrong (see Exhibit 5.3). The main idea of the theory is that people have various profiles on these five dimensions. For example, one person might tend to have high levels of value on harm and care as well as fairness and justice but low levels of value for loyalty, authority, and purity.

The following are three case studies that might cause moral reactions. Consider how you might feel if you were about to approach a session with one of these clients. Assume you are considering whether and how to use mindfulness as a part of your approach:

Case 1: Robert. Robert identifies as a 21-year-old African American, cisgender, heterosexual man. He is a star running back on his college football team. To protest the unequal treatment of racial and ethnic minorities in the United States, he has decided to take a knee during the national anthem. Robert has been suspended from his team for his actions and risks losing his scholarship. Without this scholarship, he will likely need to transfer to a community college.

Case 2: Alicia. Alicia identifies as a 35-year-old cisgender, Indian woman raising her 7-year-old daughter alone. Her parents are strongly religious and practice Hinduism, but Alicia identifies as spiritual but not religious. She and her daughter's father were never married. She recently

EXHIBIT 5.3

Moral Foundations Theory Values and Example Items

Value	Description and example item
Harm and care	Whether a person or another living thing was physically or emotionally harmed Example item: Whether or not someone suffered emotionally
Fairness and justice	Whether or not people were treated equally Example item: Whether or not people were treated differently from others
Loyalty	Commitment to one's team Example item: Whether or not someone showed love for his or her country
Authority	Respect for hierarchy and existing systems Example item: Whether or not someone showed a lack of respect for authority
Purity	Purity pathogens and contaminants Example item: Whether or not someone acted in a way God would approve of

learned that she is 2 months pregnant, but the relationship with her current partner is not serious, and Alicia does not feel that she is in the financial position to support another child on her own. She also does not want to coparent with her current partner. Alicia has decided to terminate her pregnancy.

Case 3: Marcus. Marcus identifies as a 16-year-old gay, Latino, cisgender man. He is struggling to decide whether or not he should continue to attend his family's Catholic church. Marcus recently shared his gay identity with his family. The reactions of his family members have been varied: Some have affirmed his gay identity, and others have been critical of him. Those who have not accepted his gay identity have asked that he not disclose his sexual identity to anyone at their church. Marcus is not sure how to best proceed.

Process these three examples. Notice what feelings come up for you. What moral foundations (if any) were violated? Think about someone in the past with whom you have had difficulty talking about religious or spiritual issues. Are you able to articulate how the two of you might have different priorities in terms of the moral foundations presented in Exhibit 5.3?

Differences Involving Moral Ambiguity

Some of your reactions to the preceding examples may not have fit neatly into an area of moral preference or imperative. These morally ambiguous situations can be especially difficult to navigate. Before discussing how to handle moral ambiguities, want to say more about how we are using the term. We are not referring to confusion and lack of commitment about moral values. Rather, we are thinking more in terms of how people may belong to different groups that are important to them—groups that have played a formative role in people's lives. These groups may have completely incompatible ways of viewing moral issues for a given situation.

Depending on their values and identities, therapists have different situations that put them into a moral bind within themselves. For example, a feminist therapist might struggle in working with a client who is a woman from a conservative Christian background and believes that it is her duty to honor her husband as the leader of the family—despite that his addiction to opiates has resulted in job loss and potential eviction from their home. A conservative religious therapist, on the other hand, might struggle to work with a female client who wishes to divorce her husband and pursue a sexual relationship with someone else.

Sometimes moral ambiguities arise from developmental changes as one lives and becomes a member of different communities. Perhaps in earlier parts of your life you were part of a group with a strong commitment to viewing certain things as clearly right or wrong. However, as people develop new relationships and have varied experiences, they may begin to see more room for shades of grey. Moral ambiguities are especially likely to occur when we live for long periods in communities with different commitments about certain issues, especially when communities use commitment to certain ideas as litmus tests for belonging to the community (e.g., deciding if someone is a committed liberal by using that person's stance toward abortion, affirmative action, environmental policy). For issues with strong signal value, we may have internalized the anticipated shame (or affirmation) that comes with violation (or conformity) to certain values. With moral ambiguities, we may not have fully integrated these painful experiences of potential exclusion into an integrated way of being in the world. This dynamic is similar to what some intersectional theories refer to as *living at the margins* (e.g., identifying as gay) within a marginalized group (Black Christians; Purdie-Vaughns & Eibach, 2008).

Therapy within multicultural relationships requires people to develop advanced self-regulation skills. Morally ambiguous situations can challenge one's sense of integrity. Prioritizing the client's values may feel like a breach of trust with oneself. The difficulty is that one is caught between worlds. You as a therapist may intellectually know that it is important to follow the client's values, but you may have an inner sense of disloyalty to certain communities. These situations can cause numbness, moral disengagement, or other unhelpful defensive processes. As therapists, we may not always know how to handle the potentially painful and ambivalent feelings that arise when certain issues are morally contested within different communities we value and view as central to our identity.

We do not make light of these situations. They are "easy" to resolve for people who do not hold particular identities experienced as being in conflict. But we all have potential areas that could put us into this kind of value conflict. As discussed with moral imperatives, putting language to moral feelings can begin a process that can allow greater clarification and integration. This process can, in turn, allow greater flexibility in reasoning and responding to the situation that evoked morally ambiguous feelings (e.g., J. Greenberg, 2002). Instead of impulsively seeking to get rid of the dissonance, therapists with a robust moral language can consider their options and attempt to choose their next steps carefully and wisely. When such feelings arise in therapy, MCO therapists can engage them as cultural opportunities rather than allow them to distort interactions in therapy and eventually undermine trust in the working alliance.

Consider the case example in the box that follows.

Case Example: Therapist

The therapist, a White, cisgender male, heterosexual, and spiritual but not religious, is working with a client who identifies as a Pentecostal Christian, Latino, cisgender male, and heterosexual. The therapist regularly uses mindfulness in therapy, and it undergirds his general approach to life and thinking about his work as a therapist.

In the very first session, the client directly asks about the therapist's religious background. This question catches the therapist off guard because this is the first time a client has asked him to disclose his religious or spiritual identity. He is completely surprised and unprepared to field the question, especially given his painful experience with religion and spirituality. He grew up in a Christian family but left the church and currently gravitates more towards Buddhism but in a mostly private way. Over the past several years, the therapist has engaged in a few meditation retreats but has otherwise cultivated a meditation practice primarily through self-help books and other similar resources.

The therapist's response to the situation is to evade the question and to spend the last 10 minutes of the session exploring why the question might be important to the client. The client, however, does not seem to respond well to this intervention and begins to show signs of emotional distance, such as sitting further back in his chair and crossing his arms.

This case illustrates a morally ambiguous situation. The therapist experienced competing values. For example, several of the values were related to professional acculturation. He felt like it would be inappropriate to share all about his religious background and experience with the client, but he could also discern that the answer might matter quite a lot to the client. So, he felt tremendous pressure to share something—but was not sure what to say. Furthermore, the therapist felt a strong desire to avoid explicitly addressing religious self-disclosure in the session because of his own unresolved conflicts with his religious or spiritual identity. Other reactions were related to the client's prior experiences within religious communities. In the client's own tradition, there was a strong close-mindedness toward other spiritual traditions, so the therapist anticipated the possibility of rejection from the client. He expected that if he disclosed cultural differences that existed in the relationship (e.g., that they did not share sufficiently similar worldview), doing so might cause the client to terminate therapy. We actually cannot know for sure what the client had in mind in asking the question, but it does appear that the therapist's evasion of the question did not work well and may result in the outcome that he most feared (e.g., client termination). In this case, the cultural countertransference made it difficult for the therapist to consider options that might have been better for the course of treatment, such as having an open conversation and involving the client in a decision regarding whether to consider a referral.

How would you have responded if you were the therapist in this situation? Would you have felt comfortable sharing about your own religious or spiritual identity and background? Why or why not? What would it look like to respond to this question with cultural humility?

DEVELOPMENT OF TRAINING HABITS TO INCREASE CULTURAL COMFORT

So, let's press the pause button and consider what we have learned so far. Growth in cultural comfort happens through alternating between grounding and seeking. This process is like different movements that strengthen a muscle. We want to end this chapter by suggesting lifelong habits that ought to promote growth in cultural comfort for addressing spiritual identity and its intersection with other marginalized identities. The goal—based on the MCO framework and consistent with theory on expertise—is to develop routines of training that will, over time, lead to more flexible ways of deciding if and how to use mindfulness in therapy. We have conceptualized the primary process as one of forming a strong relationship (or social bond) with clients, which is regulated by the client's perceptions of cultural humility. For our clients—who come from various identities and cultural backgrounds—to consistently experience us as culturally humble, we need to develop intentional ways of living that will make this virtue a part of our own character. We can commit ourselves to the thriving of others based on *their* terms (i.e., language) and view of thriving. Our clients will experience us as being for them when we see them accurately and also show appropriate emotional responsiveness to knowing them. For clients from marginalized groups, a core part of knowing them well is understanding and validating their experiences of injustice, which we cannot do unless we strengthen our cultural comfort. It can be difficult to sit within another person's sense of marginalization, especially when the therapist's identities interact with the client's history of marginalization.

So, our basic question is this: What are the habits that will sustain you over the course of a career and lead to greater span and comfort over time? Consider this question for yourself, and then read on for a few of our suggestions.

Build a Cultural Network

If you are living in the United States, you are being trained in an individualistic society. But building cultural humility and comfort is not an individual achievement. Humility involves an appropriate awareness and ownership of limits. Your effectiveness will depend on your ability to develop and navigate networks of cultural expertise. The MCC tradition has tended to think in what, ironically, could be described as individualistic terms: that each therapist individually possesses a certain degree of MCC. The work of therapy requires developing comfort to engage complex sources of information. It may make sense to think of expertise as a quality of systems rather than a possession of the individual therapist.

Indeed, given some of the challenges discussed in this chapter and the limits you have in time and energy, it is important to think systematically about the constellation of relationships that will be required for you to serve your clients well. With modern inventions—trains, cars, planes, telephones, computers, and the Internet—information is more accessible than ever. We need wisdom to construct relationships that will help us access contextualized knowledge quickly, accurately, and effectively. This cannot mean simply reading a lot to try to know it all. There is too much to know. We could never gain enough experience on our own. Rather, we must embed ourselves within a range of personal and professional communities that will extend our cultural span. Thus, we each need to develop networks of people that can support our cultural comfort work. A tension can exist between identifying places that and people who represent groundedness and safety and identifying places that and people who can facilitate exploration and expansion. Sometimes the same people and places represent both safety and expansion, but it is likely that to truly grow, you will need to step outside of your areas of most comfort.

Seek a Global Perspective

It may help to develop a perspective of religion and spirituality that extends beyond just the local conditions within the United States. The vast majority of the world is religious, and many marginalized groups view their religion or spirituality as an important part of their daily lives (Taylor & Chatters, 2010). At the same time, several European countries have become almost entirely secular and nonreligious. Psychologists who study religion and spirituality have become particularly intrigued by these secularization processes as well as why some countries have not followed suit during the process of secularization (Mercier, Kramer, & Shariff, 2018). Getting a sense of these various theories may help us carefully consider our biases, assumptions, and interests related to our spiritual or religious identities, loyalties, or ideologies.

Activity 5.5: Consider Religious or Spiritual Diversity in Your Local Area. If your goal is to increase your awareness of spiritual diversity in the world, a first step might be to start nearby. Thus, we encourage you to try learning more about your local community, city, county, or state. Go to the following website to explore recent polling data in your general geographical area (http://www.pewforum.org/religious-landscape-study/#geography). What religious or spiritual groups are you familiar with? Which are you less familiar with? Choose a religious or spiritual perspective that you are less familiar with and make an intention to learn something new about that religious or spiritual identity. Next, explore how that same religious or spiritual identity is practiced in another country. Does that identity hold a majority or minority status? How is the practice of that identity similar to or different from the area you initially explored?

Develop Diverse Reading Habits

Expanding your knowledge base about diverse cultural identities is an important initial step to growing in cultural comfort. A relatively simple way approach is to develop diverse reading habits. Reading provides a unique opportunity to engage the minds of others—to see the world through the eyes of the author. Multicultural orientation therapists integrate engagement with diversity into the fabric of their lives. Attending conferences, listening to podcasts, visiting spiritual communities, and traveling to other countries are also good options for expanding your knowledge. Reading widely is one way to understand the worldview of others and, with time, to consider how our own perspective may be linked. The goal is to place ourselves at the crossroads of knowledge that will grow our understanding and compassion for others. Develop a habit of not only getting a good textbook on the psychology of religion but also trying to diversify your reading list. Include books that will stretch you to see your own commitments and tradition from another point of view. Read books from people of several faith traditions who were cherished for their cultivation of a contemplative life and the associated wisdom that comes from thinking deeply.

Seek Tacit Knowledge

As we all know, there is a big difference between "reading about" and "living with" a community. It often takes many years for people to adjust to a new cultural environment. Therefore, it makes little sense to think one could ever develop fluency in every culture (indeed, it would take many lifetimes!), but spending significant amounts of time in another culture is a powerful antidote against cultural arrogance. Research with people who have lived in another country for an extended period show benefits that align with this idea (Adler & Aycan, 2018). Perhaps monoculturalism is fairly hard to escape unless one has lived like a "fish out of water" for an extended period. Otherwise, we have trouble "knowing what we don't know." We need experiences of immersion to help us see the many assumptions embedded within our cultural worldview. However, once such an experience occurs, perhaps people have an easier time accessing the depth and breadth of their cultural assumptions.

Activity 5.6: Explore Outside Your Spiritual Comfort Zone. Select a spiritual community with which you are less familiar or have an interest in learning more about. Make a commitment to attend services or events consistently (e.g., once a month or quarter). The idea is that you will begin to understand the more nuanced aspects of this cultural group. You will also be less likely to rely on stereotypes for groups with which you have had positive encounters. The primary goal is to develop the ability to form trust with a wide range of people—individuals with diverse spiritual perspectives and ideologies.

Take Responsibility for Our Field's Compositional Problems

At first glance, our final suggestion may seem counterintuitive. As clinicians, we prioritize the well-being and psychological needs of the next client to walk through our doors. Accordingly, we contend that an implication of that responsibility to serving a diverse public is that every psychologist must attend to our profession's compositional limitations. That is, to the degree that marginalized groups are underrepresented within psychology, we as a profession may have difficulty earning trust and showing sufficient responsiveness. Compositional problems create a major problem for our training systems because it is difficult for these systems to overcome biases and tendencies of self-interest—that people have a natural affinity to invest in communities to which they belong.

The problem of the racial composition of our profession is a good example. Expertise develops in part because of skillful mentoring. Research has suggested that people tend to provide critical mentorship to others who are similar to themselves (Dreher & Cox, 1996). People of color in academia often struggle to identify mentors who can support their career trajectory. They also often end up carrying a heavy load of offering support to graduate students of color (Stanley, 2006), which detracts emotional energy and increases time away from investment in developing expertise in a research program. As a result, these various barriers have a cumulative effect of perpetuating imbalances in power and making it difficult to serve marginalized racial communities well.

This problem has the potential to perpetuate itself unless people within our profession invest in a counterintuitive way. A portion of people holding privileged identities will need to invest their energies based on the logic of need rather than affinity. The logic of affinity involves people's projecting their identities onto the world and investing based on their own primary values and sense of struggle in the world (sort of the clinical version of the "research is me-search" idea). This tendency has many advantages because it is easier to form social bonds when people match with each other based on cultural values. For the power imbalances to begin to shift within our field, a growing number of therapists will need to commit themselves to being allies, which involves persisting in the difficult work of learning to build trusting relationships in contexts in which relationships are strained by power differences and a history of exploitation. Nonetheless, cultural comfort is hard earned through purposefully seeking out personally challenging contexts.

Through an MCO lens, being an ally is a relational construct—not something that can be done alone. Indeed, the word *alliance* refers to a trusting and cooperative relationship. The quality of an alliance depends on the degree to which clients feel like their interests and needs are appropriately known and prioritized within a relationship. Thus, it makes no sense for therapists to declare themselves a "good ally"; that designation comes from the individual or community with whom an individual is working (D.W. Sue, 2017). Allies demonstrate that they value a relationship strongly and remain faithful to the alliance even when—perhaps most critically when—cooperation becomes less expedient or immediately rewarding. An ally identity is not just an abstract commitment to a particular ideology in which the self is enhanced through grandiose expressions that do not amount to actions that benefit marginalized groups; rather, it is a commitment to authentic relationships. This is growing in cultural comfort.

Activity 5.7: Consider Allyship Regarding Religious or Spiritual Diversity. Consider your areas of privilege. Privilege is difficult to identify, so if you initially have difficulty naming your areas of privilege, you might consider talking with someone you trust about how that person understands his or her privilege. Once you have identified an area of privilege, consider how you might use your privilege to become an ally to a cause or community. What is critical here is not to approach this process from a paternalistic perspective. If you infantilize others or see yourself as a savior, you miss the point of allyship. People with marginalized identities are not looking to be saved; they want to be seen—as human, as equal, as worthy of the right to self-actualize.

Read the following story that current book author C. D. shares, and then consider a few questions.

A Story From Author C. D.

I distinctly remember when I became aware of my heterosexual privilege. I was in my master's program. I had a close friend who had recently come out as a gay. At the time, there was marriage equality legislation being considered, and protests were abundant. My friend and I passed a protest on our way to class. My reaction to the demonstration had been one of vague interest, but I was completely taken aback when my friend began to cry after we were safely clear of the crowd. He questioned why the group of demonstrators "hated" him. This was an example of my privilege. I had walked by this demonstration and had not had a core identity maligned. I could go through my whole life and never fear coming across a group of people protesting my right to marry the person I loved. That was the day I became an ally—or at least began the work of developing as an ally. Many pieces fell into place for me that day. First, I realized I could not fight the other oppressions that had been my focus (i.e., racism and sexism) and omit heterosexism. I used my understanding of my less privileged identities (e.g., woman of color) to inform my understanding of how I could leverage my privilege as a heterosexual person to advocate for sexual minority people.

What came up for you as you read author C. D.'s story? How might you want to use your privilege to contribute to these efforts? Another point to consider is that allyship comes in many forms. Allyship can take place in voting. It can be present in speaking up against bigotry at a family dinner. It can be marching, mentoring, serving on a school board, or influencing institutional hiring practices. Try not to be dissuaded from becoming an ally because you are not sure where to begin. The key is to begin.

CONCLUSION

The goal of this chapter was to develop a plan for cultivating habits and practices that will grow your zone of toleration for dealing with religious and spiritual diversity. If we build these structures into our lives, they will provide us with a better context for adapting to the needs of our clients.

We began by providing an initial baseline measure of spiritual comfort. Next, we drew on a model of spiritual or existential transformation and growth to describe why we often have such powerful reactions to religious and spiritual differences. We provided activities we think could be helpful for both grounding and exploring outside of yourself. We suggested that increasing your zone of toleration requires a commitment to engaging these two movements over long periods of your life and in the context of diverse communities. Finally, we suggested potential disciplines to develop so that you can build these principles into the fabric of your life and work as a therapist.

II

APPLICATION OF MULTICULTURAL ORIENTATION IN STAGES OF THERAPY

6

Assessing the Appropriateness of Mindfulness Interventions for Clients

Our task in Part II is to apply the multicultural orientation (MCO) framework to the context of therapy and work it out in the details. In this chapter, we draw on theory on the therapy alliance to organize our thinking. We consider the process of gathering information within the first session or two to make a good decision about the degree to which therapeutic mindfulness may be helpful or appropriate. Indeed, what happens before and during the first session is important for the remainder of therapy. The relationship patterns established early in the process may be difficult to change because they become more solidified. Furthermore, when it comes to clients from marginalized groups, many never even venture a first session (Betancourt, Green, Carrillo, & Ananeh-Firempong, 2003; Clement et al., 2015; Wang et al., 2007). For those who do take the risk and attempt therapy, many decide not to come back for a second session (e.g., Owen, Imel, Adelson, & Rodolfa, 2012).

Given the importance of the early relationship, we focus on the critical processes that occur in the beginning stage of therapy, especially as they relate to the potential use of mindfulness. Accordingly, we begin by describing the role of power during an effective intake interview. We then offer practical suggestions for assessing spiritual identity and its intersection with other identities. We discuss several considerations when deciding whether and how to potentially incorporate mindfulness into one's treatment plan.

http://dx.doi.org/10.1037/0000156-006
Mindfulness-Based Practices in Therapy: A Cultural Humility Approach, by D. Davis, C. DeBlaere, J. N. Hook, and J. Owen

THE ROLE OF POWER IN CONDUCTING AN INTAKE INTERVIEW

Power differentials are one of the contextual factors that make humility especially difficult (but also important and powerful) within the context of psychotherapy. The personality trait of humility, more broadly, involves the regulation of altruistic behavior when one relationally has the power to potentially exploit a relationship (for a review, see Ashton, Lee, & de Vries, 2014). Thus, it is easy to discern how humility in response to power, an inherent aspect of therapy, is important to cultivate.

By the very nature of seeking a therapist's help, clients are placing themselves in a position of less power. Even theories that strive for egalitarian power interactions in the therapy relationship acknowledge that the power differential cannot and should not be ignored; the power differential does not go away just because it is not explicitly named. The best we can hope for is for the power dynamics to be engaged fairly and benevolently (Henretty & Levitt, 2010; Prilleltensky, 2008; Vera & Speight, 2003).

Both therapists and clients bring their cultural identities and history to the therapy relationship. These histories affect how therapists and clients interpret what is happening within the therapy relationship. These histories also include an element of perceived power: Existing power dynamics related to the therapist's identity and the client's identity can and do extend into the therapy room.

The location of therapy is embedded within a larger ecological system. Therapists are situated in a clinical setting that has an existing reputation within the broader community. There are various ways the clinical setting could relate to systems of power (e.g., collusion, conformance, advocacy on behalf of clients). For example, if the counseling center has a poor reputation with a community of clients from a marginalized group, then that reputation could put the therapy relationship at an immediate disadvantage. It could be more difficult to establish trust, form a therapy alliance, and achieve positive therapy outcomes. Therefore, it is critically important to contemplate all of these levels of power during the intake interview (and beyond).

Activity 6.1: Consider Two Case Studies. As we raise a variety of themes related to power in this chapter, we want you to consider two possible cases in which you, as therapist, are considering the use of mindfulness. After presenting new information, we also pose reflection questions for your consideration.

Case 1: Monique (therapist) and Daryl (client). Monique is a psychologist at a state prison. She is a 46-year-old, African American, heterosexual, cisgender woman. Monique was raised as a Baptist, but she is not currently attending services regularly, nor is she a member of a church. Daryl, her client, is a 19-year-old, White, heterosexual, cisgender man who identifies as agnostic. He is serving a 2-year sentence for attempted robbery. He is eligible for parole and his hearing is in 2 months. Daryl is hoping that participating in counseling will lead to a more favorable evaluation by the parole board.

Case 2: Adam (therapist) and Debra (client). Adam, a 30-year-old, gay, White, cisgender man, is a licensed mental health counselor practicing in a newly formed private practice. This is Adam's second year in the practice. During his first year, he was trained by a senior colleague within the practice. Adam is currently working diligently to grow his caseload so that he is able to cover the costs of the office space and administrative support provided by the private practice. His client, Debra, is a 55-year-old, heterosexual, Latina woman. She came to therapy to develop better coping strategies for her stress and anxiety. Debra is a senior partner in a law firm. The stress of balancing her job, marriage, and children has become unbearable.

Think about each of these therapy dyads. First, consider the two therapists. Do you imagine any differences in the degree of power the two wield within the therapy dyad? Relatedly, given their respective cultural identities and those of their clients, what identity dynamics could be potentially important to consider? Also, consider the places of employment for therapists Monique and Adam. Do you think that their different places of employment as well as their roles within their organizations may impact the power dynamics present within the therapy relationship? If so, in what ways?

As another discussion point, did you notice that in both scenarios the therapist is described first followed by the client? This is typical in case study presentations and in representations of power more broadly. Indeed, our typical vernacular—"mother and daughter" or "supervisor and supervisee"—often tends to reflect the order of power and priority. If we had described the client first, do you think that would have stood out to you? Take a moment to consider other ways that language conveys power (e.g., "There is the CEO and his assistant" versus "There is the assistant and his CEO"). Noticing these seemingly small details can go a long way in conveying your own awareness of power dynamics in your interactions with clients. In light of the topic of the book, if you were supervising Monique and Adam, how would attending to these power dynamics affect how you would recommend that they present mindfulness to these clients?

Types of Power

Relational Power

Several types of power are worth attending to in the first few sessions. The power dynamic present in a relationship is termed *relational power*, which refers to all the resources a person has at his or her disposal to negotiate that person's interests and enact a change within a relationship. Although psychologists have defined *power* in various ways, one interesting approach to defining relational power comes from couples literature. Here, greater power is held by the person who cares the least about changing the status quo (e.g., Blanc, 2001; Malik & Lindahl, 2004). For example, a partner with a greater need for quality time might have lower power in that domain; a partner with a greater need for order in the home may have lower power in that given domain.

This way of understanding power makes it clear why therapists have power in their role. When they go home, they do not carry the client's problems with them (although they may carry them vicariously). Clients have greater investment in changing the status quo of their lives. Indeed, they and they alone bear the consequences for being unable to address the issues that brought them to therapy. They come to therapists willing to pay money for professional support, guidance, and skill. Many therapists drawing from an MCO framework may work to reduce this power differential, but it is impossible to fully step into a client's shoes and take responsibility for the consequences of that client's decisions. The relationship will suffer if we therapists do not honor this inherent power differential.

Societal Power

The power associated with social identities is termed *societal power*, which refers to the leverage a person may possess based on his or her holding certain privileged cultural identities (Fiske, 2001). For example, married heterosexual couples in the United States have collective interests. Their collective bargaining power has influenced various institutions (e.g., laws, how civic spaces are structured) and cultural norms (e.g., endorsement of behaviors considered more and less acceptable). Some people refer to cultural identities associated with power (in the United States) as *prototypical identities* (e.g., Purdie-Vaughns & Eibach, 2008), those identities that have become the default due to their privileged status (e.g., man, heterosexual, White, able-bodied, middle-class). Any person who holds prototypical status may receive unearned benefits negotiated on behalf of the privileged collective.

Conversely, individuals with nonprototypical identities (e.g., woman, sexual minority, racial or ethnic minority, with a disability, poor) do not have direct access to these benefits. Thus, because everyone is associated with various identities—self- and other-determined—their starting point for negotiations within social relationships may begin at a different point based on their salient identities. These social locations represent advantages and disadvantages that can accumulate over a lifetime. The benefits can manifest in many ways, some expected and others less expected. For example, because men are expected to be more assertive, they can act assertively without social penalty, but this is not true for women. Likewise, men also receive greater benefit from expressing humility and selflessness than do women (e.g., a woman must express higher levels of these traits to be considered humble; Amanatullah & Morris, 2010; Amanatullah, Morris, & Curhan, 2008; Amanatullah & Tinsley, 2013; Tinsley, Cheldelin, Schneider, & Amanatullah, 2009).

Structural Power

The power associated with institutions could be considered an aspect of *structural power*, which is the orchestration of influential forces in people's lives (e.g., financial, political). When working with clients, the organizations with which we therapists are affiliated can have a significant impact on the lives of our clients. For example, a university counseling center could be perceived by student clients as a function of the larger university system. Clients may imagine that their therapy experiences may affect their continued advancement toward a degree (which is sometimes true, such as when an administrator mandates therapy as a part of a remediation plan). Similarly, clients may participate in required counseling while incarcerated (which may determine qualification for disability or parole) or as part of a mediation process. Thus, as therapists, we should spend time reflecting on the setting(s) in which we practice and consider how these organizations can and often do represent structures of power that can have important implications for the perceived power we possess as therapists and the client's degree of felt autonomy.

Application of Power Within the Multicultural Orientation Framework

If a therapist uses power and coercion to influence a client's decision, doing so will likely harm the client's chance at achieving positive therapy outcomes. A client's counterbalance to a power differential is commitment and engagement. When clients feel a potential for exploitation or coercion, they will intuitively limit their investment in the relationship. When clients see their therapist as low in cultural humility, it weakens the social bond, which can lead to a downward spiral of lower investment and engagement that may eventually result in termination. When therapists demonstrate high cultural humility, the reverse happens. They feel more psychologically safe, which leads to a strengthening of the social bond that can lead to greater investment and engagement. Healing has a chance to occur. Rather than having to monitor the relationship for the potential for exploitation, clients can relax their vigilance and focus their available energy on the primary treatment goals.

Thus, according to the MCO framework, clients (rightfully) sense a power differential when they come to us. Although we cannot fully balance power, we can make every effort to minimize coercion. We can develop a social bond and adopt a culturally humble relational stance that prioritizes and aligns with the client's expressed interests. Therefore, a crucial intention of the early phase of therapy is to signal a desire and commitment to share power through aligning with the client's goals.

We must think about this intention when considering whether to use mindfulness with a client. As therapists, we should consider the extent to which using contemplative practices aligns with the client's goals and interests. Given how poor therapists (and all people are) at mind reading, often we assume that a direct conversation may work best. A client may not understand all of the potential benefits of mindfulness for addressing his or her presenting concerns. In this case, it is our responsibility as therapists to share the evidence for its use and our rationale for wanting to incorporate this practice in the client's therapy, including why we think it is a good fit for that client's particular circumstance. If after sharing our perspective, a client is not receptive to the use of mindfulness, though, we should be willing to consider alternative approaches with humility. Otherwise, we risk adopting a paternalistic stance that is incongruent with the MCO framework.

Consider the following case, which we revisit later in the chapter.

Case Example: Julia and Dana

Julia is a 45-year-old, Mexican American, heterosexual, cisgender woman and therapist who specializes in the treatment of anxiety. Dana is a 28-year-old, White, heterosexual, cisgender woman who presents to therapy for treatment of generalized anxiety disorder (GAD). This dialogue comes near the end of their initial session.

JULIA: Thanks for sharing some of your story with me, Dana. I know we can't cover everything in one session, but I feel like we have a good start. What do you think?

DANA: Yeah, I do too. I'm surprised I was able to lay it all out like that. Usually when people ask me what the problem is, I have a hard time explaining it in a way that makes sense.

JULIA: Yeah, I can understand that. It sounds like you have a lot going on in several different aspects of your life, so it might be hard to get it all out.

DANA: That's for sure!

JULIA: One thing I want to be certain we do as we go forward is that we keep your goals and what you are wanting from therapy front and center. Periodically, if it's okay with you, I'd like to check in with you about that just to make sure we're on track. Would that be okay?

DANA: Yeah, I appreciate you doing that. Because this is my first time doing counseling, I'm not exactly sure how everything is supposed to go.

What was your initial reaction to the dialogue between Julia and Dana? What aspects of power could you identify that are at play in the therapy room? What do you think of how Julia tried to share power with Dana? How do you try to share power with your clients? Can you see how this principle might apply to deciding whether to use mindfulness in therapy? As a basic premise, we are suggesting that the therapist has the potential to exert undue influence on this decision. It is important to keep that in mind as you negotiate the treatment plan with clients.

THE SHARING OF POWER BY ACKNOWLEDGING LIMITATIONS

Clients enter therapy not knowing whether their therapist will fully align with their goals. The MCO framework focuses our attention—as therapists—on ways of intentionally putting the client's wishes first through expressing culturally humble behaviors. We cannot erase our power, but we can show ourselves to be trustworthy when in a position to potentially exploit our influence. Expressing culturally humble behaviors becomes even more important when the client holds marginalized identities.

An occupational hazard of being a therapist is the tendency to think we control more than we do. Early in our training, we learn to develop a case conceptualization, which is supposed to give us a story about the causes of the client's presenting concerns that also implies a treatment plan for addressing the issues. Reality is rarely that simple, however. Cultural humility would tell us that this conceptualization is only one possible hypothesis among many. We could be wrong. This process of coming up with a conceptualization and hypothesis is good as long as we do not imbue our "storytelling" with magical powers or believe our conceptualization represents an absolute truth. To perhaps state the obvious: We cannot actually know the past perfectly, and we cannot predict the future. We have to keep in mind that our stories and hypotheses are inherently limited. They gain power as they adjust and conform to the ongoing reality of the client's situation and are receptive to the client's investment. It seems possible that these stories work best when they invite clients to add themselves into the story—to cocreate the narrative and use it to structure some of their decisions.

This emphasis on the limits of "problem-solving" ways of engaging life align squarely with theories of therapeutic mindfulness especially found in acceptance and commitment therapy. The power to analyze and plan is effective for some purposes, but clients need therapists who are willing to temper their desire to plan and control with receptivity, openness, and tolerance of ambiguity. This idea also aligns with fundamental teachings of Buddhism and the nature of suffering. Life is in flux and changing, and failure to acknowledge that reality leads to an illusion of control that does not work well and amplifies distress. Thus, an important aspect of cultural humility during the assessment process involves having a relatively accurate sense of how little in life we can actually predict or control. This sense not only aligns with mindfulness practice but also helps ensure that the process of conceptualization remains flexible and responsive to new information and ongoing interactions with clients. Conceptualization involves making reasonable guesses that we then check out and update over time.

Activity 6.2: What Do You Think? Read the following story from current book author J. N. H. and then think about your own development. When have you noticed important shifts in your awareness of overconfidence in your work as a counselor?

A Reflection From Author J. N. H.

I remember that when I first started to supervise beginning graduate students in counseling, they were focused on finding a solution to the client's problem right away. A trainee would talk with a client for only a few minutes and would already have a hypothesis and be working toward a potential solution. I tried to urge my supervisees to slow down and take their time. "I'm not sure we have a good sense of the problem and what is causing it yet," I would tell them. But, if I'm honest with myself, I was the same way as a beginning therapist. I was so focused on "being helpful" or "being successful" that I rushed through the process of therapy. I thought that I had figured out the right direction to go, and I was off to the races, whether the client was coming with me or not.

It took me some time to realize that my hypotheses weren't always right and that it was disrespectful to think I had my client's situation pegged after just a session or two. Even if my instincts were right, I had to learn to slow down. I had to take my time to get to know my client, develop a connection, and see where my client wanted to go. I had to journey with my client, rather than trying to lead the client in a particular direction. If I had a hypothesis, that was fine, but I needed to learn to keep my hypothesis in my back pocket, ready if I thought it would help the therapeutic process but waiting to see if it would be supported by future data.

BARRIERS TO CULTURAL HUMILITY IN EARLY SESSIONS

Cultural humility involves cultivating an awareness and ownership of limitations in several sources of knowledge (Whitcomb, Battaly, Baehr, & Howard-Snyder, 2017). On the basis of recent theory and research on intellectual humility, we developed a heuristic for considering limitations that could bias a therapist's decisions during the assessment process. Each circle represents a lens for viewing the client's situation. Alone, each domain has limitations; however, using all the lenses simultaneously allows therapists to place greater weight on areas of convergence and consider areas of divergence more carefully. We provide an overview of each domain as a caution to attend to the limitations associated with authority sources within clinical decision making.

Beware of Scientism

Science is an observational process in which one uses a theory to make certain predictions and then seeks to create conditions under which those ideas can be falsified (Popper, 1974). Psychological scientists spend much of their time and energy investing in ways of thinking and tools for testing (and falsifying) ideas about how therapy works. However, when it comes to translating science to clinical decision making, many inferences are precarious. First, many aspects of a theoretical orientation cannot be falsified, so scientists are already making an error in assumption when they attempt to use science to demonstrate evidence for ideas that cannot lead to falsifiable tests. Second, most research on therapy addresses decisions in the aggregate. The process of therapy, which involves repeated interactions with one person, does not align with the method of observing lots of people. For example, the decisions researchers make to test therapies in clinical trials tend to weaken the external validity of the study (e.g., excluding comorbid diagnoses).

Even studies that are conducted in the "real world" have limited validity for telling us what to do with our particular client. Therapy happens one person at a time and unfolds gradually, which aligns poorly with the typical method of aggregating across people and drawing inferences based on simplified statistical models. Even with the "best" approaches, some clients do not benefit and may even be harmed (Lilienfeld, 2007). Thus, although it is nice to know that therapy generally works, we should not overgeneralize this fact. Each client is a new and unique challenge. As we touched on in Chapter 2, this principle also extends to the use of mindfulness in therapy. Research has only recently begun to consider factors that can amplify or detract from the effectiveness of therapeutic mindfulness (e.g., client demographics, personality traits, history). Therefore, although research on the use of mindfulness in therapy has been promising, therapists need to recognize the limitations of the research to date and not assume its effectiveness with all clients and all presenting concerns.

Beware of Theoretical Orthodoxy

Another pitfall is theoretical orthodoxy. To learn a theoretical orientation, we often submit ourselves to an authority structure within a tradition. Only parts of this training structure align with the scientific process. We also commit to belonging to a professional culture that has established ways of being, knowing, and doing. If we train long enough within a tradition, we begin to internalize certain ways of viewing the process of therapy.

A good theory provides a coherent story about why a problem exists and persists as well as a course of action for moving forward and healing. The story functions to expand on particular aspects of the case while it also diminishes focus on other possible aspects. Thus, the story has to be simple enough for clients to retain—even under duress—so they can learn new ways of thinking and being that they can live out independently.

But theoretical traditions have limitations, especially from a multicultural perspective. Theories develop within a community of professionals and within the particular worldview and social contexts of the developer(s) of the orientation. For example, some scholars have argued that Sigmund Freud's theories (e.g., the Oedipus complex; Freud, 1924/1961a) reflect his unusual family and cultural constellation growing up in Vienna, Austria. His household included his mother, who was the second (or third) wife of his father and 20 years his father's junior, and half brothers who were closer to his mother's age than his father's. These relationships could have created complex relational dynamics that were difficult for a young Freud to understand. Furthermore, Freud's focus on the male anatomy for the healthy development of women and men likely reflects the sexist beliefs of his time that restricted the roles of women and valued their contributions and potential less (Murdoch, 2013).

Thus, although psychological theorists attempt to ground their thinking in science, they also adopt values and take leaps of faith that are not grounded in science (Wampold & Imel, 2015). Theory-making is a human process. With all their history and experiences, the theorists, put their intuitions on the page. They can never know all the factors that may have influenced their ideas. It is for future psychologists to consider potential limitations and biases that may have been intertwined with their ideas. Furthermore, the theory becomes a living and evolving entity as a community of practitioners continue to use it to inform their work.

Of course, these various factors can undermine the validity of a theory's applicability to people with marginalized identities who likely were not part of the discourse and had less influence on the development of the professional community (e.g., through underrepresentation in the profession). Even though many prominent theorists made grand claims that their theory had universal application, we now know to view such agendas with caution.

Activity 6.3: Engage in a Thought Experiment. Cultural humility may require creativity as we seek ways to imagine or otherwise bring to our conscious awareness cultural assumptions that may not hold for clients with marginalized identities. With these efforts, practices and ways of doing things that may seem inevitable and part of the inherent structure of our profession might seem less inevitable and inherent. We attempt to illustrate the point with a few simple thought experiments. Consider the following questions:

- Why does most therapy involve a weekly individual session for 50 minutes rather than, for example, a 2-hour session with the family present?
- Why do we conduct therapy in offices where we expect clients to come to us rather than conduct therapy in a client's home, place of work, or church?
- Why does our field generally frown on dual relationships in which a therapist belongs to the same salient community as the client rather than encourage these multiple roles as a means to developing trust?
- What if therapy routinely occurred within teams of therapists and one client rather than the reverse (e.g., group therapy)?
- What if the prominent theorists embraced in our field were Black women rather than primarily White men?
- What if the dominant version of psychotherapy developed in India rather than Europe and the United States?

You may have heard these ideas before, especially in your multicultural training. But they have not necessarily been integrated into scholarship on mindfulness. What assumptions were challenged for you in this exercise? What biases came to awareness about how you understand the parameters of "good" therapy? Now, consider the current community invested in promoting and disseminating mindfulness in psychology. Do you see any potential problems?

Beware of Self-Preoccupation

Our awareness of the present moment is another lens we can use to understand what is occurring for our clients. This lens builds on converging work that emphasizes the importance of increasing the quality of therapeutic presence with (or attunement to) clients and their salient identities and values (Geller & Greenberg, 2012). Even so, just attending to the present moment does not guarantee that therapists will make wise decisions.

Illustrations of this point come from critiques of Western approaches to mindfulness (e.g., C. G. Brown, 2017; Purser, 2015). Attending to one's current flow of consciousness in an accepting way can lead to unethical and unwise behavior if not practiced within an appropriate larger framework. Within Buddhist traditions, mindfulness is a beginning practice that is contextualized within a larger meaning-system having specific goals and ways of understanding the world and the relationships between the self, other people, and the material world. These traditions have scriptures that attend to the tendencies of humans to engage with others and the world in unhelpful ways, and these tendencies flow from problematic ways of relating to one's internal experience.

Relating wisely to the complexity of clients' lives may require more than just teaching a meditation technique. For example, one can present mindfulness to a client who is experiencing racial trauma, but that presentation might amplify distress and internalization of racism (DeLuca, Kelman, & Waelde, 2018; Proulx et al., 2018). Also, some ways of presenting mindfulness might collude with unwise avoidance patterns of the client. Depending on the client's presenting problem, his or her situation may require immediate action and problem-focused coping. (Mindfulness may be introduced later, if at all.) Therefore, effective therapists must develop a practical wisdom about human nature that informs how to effectively respond to the challenges people face in their daily lives and how to come alongside clients in a way that will empower them to make decisions that enhance their wellness.

Beware of the Influence of Relational History

We also interpret our client's situation through the lens of our history within relationships, including our current belonging to a diverse and pluralistic professional community. Indeed, each therapist has a rich history of memories.

Therapists have encountered a range of complex situations; attempted to engage their environment; and, based on how those encounters and engagements transpired, developed a general sense of how to work toward goals. Having a strong professional network provides therapists with the ability to access much more than just their own perspective. With an email, a phone call, or Google search, they can gain access to a broad assortment of perspectives and cultural viewpoints. Ideally, this network would include people with diverse identities (e.g., race, gender, sexual orientation), theoretical orientations, political orientations, work environments (e.g., academic, private practice, community mental health center, detention center), and settings (e.g., urban, suburban, rural).

However, we all have gaps in accessible perspectives or biases in our history and current professional community. We tend to gravitate toward relationships with people who have shared values, interests, and commitments. For example, some groups may have a higher degree of mistrust for the integrity and trustworthiness of the scientific community. This caution can help hold the scientific community accountable because it is not immune from error, as evidenced by the recent replication crisis in psychological research that has called into question the findings of many foundational social psychological studies (e.g., Maxwell, Lau, & Howard, 2015). Another example is that many professionals prefer to live near cities or in middle-class or upper-class neighborhoods. As a result of these trends, we must be careful to not assume that our professional network provides an unbiased perspective. As an MCO therapist, one must make a concerted effort to create a broad and diverse network.

Activity 6.4: Map Your Professional Network. Map your professional network using the diagram shown in (see Figure 6.1). You'll see a set of concentric circles. The inner circle (Level 1) represents those colleagues with whom you have the closest, most vulnerable, and trusting relationships. The second circle (Level 2) represents the group of colleagues next closest to you and could include supervisors (peer or otherwise) or individuals with whom you work. The third and outermost circle (Level 3) could represent colleagues with whom you have more intermittent contact but still access for consultation. Write the names of your colleagues alongside each circle.

Now that you have mapped out your professional network, consider the demographic characteristics (e.g., race, ethnicity, social class, sexual orientation, religious or spiritual identity, gender identity, ability status), worldviews (e.g., collectivistic, individualistic), perspectives and knowledge of mindfulness practice, place of work (e.g., hospital, university counseling center, private practice), primary theoretical orientation, professional roles (e.g., staff psychologist, professor, administrator), and professional level (e.g., trainee, retired) of your network. Do you see any trends, patterns, or omissions? It may be particularly important to consider worldviews, identities, and theoretical approaches that may be missing from your network because people tend to complete goals that are clearly articulated.

FIGURE 6.1. Professional Network Spheres

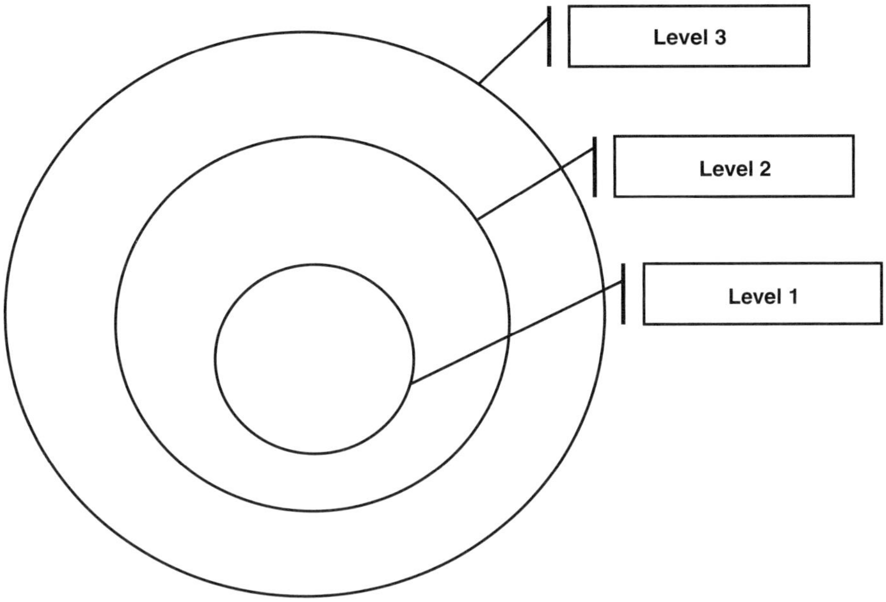

As discussed in Chapter 5, our training habits end up shaping our professional lives. What would it look like for you to make a subtle shift that would begin to increase the diversity of your current social network? For example, could you plan to add at least one new person to your network within the next month? As it relates to the theme of this book, the MCO framework aims to increase accountability and responsibility for gaps in one's social network. On one hand, we are not asking you to be overly self-punitive if your current network involves minimal exposure to different perspectives on contemplative practice. On the other hand, awareness comes with responsibility. So, as a step of commitment, we encourage you to identify your plan of action to identify and contact that person. Send the email, make the phone call, or write down your next step on your to-do list. Once you have done that, move on to the next section.

PRE-INTAKE PROCESS INFORMED BY MULTICULTURAL ORIENTATION

Even before stepping into the therapy room, we have learned to adopt a humble stance toward sources of knowledge. As you begin the session, it is also important to adopt a curious and receptive stance. The quality of our listening behavior is one of the primary indicators of cultural humility. As discussed in Chapter 4, listening well requires attending to our own experiences (i.e., use of self). If we are numb to our own thoughts and feelings or be carried away by forms of reactivity, then we will not have good discernment within the session. We will give too much attention to some things and too little attention to other things.

Expert therapists cultivate cues that allow them to optimize attention to the client and the development of insights that emerge from their knowledge and experience (Geller & Porges, 2014). Of course, having a long to-do list can take us away from listening well. A long list is precisely what we have when we conduct an intake interview. Especially early in our training, it can be challenging to mentally juggle this list of responsibilities (e.g., gathering information, making an accurate diagnosis) with the crucial task of listening well and forming a strong emotional bond with the client. Nonetheless, there may not be a second session unless the intake process happens with sufficient quality.

In this regard, it is important to have a good plan for assessment, which can help increase receptiveness because it allows us to trust that we have an effective process in place for gathering information. We only have so much capacity in our short-term memory, and the intake process certainly strains this capacity. Checklists are one of the ways that a variety of industries (e.g., pilots, construction project managers) have supplemented limitations of the human mind. Surgical errors are an area in which the use of checklists has dramatically improved outcomes (Gawande, 2009). We suspect that attending to the complexity of cultural issues in the first session is another area in which checklists could be helpful.

An intake form is like a checklist. You have prompts that keep the session on course, and the structure also gives you a sense of the pacing (e.g., if the first question takes 15 minutes, you know you will somehow need to make up ground or possibly consider having a second intake interview, if that is permissible within your setting). Therefore, checklists are a structure that shape what we prioritize with our time in the intake. As it relates to the topic of this book, most intake processes do not include information that would be most helpful for considering how to contextualize the use of mindfulness to the client's cultural background.

Activity 6.5: Develop a Multicultural Orientation Intake Form. Most sites have a standard intake form that all associated therapists are expected to use. Consider the intake form used at your site. With MCO values in mind, what changes would you make to this form? Would you add items? Take time to thoroughly review your intake materials with a particular emphasis on cultural identity and worldview. You might consider demographic variables, such as race, ethnicity, or spiritual identity, but you may also consider more nuanced information. This information could include immigrant status, nationality, racial identity, acculturation level, region of the United States with which the client is most familiar, family and cultural views of participating in therapy, and how your client defines *family*. As a therapist, we often need to strike a balance between gathering information and developing initial rapport all while attending to the time constraints of an intake interview. With practice, we can identify cultural opportunities and explore our client's cultural identities more deeply if we set that intention from the outset.

Now that you have considered your own intake form, read the statements in the following three examples. They describe how you could more deeply explore your client's salient cultural identities with questions and responses typical of an intake session.

- ***Example 1:***

  THERAPIST: I see that you checked "African American/Black" on your intake form.

  CLIENT: Yes. I identify as Black.

  THERAPIST: You know, I appreciate your specifying that. I am aware that identifying as Black versus African American can have important meaning for some people. Does that feel important to you?

- ***Example 2:***

  THERAPIST: You indicated that you identify as "Questioning" on our intake form. I was wondering what that means for you.

  CLIENT: I am still not sure about my sexual orientation. I think I may be attracted to all genders, but I haven't really explored that very much so far.

  THERAPIST: That makes sense. I really appreciate your sharing where you are with me. Is this something you would like to explore in therapy, or is the test anxiety you mentioned more of a priority right now?

- ***Example 3:***

  THERAPIST: We don't ask about family in our intake, but that is something that can be important for some people. Would you say that is true for you?

  CLIENT: Yes, definitely.

  THERAPIST: Okay, could you tell me more about yours? And, let me say that I think family can mean a lot of different things for different people, so please share whatever feels important to you.

In MCO language, the entire intake process is one large cultural opportunity. Most clients expect you to take the lead. It sends an important message if and how you engage cultural topics during this first session. For example, there is debate within the multicultural literature on whether it is important to explicitly address identities within the first few sessions. There also are mixed findings regarding whether rigidly having therapists raise a marginalized identity in their first session is helpful (Huey, Tilley, Jones, & Smith, 2014). In general, we tend to favor bringing up the topic so that clients can discuss their cultural identities if they so choose. But it is not just important that the therapist broaches identity topics; it also is important how this happens. For example, abrupt transitions can be unsettling for clients, so when therapists talk about cultural identities using smooth transitions, that contributes to trust in the relationship. For example, linking discussion about the client's cultural identities to the client's presenting problem, values, or possible sources of support can be helpful.

APPROACH TO THE USE OF MINDFULNESS

We extend a similar line of thought to how we might approach a client about the potential use of mindfulness in therapy. These conversations could happen in a first session or later in the therapy as your working relationship deepens. Remember, what matters most is *how* these conversations happen. In the following section, we outline general skills and considerations to inform your process. As we work through the steps, we refer to the case introduced near the beginning of the chapter: Julia (45-year-old, Mexican American, heterosexual, cisgender woman and therapist who specializes in the treatment of anxiety) and Dana (28-year-old, White, heterosexual, cisgender woman who presents to therapy for treatment of GAD).

Open-Ended Questions

A foundational principle we learned early in our helping skills courses was that open-ended questions have advantages over closed-ended questions for eliciting more complex emotional content. The three examples in Activity 6.5 illustrate the importance of open-ended questions and how therapists can use them to create smooth transitions between questions. Open-ended questions are especially important for broaching cultural topics. Given the focus of this book on attending to spirituality and its intersection with other identities, we want to illustrate this principle with how one might assess for the client's spiritual identity.

The reasons we suggest explicitly addressing spiritual identity in the first session is that we know that mindfulness has spiritual meaning and implications for many clients (Stratton, 2015). We also know that even for spiritual clients, many of them do not want to address spiritual themes in their therapy (Cornish, Wade, & Post, 2012). Therefore, we conclude that the way to determine the client's preferences is to ask the client. The approach could be as simple as asking three questions: (a) Do you identify as spiritual or religious? (b) If so, how important is spirituality or religion in your life? and (c) Is your spirituality or religion something you would like to discuss in therapy? (Cashwell & Watts, 2010). Many therapists include questions like these in their intake paperwork and review them before the session, which seems like an excellent idea because the client's preferences matter.

The type of language we use also matters. Carefully wording your questions can send a message of acceptance or inclusiveness (e.g., if the language does not assume a theistic spirituality). The importance of language is true for a variety of identities but especially true for spiritual identity. What feels like inclusive language for one client may be a sign of threat for another, so you need to carefully attend to nonverbal cues of how the client is responding to your interventions.

Spirituality is often connected with other identities. When engaging spiritual themes, cultural opportunities abound. The client's sense of gender, race, family, sexual orientation, and so forth may all be linked so be ready to listen for potentially important content. What exactly are we listening for? Probably at least two things: (a) content that is clearly important to the client based on signs of emotional connection and stated significance and (b) content that is potentially important because the client has emotional aversion and potential pain related to the that content. To show that we are present, we should regularly reinforce that we have heard the topics that clearly are emotionally significant to the client. Careful discernment, though, is required when confirming that we have heard content to which a client has emotional aversion and pain. For example, we might note that we are aware of the pain but show that we will be cautious and compassionate related to the topic that is potentially painful.

As the client is talking, it may help to keep a few open-ended questions in mind (e.g., How does the client's existential worldview both help and potentially interfere with that client's treatment goals?) to help you attend more closely to how the client's spiritual life may relate to his or her presenting problem. Spirituality is an area prone to splitting cognitions both for clients and therapists. Concepts of good and evil often promote binaries. The idea of the Sacred amplifies the significance of content and emotional reactions. Nonetheless, it is important to resist the urge to carve the world into binaries. Robust research has documented that religion or spirituality can provide a powerful source of coping for many clients and also amplify sources of suffering when people enter spiritual struggles (Exline, Pargament, Grubbs, & Yali, 2014). Even when therapists feel a pull to idealize or devalue, we can return to a cultural humble stance of interest and curiosity, which will model a similar stance for the client and promote greater integration rather than cognitive splitting.

Activity 6.6: Practice Assessing Spirituality and Its Intersection With Other Identities. Imagine that you are Julia working with Dana in therapy. You notice on Dana's paperwork that she checked the box indicating that she identifies as Christian. With the intake information available, how might you proceed to address gaps in your knowledge about Dana's salient identities? An important thing to keep in mind is that frequently practical suggestions are available, so you don't need to start from scratch.

To generate ideas, we have included in Exhibit 6.1 (Saunders, Miller, & Bright, 2010) other open-ended questions you could use to explore Dana's spiritual identity. First, answer these open-ended questions for yourself to get a sense of what it might feel like to have these questions posed to you. Then, ask yourself two questions: (a) Would you make changes to how these questions are asked that would make the questions more relevant to you? and (b) Are there questions you would avoid or ones you would add? Next, pose the open-ended questions in Exhibit 6.1 to two other people, including one person you feel comfortable with. It might be helpful to ask someone who has a different cultural perspective than you do. Then, ask these two people that same two questions we presented to you: Would you make changes to how these questions are asked that would make the questions more relevant to you? Are there questions you would avoid or ones you would add?

EXHIBIT 6.1

Possible Questions for Assessing Spiritual Identity

General Questions About Beliefs and Behaviors

- Are you a religious or spiritual person?
- How important is spirituality or religion in your daily life?
- How has spirituality or religion been important to you in your life?
- What things are most important to you?
- Are there things in your life that are sacred to you?
- What give your life purpose or meaning?
- Do you believe in a higher power?
- Are you part of a spiritual or religious community?
- Do you practice a religion currently?
- Are there spiritual or religious practices that you follow regularly?

The Relationship Between the Problem and Spirituality or Religion

- Has your current problems affected your relationship with your higher power?
- Has the problem for which you are seeking help affected your religious or spiritual life?
- Are spirituality or religion important to this problem? How?
- Has your religion or spirituality been involved in your attempts to deal with this problem?
- Are you worried about possible conflicts between your beliefs and your treatments?

Potential Resources

- Are members of your spiritual or religious community (such as a spiritual leader) a potential resource for you in trying to deal with this problem?
- Is there someone you can talk to about spiritual or religious matters as they relate to this problem?
- Is there anything that I can do to help you access such resources?
- Would it be helpful if I consulted with your spiritual leader?

Note. Adapted from "Spiritually Conscious Psychological Care," by S. M. Saunders, M. L. Miller, and M. M. Bright, 2010, *Professional Psychology: Research and Practice, 41*, p. 359. Copyright 2010 by the American Psychological Association.

After doing this preliminary work, how do you think it might this inform the questions you may be ready to ask Dana in this case? What areas do you think might be painful or uncomfortable for the client? Are you aware of any aspects of this conversation that might feel more uncomfortable for you?

Assessment of Possible Contraindication

The last theme to address in this chapter is assessment of potential problems with using mindfulness with a client. In Chapter 2, we introduced research on contraindications. Given how limited that research is, we must rely heavily on discernment and careful reasoning. If you are making a checklist for yourself, as we have proposed, then the following areas are good candidates for that list: side effects, the potential for difficulty engaging in practice, the potential for religious resistance, and opportunity costs.

Side Effects

Meditation has some known—albeit rare—potential side effects, so it makes sense to ask clients if they have ever had any of these problems as a result of engaging in meditation. Common difficulties include boredom, irritability, or intrusive thoughts. Meditation practices can assist people to become less reactive to mild to moderate psychological discomfort with a new way of being. However, in beginners, meditation can also make things worse before they get better. Perhaps for the first time, people are giving more space and attention to their inner life, which can result in greater awareness of unconscious thoughts and feelings (see A. M. Hayes & Feldman, 2004). In addition, although uncommon, some clients can experience more severe side effects, such as intense anxiety and stress, depersonalization, or other psychotic symptoms (Lindahl, Kaplan, Winget, & Britton, 2014; Shonin, Van Gordon, & Griffiths, 2014). Unfortunately, we have limited research on adverse effects in general and especially for marginalized groups (Van Dam et al., 2018). We would be wise to assume that distress will impair the client's ability to cope with meditation-related difficulties. For example, consistent with principles of treating trauma (Park, Currier, Harris, & Slattery, 2017), it would be unwise to assign mindfulness activities to clients dealing with trauma symptoms until they have sufficient skills to regulate their distress.

In our example, if Julia thought it might be helpful for Dana to incorporate mindfulness exercises as part of her treatment for GAD, she might—at intake—ask Dana about any prior experience she may have had with mindfulness and meditation, including side effects. If Dana has had little or no experience with mindfulness, Julia would talk about potential side effects and keep those side effects in mind as therapy progressed.

Potential for Difficulty Completing the Activities

Some clients may experience challenges in practicing mindfulness and building this practice into their daily lives. For example, typical mindfulness activities require cognitive skills related to introspection and abstraction. Accordingly, clients who may have a hard time sitting for long periods may find mindfulness difficult. Just like we would not assign highly introspective tasks to small children, we may want to consider other factors (e.g., personality, gender, cognitive or physical disabilities) that may interfere with a client's ability to engage in mindfulness activities (Bluth, Roberson, & Girdler, 2017). At the same time, practitioners have developed creative ways to use mindfulness, even with clients who may struggle with developing a practice (for a review of mindfulness with clients with attention-deficit/hyperactivity disorder, see Mak, Whittingham, Cunnington, & Boyd, 2018).

In our example, Dana did not have prior experience with mindfulness or meditation, but she appeared to have average to above-average cognitive skills related to introspection and abstraction. In her intake session, nothing indicated to Julia that Dana was likely to have difficulty completing the mindfulness activities, but she resolved to revisit potential challenges and continue to attend to indicators of difficulty moving forward.

Potential for Religious or Spiritual Resistance

The research and clinical literature on mindfulness are replete with warnings about religious or spiritual resistance to mindfulness. Despite minimal attention for other identities, this area does seem to have generated multicultural attention. For example, the newest manual for dialectical behavior therapy includes more explicit instructions for therapists on how to address potential reservations about the links between mindfulness and Eastern spiritual traditions (Linehan, 2014). We also see specialists advancing religiously accommodated versions of acceptance and commitment therapy (for a review, see Rosales & Tan, 2016).

For clients with a strong religious commitment, it is reasonable to assume they may view most aspects of their life through a religious or spiritual lens (Worthington, 1988). This strong religious or spiritual salience increases the chance that a cultural rupture could occur if therapists present mindfulness in a way that is insufficiently respectful of and compatible with their clients' religious or spiritual traditions. Thus, for some clients, it is probably important to have an explicit conversation exploring their attitudes and ideas about mindfulness. As discussed in Chapter 5, some clients may possess a narrower cultural span, and a person's span tends to be narrower under duress. Clients with painful and ongoing experiences of spiritual struggle due to prior exclusion and marginalization may have more brittle reactions to value differences.

Regarding the case involving Julia and Dana, because Dana had indicated that she was a Christian, Julia had a conversation with her about her faith. Before progressing with integrating mindfulness practice into treatment, Julia discussed with Dana how her faith might align (or not) with mindfulness activities. Here is an example of their dialogue (see box).

JULIA: We've talked a little bit about your Christian faith and how it is an important part of your life. I did want to check in with you about something. Sometimes in my work with clients who want to work on their anxiety, we work through some mindfulness activities to help you get in touch with your anxious thoughts and see if there's a way to approach them in a different way that can leave you with more peace and space to do what you want to do in life. Have you heard of mindfulness?

DANA: A little bit. My brother got into it awhile back and was using an app on his phone pretty regularly. It seemed to help him some, but I haven't explored it much.

JULIA: Yeah, it seems like it's everywhere on apps nowadays. One of the things I wanted to check in with you about is that mindfulness is based on Buddhist approaches to meditation. The approach I use attempts to draw on those ideas in a way that is compatible for people from a variety of cultures, including people who are not religious. If we did incorporate some of these activities, I would want to make sure the activities were consistent with your own beliefs and values. Do you have any thoughts about that?

DANA: I appreciate your saying that. Sometimes I do get wary about some of that "new age" stuff—not that that's what you're doing, but sometimes with that stuff I'm not always sure if it aligns with my faith, you know?

JULIA: Definitely, and I wouldn't want you to do anything that is counter to your faith. Why don't we keep that in mind, and if I think it might be helpful to incorporate some mindfulness practices, we'll walk through the activity together and see how you feel and if you are comfortable with it. How does that sound for a plan moving forward?

What did you think about the dialogue between Julia and Dana? Did you think that Julia addressed Dana's concerns about mindfulness in a culturally humble manner? What did Julia do well? What did Julia not do well? If you were in Julia's position, how might you have responded to Dana?

Opportunity Costs

It is important to consider whether mindfulness is currently the client's best use of time and energy. Even if mindfulness could be helpful, it may not be the highest priority for therapy. Indeed, any time (or emotional energy) spent on mindfulness is time not spent on other potentially important activities. Nonetheless, there are numerous potential reasons to consider using mindfulness. Early in therapy, it might help the client tolerate the work of therapy. Preparing for termination, it might help the client build skills that will help the client maintain progress. Research data are sparse for evaluating opportunity costs, and data on treatment moderators are limited (Van Dam et al., 2018). For example, presumably, if clients are already high on trait mindfulness, perhaps they have less to gain from focusing on mindfulness. Mindfulness has stronger evidence for some presenting problems than others. As we wait for more systematic knowledge, we can still use our best judgment.

In our running case example, Julia would have to weigh the benefits of mindfulness with engaging in other types of therapeutic activities. What do you think? Given Dana's presenting problem and diagnosis, what other activities might Julia consider in addition to mindfulness? Given your theoretical orientation, what other activities would you consider prioritizing?

To Use or Not to Use Mindfulness?

In many settings, after the first session or two, there is a formal or semiformal process of consolidating information into a conceptualization and treatment plan. The MCO framework focuses therapists' attention on how to contextualize our approach to the client's cultural identities to optimize the therapy alliance. We do so by owning our power in the relationship and using it to orient ourselves with the client's identities, values, and interests. When we say *orient,* what we mean is that we align ourselves with clients and what they want. We also put our available emotional energy toward strengthening an emotional bond.

Therapeutic presence is one of the key ways we orient. We attend to our own experience, which makes us receptive to the client. Then, we trust ourselves to respond in the moment. We remain open to feedback and the potential need for adjustment. This point about remaining open to the need for adjustment is crucial and can be where lapses in our therapeutic presence could cause major problems in the relationship. Imagine what would happen if you fell asleep at the wheel of a car even for a few minutes. When clients are in severe pain, we cannot afford to let ourselves fall asleep at the wheel.

Let's put all the pieces together from this chapter. For the case of Julia and Dana as well as the additional information gained in the intake interview process, what do you think? Would you decide to consider mindfulness as part of the treatment plan? How would you balance various sources of information and their limitations? Which "beware" statements would you rely on most heavily to guide your decisions? How confident are you that you could connect with Dana if she were your client? What things might you think about or do to make yourself emotionally available and responsive? Related to your own life, are there any other potential biases you are aware of that might cause problems for your decision?

CONCLUSION

This chapter focused on the process of forming a relationship with a client and deciding whether and how to integrate mindfulness into the treatment plan. We used this specific context to explore how someone with a strong MCO orientation might move forward with a balance of structure and responsiveness to the client's priorities. Based on the contextual model and the MCO framework, especially theory and research on the therapy alliance, we asserted that therapists should prioritize the client's perspective and interests as they emerge in the process of therapy. Rather than relying too heavily on cultural categories (e.g., race, gender, religion), which can lead to stereotyping and a lack of flexibility, we illustrated what it might look like for therapists to optimize their attunement to the client and quality of emotional engagement with the client.

A commitment to these behaviors builds a strong foundation for a relationship bond in which the client can feel confident that his or her therapist is truly and deeply "for me." This foundation of trust is needed in subsequent stages of therapy.

7

Negotiating the Plan

In Chapter 6, we talked about the initial stage of therapy and focused on the assessment of whether it was appropriate to incorporate mindfulness into therapy. This chapter assumes you have made it past the first session or two and have decided to integrate mindfulness into therapy. The key question we are tackling in this chapter is, How do I include mindfulness in a way that will work with *this client,* considering his or her cultural background and experiences in relationships? In this chapter, we revisit the tensions and dialectic introduced in Chapter 3 between contextualizing mindfulness to the individual client and honoring the cultural traditions that brought us therapeutic mindfulness. We are curious if the language and ideas of the multicultural orientation (MCO) framework can help us begin to think about how to hold these two multicultural values in tension as we tailor how we use mindfulness in therapy.

Our ideas for the current chapter are based on the *social oil hypothesis of humility,* which predicts that humility reduces the wear and tear of relationship factors that can cause deterioration in trust and commitment (Davis et al., 2011). As such, humility functions like oil to a car engine: It protects relationships from breaking down as a result of repetitive behaviors that undermine cooperation. Early examples of the social hypothesis came from scholarship on business leaders that suggested that leaders are selected for their positions based on competitive traits, such as high performance or even some degree of grandiosity. Humility can buffer the potential for negative

---

http://dx.doi.org/10.1037/0000156-007
Mindfulness-Based Practices in Therapy: A Cultural Humility Approach, by D. Davis, C. DeBlaere, J. N. Hook, and J. Owen

interpersonal consequences resulting from these qualities (Owens, Wallace, & Waldman, 2015).

Under the umbrella of the MCO framework, the social oil hypothesis has also been demonstrated in psychotherapy. When therapists missed opportunities to connect with their client's cultural identities, these missed opportunities were associated with worse therapy outcomes (i.e., lower alliance and self-rated improvement in therapy). However, cultural humility buffered this negative relationship (Owen et al., 2016). These findings point to the important role of demonstrating cultural humility to provide resources so that the therapist–client relationship can handle potential challenges or even cultural ruptures.

In the current chapter, we extrapolate the social oil hypothesis to consider how therapists might negotiate the use of mindfulness with their clients given that negotiating the tasks and goals of therapy can potentially cause conflict (Davis et al., 2018). This potential is amplified by the presence of cultural differences. As a result, clients from marginalized groups have good reason to wonder whether their therapist will put their needs first. These clients may approach the new relationship with cautious optimism and then be pleasantly surprised if their therapist demonstrates ease, interest, curiosity, flexibility, caringness, compassion, and faithfulness when engaging cultural diversity and intersections of identity (Davis et al., 2018; Hook, Davis, Owen, & DeBlaere, 2017).

It might help to think of this as a two-step process. In Chapter 6, we considered a first phase of information gathering and assessment. This chapter focuses on a second phase of collaboratively determining the plan. For clients from marginalized groups, it is important to attend to indicators of potentially exploitive relationships. We cannot just tell our clients we will put them first; they will watch our behavior for signs of trustworthiness. Actions matter more than words. For example, research with cross-racial dyads showed that when a person says one thing but does another, that action hurts outcomes (e.g., Jacoby-Senghor, Sinclair, & Shelton, 2016). Put another way, incongruence between stated and expressed goals negatively impacts a dyad's ability to complete a shared task like therapy. Consequently, to maximize the therapy alliance, therapists must increase awareness of biases so that they do not submit to them unintentionally.

Clients wondering about the responsiveness of a new relationship will often look for clear signs that a relationship is trustworthy. Whether we pay attention to it or not, the process of cocreating the goals and tasks of therapy is one of the first tests of a developing therapy relationship. Clients may pull away if they feel coerced or manipulated. Alternatively, they may invest deeply in the relationship when they sense that their identities and deepest values are honored, respected, known, and valued. Accordingly, this chapter is organized to address potential telltale signs of cultural humility. We describe four practical recommendations. We also provide an opportunity for you to practice with a case involving a client with a strong religious or spiritual identity. We also have you consider how to weigh critiques about appropriation. As in the preceding chapter, we introduce a case example and use it to illustrate various themes along the way.

RECOMMENDATION 1: ACCEPT INFLUENCE TO PROMOTE A COLLABORATIVE RELATIONSHIP

The first recommendation is to accept influence from our clients. Trust is the rate-limiting factor of the therapy relationship. So, during the early phase, therapists should seek to optimize trust. This investment will provide a foundation for working to address the presenting concerns and protect the relationship from misunderstandings that may emerge over time. How will clients feel like they have been put first if we do not listen carefully to what they want from therapy?

For clients from marginalized groups, we cannot assume that we agree on how therapy is supposed to work. Consistent with a contextual perspective, research on the effectiveness of culturally adapted therapies indicated that interventions work better when aligned with the client's *cultural myths* (see Benish, Quintana, & Wampold, 2011, for a meta-analysis), the stories therapists or clients have about the presenting problem and how it might be addressed (Frank & Frank, 1993). The use of the word *myth* acknowledges that aspects of a theory of change are unfalsifiable scientifically but still important for the process of achieving a shared trust by clients and the therapist. Two-person theories, for example, frame therapy as a process of cocreating and enacting a cultural myth (Wachtel, 2008). We can try to accept influence in several ways while developing a plan.

A helpful intervention can be to offer the client a jargon-free conceptualization and treatment plan and then seek the client's feedback. Clients come to therapists in distress and may not have the energy and resources to internalize an overly complex plan. Therefore, it's important to distill the logic of our theory down into its key movements. For example, in a cognitive conceptualization, the ABC (i.e., antecedent [A], behavior [B], and consequence [C]) model helps clients remember that antecedents lead to beliefs, which in turn influence consequences—a cognitive conceptualization in a nutshell.

In qualitative research, it is customary to conduct validation or verification checks. A similar approach is warranted to confirm a strong therapy alliance. Therapists can offer their perspective in plain language and "check out" their ideas for fit with the client's own perspective. Sometimes this approach can happen explicitly and with words but should happen implicitly as the therapist looks for potential cues that things may not be going well. For example, through subtle cues such as closed or protective body posture (e.g., arm crossing), clients may insinuate that they are not feeling connected with the therapist. When we therapists fail to attend to these subtle cues, we may see a much less subtle cue: termination of therapy. Checking in with the client communicates respect and caring. Imagine how you might present your approach for the following case, which occurs in the third session.

Case Example: Curtis and James, Session 3

Curtis, the therapist, is a 52-year-old, African American, cisgender man. He has a PhD in clinical psychology and has worked in private practice for 19 years. He is married with two children, and he identifies as heterosexual and agnostic. James, the client, is a 22-year-old, White, gay, cisgender man, and Catholic. He is going to school part time to earn a bachelor's degree in English. He is out to some of his friends but not to his family or church community. He is attending therapy to help with stress and anxiety related to school and work as well as his religious and sexual identities. This dialogue is from their third session.

CURTIS: I was wondering if we could talk a little bit about where we want to go in therapy now that I've had a chance to meet with you a couple of times and get a sense of your background and what you're wanting from counseling.

JAMES: Sure, that sounds good. I'm not sure if I know exactly where I want to go or how to get there, so it will be good to talk about it.

CURTIS: From our sessions so far, it seems like you're in a place where you're trying to figure out some key aspects of your identity—you're trying to figure out what you want to major in and what your work identity is going to be. And there's the conflict between your religious and sexual identities that you've been trying to work out. And there's also the social part of your identity—how do you want to be with your family and your close friendships. These are some big questions to figure out, and it seems like it's causing you stress.

JAMES: Yeah, I think that sounds about right. There are a lot of things I'm trying to figure out right now, and some of them seem pretty major like they could alter the course of my entire life, you know?

CURTIS: I agree. They do seem like key aspects of your life. I do want to say that it's a big deal that you took the step to come to therapy to work on these things. Not everyone takes the initiative that you did to make a change. But you're really working to think about some of the deeper things in life. That's admirable.

JAMES: Thanks.

CURTIS: As I mentioned a bit in the first session, I tend to think about people's problems through a lens called acceptance and commitment therapy, or ACT. Put simply, through ACT, we don't necessarily try to get rid of all your problems and stress because that would be impossible. You're tackling some big things right now, and it would be impossible to just totally remove those problems from your life. The focus of this approach is on clarifying what is most important to you and letting that guide your responses, rather than spending emotional energy trying to control or fix the problems in your life, which can backfire. So, the goal is not to fix your problems per se but to develop a new way of relating to problems. Keeping in mind what you really want in life is a concrete way to change how you see your problems. How does that sound?

JAMES: I like the idea of identifying my values and working toward them. I think that might really help me sort out what I'm wanting in the various parts of my life. I'm not sure I'm quite understanding what you mean by relating to my thoughts in a different way, but I'm open to that.

What do you think of the dialogue between Curtis and James? Do you think Curtis and James were able to discuss James's presenting problem in a collaborative way? How could Curtis have been more culturally humble in his discussion with James? If you were Curtis, what might you say next?

RECOMMENDATION 2: SHOW RESPECT FOR THE CLIENT'S RIGHT TO CHOOSE

A second recommendation related to expression of cultural humility is to respect the client's autonomy during the process of negotiating the plan. In any relationship, emergent goals can eclipse the priority of the emotional bond. In therapy, treatment planning is a phase during which therapists may gravitate toward putting their own needs ahead of their clients', especially new therapists who have a strong desire to perform well and prove their competence. We have our own ideas about what is wrong and what might help, which is okay. But the process of reconciling our perspective with the client's perspective is fundamental to a strong therapy alliance. Clients rely on us to seek alignment with great skill and without relying on coercion or use of power, as described in Chapter 6.

Consider the following example: A psychologist who is promoting a mindfulness intervention in public schools intentionally camouflages that mindfulness is rooted in Buddhism and other world religions. Among the team, concealing the cultural roots of the practice is explicitly discussed. The strategy is used primarily to avoid potential parental concerns and to allay the fears of school administrators concerned about parental resistance. How would you feel if you were a parent and school instructors—to avoid a conflict—intentionally concealed information about the cultural roots of an intervention? Would you generally favor the strategy? What problems do you see with this strategy?

You might align more with a parent who feels that such education falls outside the charter of the public school mission. Separation of church and state dictates that schools err on the side of caution when it comes to teaching religious content, and this decision to conceal the historical roots of the practice helps align with this principle. On the other hand, you might view the reactions of some parents as potentially too restrictive. For example, one could argue that mindfulness is actually a psychological concept—not the possession of any one religion. Many religions have teachings related to encouraging one's children, but we would rarely view the teaching of such a practice as primarily religious or spiritual in content. You may feel that it is a weakness of school systems that they are so limited in exposing children to more diverse cultural perspectives.

In the moment, it may seem innocuous to use our power in sessions to influence the direction of therapy. However, the problem is that using our influence against the client's wishes perpetuates societal dynamics of power and control within larger society; the therapy room becomes a microcosm of the dynamics of power and privilege in larger society. The MCO framework reminds us to view the therapy relationship with an awareness of larger systems of power so that we can use power to align our goals with those of our clients. Indeed, as should be clear by now, we do not view power as something one can "give up." The closest thing we can do is align our interests with the client's. Think of when a plane is flying in the direction of a tailwind versus against it. Not only is the flight shorter and more efficient, it can be less bumpy along the way. We can use our influence to help clients get where they want to go more effectively.

Activity 7.1: Think About Respect in Relationships. When you consider your own relationships or therapy experiences, what actions or phrases have others used that made you feel they respected your autonomy? Conversely, what have they said or done that made you feel that they did not respect your autonomy? List each of these phrases or actions. Now, how can you apply these experiences to your work with clients? What can you do or say, and what can you avoid?

One approach to protecting your client's autonomy is to present mindfulness as one of several possible ways of approaching his or her goals rather than a singular option. Even little kids like to have choices—as do independent and autonomous adults. One of the authors (D. D.) has a daughter who tends to be very autonomous. Rather than getting embroiled in power struggles, D. D. often will present her with at least two possible choices. This strategy has helped protect their relationship from conflict. It also has given him insight into her decision-making process, which has helped them to develop a stronger relationship through collaborating on decisions together. In a healthy parenting relationship, there is an element of power that decreases over time. Similarly, good therapy involves a power differential, but, ideally, the therapist collaborates with the client to foster independence.

Decisions in therapy require navigating similar power dynamics and the need to collaborate to share power. One strategy to avoiding coercion when proposing mindfulness is to generate at least one viable alternative option for whatever the treatment goal might be. For example, if the goal is to help the client reduce stress, mindfulness could be presented alongside other activities that could help the client reduce stress through avoiding rumination (e.g., exercising, journaling, talking with a friend). If the goal is to reduce time pressure and perfectionism, mindfulness could be presented alongside other behavioral strategies (e.g., making to-do lists at the beginning of each day to establish priorities).

A story about the Dalai Lama that is now part of the folklore about Western mindfulness (Hickey, 2010) illustrates the point. The Dalai Lama was invited to a meeting that included talks on the scientific evidence for mindfulness. With muted enthusiasm, he noted that mindfulness is good, but he prefers analytical meditation or getting a good night's sleep. The point being, perhaps, that mindfulness has many benefits, but it is not a cure-all, and part of the process of living well involves increasing one's flexibility to consider an array of potential options and wisely choose how to respond to one's current situation. Failing to offer options limits the client's choices and can violate the client's autonomy. Having mindfulness become part of the mainstream culture can lead to potentially dangerous problems, such as unrealistic expectations or clients' feeling pressure to try mindfulness. No matter what happens in popular or social media, therapists should never come across as "mindfulness missionaries" (e.g., Grant, 2015).

Activity 7.2: Think of Alternatives. Create a list of the presenting problems you imagine you might address using mindfulness as an adjunctive technique. Once you have created this list, see if you can think of at least one alternative approach to address the same issue or challenge. What is the best alternative you can think of? This simple practice may help you avoid becoming rigid in your promotion of mindfulness.

Activity 7.3: Practice Introducing Mindfulness. Let's return to the example of Curtis and James. During the fourth session, Curtis notices that James appears to be experiencing strong thoughts that come and go quickly and are causing him distress (e.g., "My family will never accept me as a gay man," "I can't figure out what I want to do in life," "My partner doesn't love me"). Curtis would like to introduce James to an exercise in which he pictures each thought, feeling, or sensation that comes to him like a leaf floating by on a stream. The goal of the exercise is to increase mindfulness of one's thoughts, feelings, and sensations and also to create distance between the self and the particular experience by labeling it as a thought, feeling, or sensation. How might you introduce this exercise to James in a way that respects his autonomy?

RECOMMENDATION 3: RESPOND TO CULTURAL BIDS

A third way we can express cultural humility during the negotiation of the treatment plan is through following up on *cultural bids,* an example of a cultural opportunity within the MCO framework. We are also borrowing from some of John Gottman's language for working with couples (Gottman & Driver, 2005). On the basis of his research on how couples interact with each other, Gottman observed a key difference in how happy couples respond to each other relative to unhappy couples. He coined the term *bids* to describe this difference (Gottman & Driver, 2005). In relationships, almost every moment is rich with opportunities for possible connection and bonding. More specifically, Gottman and Driver (2005) noted that happy couples would consistently respond positively to relationship bids—no matter how small—by their partner. For example, one partner might say, "Look at that red bird! That is stunning." With a happy couple, the partner might respond, "Wow, that is beautiful." However, with an unhappy couple, the partner might grumble something back, ignore the comment, or say something undermining (e.g., "I prefer blue birds").

Clients make bids too, and often the bids have a cultural dimension. Cultural bids are a type of cultural opportunity. As a good partner responds with positive emotional engagement to various bids, the MCO therapist should respond with emotional engagement to his or her client's various cultural bids. We want to cultivate a mind-set that sees each session as having many potential bids, but often we have to slow ourselves down to see a session this way. The truth is, clients take a risk every time they share something about themselves with us. We want to honor each of these little risks as much as we can. Each time we respond with interest and curiosity, we strengthen the emotional bond. The reverse is true if we respond with minimization.

Activity 7.4: Practice Attuning to Bids. Responding to emotional bids requires consistent practice. Think of a relationship or role in your own life with which you can practice attuning to emotional bids. What are the things you will need to do to create internal space for this kind of shift in attention? Read the following example of attuning to bids from book author D. D.

Author D. D.'s Example of Attuning to Bids

Cultivating a responsiveness to cultural opportunities is a way of being more than a way of doing. As my career has developed, I have felt roles and responsibilities pile up. Sometimes my life at work feels like a variety of lists—long lists. I have lists of papers to write, people to call, e-mails to send, people to meet, and so on. Sometimes these lists can cause me to feel anxious and afraid I am not doing enough. I feel an inner striving.

In contrast, I think about what it feels like when I can set aside my lists and enjoy being with my three kids, Adam, Catherine, and Emerson. They make bids for my attention and want to play with me. They want to play with me at their level. I feel guilty about it, but sometimes I don't always really want to play at first. I have to turn my mind toward them and quiet down my strivings. I turn down the volume on the "listing" part of my mind and its sense of being behind. I turn as much of my being as possible to my kids and their desire to play with me and be with me. I have found that therapy seems to require a similar mode or mental frame of mind. I cannot go into a session with lists; I have to settle into a different space that is less effortful and more willing and receptive.

Attune to the Client's Situation With Humility

Responding to cultural opportunities necessitates that the therapist similarly turn the mind. Although the therapist has plenty of things to do, the work of therapy requires a responsive and attentive frame of mind, and the healing aspects of therapy warrant quieting the mind's "doing mode." We want to cultivate an inner space for curiosity and interest. As we stir these emotions, we allow a space for flexibility and warm and accepting attention. These qualities extend an emotional tone to the relationship that can provide clients with respite from the stress and loneliness of their daily lives (Topor, Bøe, & Larsen, 2018). When they share their worries and concerns with us, they do so in a new environment. They are now with someone who cares deeply about them and expresses this care through careful attunement.

Consider the following dialogue from Curtis and James's fifth session. Pay attention to how Curtis responds to James's cultural bid. How culturally humble was Curtis's response?

Case Example: Session 5

CURTIS: Let's check in about our homework from the previous week. What thoughts came up for you that were most painful?

JAMES: To be honest, it was a really tough week. I was so overwhelmed; I didn't really get around to writing down my thoughts. I'm sorry.

CURTIS: That's okay. What happened that made the week so tough?

JAMES: Well, I went out this weekend and saw my ex. He was drinking and dancing and having a great time, and I just got so upset. I'm not over him, and I want to be, and I just don't know how to do it. Anyways, I ended up getting drunk and going home with some guy I didn't even know. Then I felt guilty, so I went to church the next morning, and the pastor was talking about lust and how bad it was, and I sat there thinking, "If they only knew what I was doing 6 hours ago." And I just felt more and more depressed because I'm such a different person everywhere I go. No one really knows the whole me.

CURTIS: Yeah, I can see how that would be tough. You're not over your ex, but it seemed like he was doing just fine. And then there's the various identities conflicting again. You can't be completely yourself anywhere you go. How does it feel when you have to mask part of who you are?

What did you think of Curtis's response? Did you view what James shared as a cultural bid? Why or why not? If you were Curtis, how would you have responded to what James shared?

Reframe Our View of Cultural Ruptures

Even conflict can provide an opportunity to strengthen the relationship. Criticisms or resistance in therapy can be viewed as a potential cultural bid. Indeed, miscommunications or hurts happen even under the best of circumstances, and stress and cultural differences make them even more likely. We make mistakes. We may reinforce a stereotype, remind a client of a past hurt, or miss a cultural bid. That these ruptures happen is not the primary problem.

What matters most is how we respond to cultural ruptures. Cultural ruptures are painful (Safran & Muran, 2006), and many clients do not address them verbally until they are on the verge of terminating (Binder & Strupp, 1997). One way to help make sure the relationship can handle misunderstandings is to invest in the relationship with high responsiveness and engagement. That way, both people will notice and grieve the momentary loss of connection when it happens. Both will be invested in getting things back on the right track. A strong bond helps us notice when a shift in the emotional tone has occurred. The client will be more likely to tell us if there is a problem. Even if the client does not tell us directly, we are more likely to pick up on the indirect signs of a problem.

Although it can feel uncomfortable to be confronted by our clients with our bias, prejudice, or discriminatory actions, it is critical to consider these confrontations as gifts. Clients take a significant risk in sharing the vulnerability of being injured by our words or actions: They risk rejection, apathy, and invalidation (all things they have likely experienced numerous times before in relationships that were both less and more significant than their working alliance with us). The key thing to remember is that by sharing their experience with us, they are making a bid to repair and strengthen the working relationship. After all, if they were giving up on the relationship, they likely would say nothing and terminate.

As therapists, we grow in cultural humility as we continually practice and sharpen our listening and communication skills. We can reduce our attunement and responsiveness to clients in many ways. Can you think of times in your clinical work when you were less engaged and responsive to your client because you were distracted by your own needs? For example, perhaps you bombarded your client with questions about how things were going without taking the time to fully explore any response. In turn, the client correctly surmised that the primary impetus for the interaction was not their needs but some need of yours (e.g., need for assurance, sense of self-efficacy, self-determined agenda). The next activity is intended to assist you in further developing your own listening skills.

Activity 7.5: Spend Time With an Exceptional Listener. Draw to mind your own experiences of being with exceptional listeners. Think of the best listener you have ever known. What was that person like? What was the person like when busy and stressed?

We as a group of coauthors considered qualities that we admire in good listeners. They have the ability to conceal their degree of stress. It is not that they suppress their feelings, but they are able to momentarily set aside their needs to put others first in the moment. This ability allows them to offer and maintain strong presence to others. Even in emotionally chaotic situations, they seem to have quiet egos. Also, they stay emotionally engaged in life and what is happening around them. They apologize quickly after mistakes rather than get defensive and escalate conflict. Their consistency across all domains of life helps them offer a relatively unmitigated sense of presence and engagement. They also help us integrate our feelings into our awareness of the present moment. They notice things about our body language that help us develop insights. They listen carefully to our nonverbal communication and body language. In addition, they are careful and disciplined in how they express anger or resentment. For example, they choose their words wisely, are slow to speak, and rarely draw extra people into conflict. Indeed, these great listeners have cultivated habits of presence. Something about this gift of presence is powerfully healing, especially when combined with attitudes of acceptance, caring, and compassion. Overall, they consistently practice kindness and compassion in their interactions with others across situations and relationships.

Think of your own listening heroes. List the characteristics and manifestations of your great listeners. Commit to practicing incorporating these skills, words, and actions into your own practice. You might consider developing a plan of action whereby you work on one skill or action per week in your own clinical work.

Taken together, our ability to attend well to clients requires that we stay connected to the present moment rather than get lost in a pattern of reactivity and analytical thinking about the past or future. It is when we prioritize wanting to have a sense of control, be right, or impress ourselves, our supervisor, or our clients that our work as therapists can shift from being attuned and truly listening to an ego-focused exercise.

RECOMMENDATION 4: SHOW AN AWARENESS OF SPIRITUAL AND EXISTENTIAL DIVERSITY

A fourth recommendation for negotiating the use of mindfulness with cultural humility is to show an awareness and sensitivity to spiritual diversity. We serve a diverse and pluralistic society with broad values, beliefs, practices, and cultural identities. Our clients vary in their degree of religious or spiritual commitment as well as their engagement of intersecting identities. Their communities vary in their knowledge about and receptiveness to the mainstream interest in mindfulness within the West. Cultural humility dictates that we cultivate flexible ways of thinking and talking about mindfulness. Using our case from this chapter, we illustrate several suggestions for expressing cultural humility by demonstrating greater awareness of spiritual diversity.

Prepare for Questions

Given that many clients view mindfulness as a spiritual practice, they may ask direct questions about mindfulness, so it is good to anticipate them. For example, consider how you might handle the following situation if you were Curtis:

JAMES: So, it sounds like you think mindfulness may help me handle some of the stress I have. I'm interested in hearing more. However, isn't mindfulness a form of Buddhist prayer? I am not sure I want to pray in therapy. Are you Buddhist? Is that why you use mindfulness as a therapist?

What would you say next? Your theoretical tradition might give you guidance on how to handle the risks of self-disclosure. Sharing too much might burden the relationship with additional dynamics but sharing too little might come across as unresponsive to the client's concerns and reasons for wanting to get to know his or her therapist better.

Regardless of what you decide, the MCO framework suggests that it is important to seize upon this cultural opportunity. You may decide to hold a firmer boundary, but the goal is to provide a warm and engaged emotional response that attends to the heart of the client's concern. For example, here are potential responses:

- "I'm willing to answer that question, but before I do, would you be willing to share how it would be helpful for you to know whether or not I am Buddhist?"
- "You asked if mindfulness is a form of Buddhist prayer. That's a great question. It can be, but how we plan to use mindfulness in our work together will focus less on suggesting ideas on which to pray and more on understanding how you are engaging your life in the present moment."
- "You asked a lot of questions there. Which one feels most important to you for me to answer?"

The MCO framework has no rigid formula for responding to such situations. To decide how to respond, you need to rely on a combination of your theoretical orientation, prior training, and intuition in the moment. However, the MCO framework can guide how you might frame the problem. The client is making a cultural bid. If you get defensive and stand behind a veil of authority, the bid will go unanswered. The client took a risk. The response will require its own type of risk. If we show rigidity and fail to address the client's concerns and needs, we may quickly reach a cultural impasse. Therefore, this example interaction indicates that even challenging and surprising situations give us a chance to strengthen our relationship with clients.

Without question, holding appropriate limits and boundaries is a crucial aspect of therapy, but how we hold those boundaries also sends an important message about our cultural stance. Cultural humility involves softening our values and routines (i.e., our way of doing things, even professionally) to find a way forward with our clients. Clients will experience rigid responses as a lack of cultural comfort. When we respond defensively to cultural bids, clients may lower their expectations in that area of their lives (with us and potentially others), which is not at all what we want.

Choose Language Wisely

Remember that language matters. Clients use language as a clue to understand our loyalties and identities. The inclusiveness and specificity of our language can provide information about our identities. As we talk with our clients, we can increasingly seek to calibrate our language with theirs, which communicates responsiveness. For example, using overly inclusive language (e.g., "We are all spiritual beings") may not fit for a conservative religious client. A lack of inclusive language (e.g., using specific religious terminology, such as "God," "Jesus," "sin") may not fit for a client who is spiritual but not religious. Consider the following dialogue from Curtis and James's ninth session.

Case Example: Session 9

CURTIS: It sounds like you have been struggling with your faith this week. Can you tell me more about that?

JAMES: Yeah, it's just been on my mind lately. I don't know if it's so much my personal faith that I'm struggling with but more the community aspect of it. I can pray to God by myself, and I know he loves me, but it's not the same as being with everyone. I haven't been to church for a while, and I know why I haven't been back, but there's so much there that I miss, even though being there hurts so much because they don't accept me. It's weird.

CURTIS: It doesn't sound weird. It sounds like your Catholic faith is an important part of your identity—especially the community part—and there's a sense of loss when you aren't engaging with it. As I said before when you asked me, I'm not a religious person myself, but I know that religion is an important part of many people's lives. So, I want this to be a place where we can discuss and unpack your religious faith to see if there's a way that you can engage your faith in a way that works for you.

JAMES: I appreciate your saying that.

What did you think of the exchange between Curtis and James? Did you notice how Curtis used the word *faith,* which led to James's being more specific about what was bothering him about his religion this week? Our clients use our language to surmise our values, potential biases, and what we understand about their worldview. Just like people can use facial expressions to detect subtle emotions, they also can use language to discern someone's values, ideology, political loyalties, and other identities. Therefore, it is important to be conscious of how language can affect our developing therapy alliance with clients.

Listen for Existential Assumptions

Just like our clients carefully scrutinize us early in therapy, we also can listen with a third ear. In particular, listen for the client's existential assumptions. If we ask the right questions, we can begin to align our language with the client's own language—which is generally a good approach. As clients tell their story, we can listen for clues about their meaning system. Later, you may decide to conduct a more structured assessment processes; but, before that, be patient and determine what you can glean from listening closely. Most people will convey their salient identities within a few minutes of talking about issues that are important to them. Through reflecting back affect, and with a little trust, people may naturally begin telling you about what matters the most to them.

Clients' language provides hints about how they view the world, sources of authority, and primary sources of belonging. These hints become even clearer if we ask the client about values and sources of meaning and purpose. By showing curiosity about purpose and values, therapists can begin to see how clients construct their sense of meaning and purpose in life. Then, we can consider how to align ourselves with the client's sources of values, strength, and other cultural structures. For example, a client might mention experiencing certain events in life as a "blessing." These questions can help delve into existential issues:

- Do you feel you have a purpose in life?
- How do you believe we come to know our purpose?
- What support, if any, do we receive about understanding our life's meaning and purpose? Who or what supports that understanding?
- How do you know if you have deviated from your purpose?
- What consequences do you see associated with deviating from your life's meaning or purpose?

These are some questions we sometimes find helpful. Do any of them resonate with your style? Of course, you will need to modify them for use with your own clients.

Keep in mind that the very act of asking these types of questions communicates to your client that discussing issues of spirituality, purpose, and meaning are appropriate and welcome topics of exploration in therapy. Consequently, even if your client is not yet ready to discuss these topics or does not want these topics to be the focus of therapy at the moment, there is value in your client's simply knowing that they could be. Furthermore, because the therapist is conveying an openness to discussing one cultural identity, such as spirituality, it is likely that the client may perceive that the therapist is open to exploring other cultural identities as well.

Show an Awareness of Existential Limitations

Cultural humility calls for a willingness to acknowledge and own limitations in our perspective. So, regarding spirituality and its intersection with other marginalized identities, it is important to show a willingness to examine our existential assumptions—and own our limits in that regard. This work helps us avoid getting defensive around cultural themes that make us uncomfortable.

We all have ideological commitments that guide our way of viewing and responding, including our theoretical orientation. From research on alliance ruptures, we know that therapists often respond poorly. Sometimes they even fail to notice a problem. When they do notice, they often double down and do more of the same rather than be flexible (e.g., Castonguay, Goldfried, Wiser, Raue, & Hayes, 1996). When a cultural problem happens in therapy, the therapist and client have to work together to find a way forward. Consider the following questions for self-reflection:

- What training commitments might lead to a lack of flexibility in your work?
- Have there been experiences or times in your training in which you could have demonstrated more responsiveness to feedback from your client when he conveyed feelings that therapy was not progressing well?

Let's return to our running case example. Consider the following conversation following James's agreement to engage in sitting meditation exercises.

CURTIS: How did the homework go last week?

JAMES: Okay. I wasn't that into it.

CURTIS: Oh, really? What happened?

JAMES: It's not important. I tried it, but it felt like prayer, and me and the Big Man aren't on good speaking terms these days. Let's get to the session. What's on the agenda today, doc?

If you were Curtis, what would you do next? Things are not necessarily going according to plan, and you are picking up clear signals that the client wants to avoid talking about what happened. How could you respond to this situation?

PRACTICE ENGAGING SPIRITUALITY IN THE PRESENTATION OF MINDFULNESS

We just described four recommendations for expressing cultural humility in how one negotiates the use of mindfulness with clients. These recommendations apply to any client regardless of his or her spiritual identity. In the following section, let's practice presenting mindfulness to clients who have a strong spiritual identity. We describe four steps and illustrate each with the running case example presented earlier.

Respond to the Client's Preferences

First, we must demonstrate respect for the client's preferences regarding integration of spirituality into therapy. Many clients see mindfulness as a spiritual practice, so it makes sense to proceed with caution with clients who identify as religious or spiritual. (The same probably holds for clients who say they do not want to discuss spirituality in therapy because they may view mindfulness as a spiritual activity akin to prayer.) Returning to the case example of Curtis and James, Curtis might say something like the following to explore the client's potential receptiveness to mindfulness:

CURTIS: One thing I'd like us to explore is mindfulness. I think it might be helpful to you. Although some people think of mindfulness as a spiritual practice rooted in the Buddhist tradition, a secular approach exists and has helped a lot of people. We've talked quite a bit in therapy about your Catholic faith and how aspects of your religious background have been harmful to you. From what I understand, there are very similar practices within Catholicism, such a Lectio Divina ["Divine Reading"] or other centering prayer approaches. I don't want to introduce something to therapy that might be uncomfortable to you, but I was wondering if you'd be interested in or open to learning about mindfulness from a more secular perspective. Or it would require some learning on my part, but I would be open to exploring options that might align with your own faith tradition.

In the preceding statement, Curtis, the therapist, first acknowledges the client's perspective, which conveys to the client that his preference was heard. After this acknowledgment, the therapist tentatively introduces the possibility of using mindfulness. The intention is for the therapist to gather additional information that can facilitate a collaborative decision-making process about whether or how to incorporate mindfulness into the treatment plan. Sometimes clients may show clear interest and indicate little ambivalence, which would support moving forward. Other times, clients may seem hesitant, in which case it would be wise to stop and explore the hesitation. If a client is very hesitant, it might be a good time to introduce one of the alternative treatments you generated earlier to pursue similar treatment goals.

Rather than being hesitant, other clients may feel enthused about mindfulness and may have a strong preference and expectation that the therapist integrate spirituality into sessions. For such clients, we suggest having a conversation about the degree to which mindfulness aligns with the client's cultural identities. Questions might focus on issues related to appropriation as well as spiritual alignment. This conversation is, in and of itself, a cultural opportunity to get a better understanding of the client's spiritual life and how it relates to other salient identities.

Own Your Limitations

Therapists from an MCO perspective will want to acknowledge and own their limitations to themselves and possibly to the client. Working with spiritual diversity is humbling, and we can quickly run into limits of our background and experience. For example, as authors interested in multiculturalism, we have taken steps to increase our exposure to a variety of spiritual cultures. Each time we meet a new client, student, or colleague, however, we are starting something entirely new. Each person grew up in a different family, time, and social location and has a unique configuration of identities. Awareness of how much we still have to learn can be daunting. The MCO framework reminds us that we have to learn to be comfortable with uncomfortable feelings. We can learn to be curious and interested with even painful emotions and experiences. In addition to learning about different cultures, we must increase our flexibility and responsiveness to navigating the unknown. MCO therapists learn to recognize patterns and dynamics that promote connection and trust even under precarious conditions.

If we know a lot about a particular cultural background or share a cultural identity with a client, we have to be careful not to assume we understand too much. Each new relationship requires a beginner's mind (i.e., as if we are encountering the situation for the first time). Where our cultural experience may be most helpful is through making us aware of variability within an identity: We have an intuitive sense of how different personalities and intersecting identities can affect relationships. When it comes to spirituality, each person is on a unique journey.

Given the immense spiritual diversity present in the world, how should we approach new relationships? "Fake it until you make it" is a common strategy, but we advise against it. First, it is hard to maintain a façade for long. Once the charade is revealed, the client will have good reason to wonder if you can be trusted. Second, if you are honest in your presentation, you model vulnerability, which may deepen your connection with the client. Third, the situation gives an opportunity for you to show your investment in the relationship. It is not the client's responsibility to educate you. If you acknowledge your gap in knowledge, you have a chance to take responsibility for that gap and earn the client's trust by taking reasonable steps to educate yourself. When you follow through, it will further strengthen the therapeutic bond.

It is certainly possible to make mistakes at either extreme—acting like we know more than we do or putting too much responsibility on clients to educate us. If we prioritize the process constructs within the MCO framework (i.e., cultural humility, cultural comfort, and cultural opportunities), perhaps we can chart a middle way that balances these extremes and nondefensively acknowledges one's current knowledge while conveying an investment to learn quickly and be responsive to the client's willingness to risk vulnerability. Indeed, we want to present with openness and comfort to explore the client's spiritual identity and perspective, even if we cannot know where that journey may lead.

In the running case example, a therapist who has little exposure to Catholicism might say something like the following:

> I am not as well-versed in the Catholic tradition as I would like to be. I am looking forward to doing some research on my own about it. In the meantime, how do you see your spiritual identity impacting what we're talking about?

When we engage the client in this way, we welcome the process. We do not have to be pulled this way and that by avoidance or fear of failure; these ego motives are at ease within us. When we feel them stir up, we can calm them through our own practices of grounding. We can attune ourselves to the client. We proceed in therapy, bringing as much of our attention and energy to understanding the client's meaning.

Demonstrate Responsiveness to Client's Cultural Identities

In addition to coming to terms with your limitations and associated feelings, it is important to begin demonstrating investment in the client's identities, named and unnamed. Our investment has to be real. We have to cultivate a sincere interest in helping our clients thrive. When our clients feel like we sincerely care about them, they will feel a deep sense of trust and psychological safety, which is a prerequisite for experiencing potential integration of marginalizing experiences. Therefore, this is a practical way for us to show we are just as invested as the client in promoting a positive relationship and helping the client work toward his or her goals.

Perhaps the best way to illustrate this point is to have you think of an exemplar of cultural humility in your own life. Think of what it's like to talk with them—to be with them. It takes less work to feel understood. With most people, it is difficult to share certain painful experiences. Some behaviors make you feel even more stifled, such as when listeners fail to provide sufficient affirmation and validation. Also, it is hard when people seem slow to connect the dots, or when they get activated by your sharing so that you have to devote energy to taking care of them.

Activity 7.6: Imagine How to Demonstrate Priority. We can empower our clients if we figure out a way to show that we care almost as much as they do about their problems. Imagine you are going to see a therapist. What kinds of behaviors would indicate that your therapist was willing to learn about the most important and salient aspects of your identity? Alternatively, what kinds of behaviors would indicate that the therapist had never really owned his or her power and was sitting comfortably—not really sharing the burdens of his or her clients?

Set Appropriate Expectations

Make sure to carefully manage expectations. Some clients might bring idealism to their ideas of mindfulness. After reading popular press articles that present mindfulness as a panacea, they may hope mindfulness is that cure-all. The expectations might lie dormant until just the wrong time unless we intentionally and skillfully set them early in the therapy process.

Religious or spiritual themes can sometimes amplify people's idealism. Indeed, the topic of spirituality and people's concept of the Sacred often involves inherent ideals, which guide people's lives and values (McCullough & Willoughby, 2009). For example, they may hope that developing their spiritual lives will bring a greater sense of integrity and healing. These hopes are potentially good, but we may want to double-check that clients' hopes match what we can offer them. If they want mindfulness deeply accommodated to their religion, we may or may not have the experience and expertise to do that.

Some therapists accommodate therapy to the client's religious or spiritual culture (Vieten et al., 2013), but explicit integration of this kind requires considerable skill and experience. The challenge is dealing with the particularity of many religious or spiritual groups. Under ideal training circumstances, you might need to live within the community, read widely, follow various conversations within the tradition, and obtain supervision from another professional also knowledgeable of the tradition. It may take years to master such contextualized and tacit knowledge. What precisely are the key skills you might earn through such a rigorous process? Eventually, you would begin to internalize a more refined working model of how individual differences in experience, personality, presenting problem, and other identities (e.g., gender, race, sexual orientation) intersect with the client's spiritual identity. This model would include a contextualized sense of how different ways of being and acting work within this community.

Thinking of the best-case scenario raises a final point related to appropriate expectations. How can we set appropriate expectations for our clients if we cannot set them for ourselves? Therapists already have hours of paperwork to complete, so it is unrealistic to think that we can add 2 to 3 hours of work for every new client that we see. So, we need to develop routines and habits of learning that over the course of our career will help us grow and learn. As MCO therapists, we are perpetually in training. We work the concept of training into our rhythms of life. For example, a pragmatic strategy might involve having cues about when to seek additional learning and support. Take a moment to create a list of things that let you know that you may need to spend additional energy preparing yourself to work with a client.

Another way we can have realistic expectations of ourselves is through continuing to invest in a broader vision of how we will seek to grow in cultural expertise. This plan requires an awareness of limits: We cannot become an expert at everything. Realistically, we have limits in our ability to increase our experience base. We may only have time to truly embed ourselves within one or two communities. Most people tend to find community in alignment with their salient identities, which is unsurprising, and the processes are connected with one other. We begin to view belonging to a collective as an important part of who we are. We come to view the interests of others within our community as connected to our own.

So, where will you invest your efforts? Recall what we discussed in Chapter 5 regarding allies. Consistent with the virtue of cultural humility, use the logic of need rather than just affinity. Consider the following questions: What will happen if you keep doing what you have done to this point? Are you embedded within communities that may need additional resources and responsiveness from our profession? What communities may need additional responsiveness, and what can you do to be a good citizen and help increase the field's responsiveness to everyone we serve? What are some ways that you can encourage norms of sharing and collaboration? What do you think? Is it possible for groups to promote investment in groups that fall beyond the typical boundaries of psychological affinity?

Activity 7.7: Practice. Three case descriptions follow. Imagine that you have received each case as a new client. You only have 1 week to prepare for your next set of sessions. What is a reasonable and sustainable strategy for getting up to speed on each client? Based on the details of each case, use the heuristics described earlier in the chapter to consider what you would do between sessions to ensure that you are adequately prepared to effectively work with these clients.

Case 1: **Ariana.** Ariana is a 35-year-old, Chinese American, cisgender woman who identifies as Buddhist. You recognize the potential for offense if you do not have an open conversation about the perspective of cultural appropriation of mindfulness and what it might look like to integrate mindfulness into treatment.

Case 2: **Daniel.** Daniel is a 19-year-old, White, cisgender man who identifies as a Conservative Jew. His family has expressed concerns about any behaviors that may not align with their faith. Daniel is currently dating a woman who is not Jewish, and he is concerned about what using mindfulness might indicate about his devotion to his religion and connection to his family.

Case 3: **Elyse.** Elyse is a 61-year-old, cisgender, African American woman who identifies as atheist. Elyse was raised in a Southern Baptist family and continues to attend church. She has not shared her atheist identity with her family or close friends.

Revisit Concerns About Appropriation

As you have worked through this chapter, we wonder how much you were thinking about some of the multicultural concerns raised in Chapter 3 about appropriation of mindfulness. Before we conclude, check in with yourself and your values in this regard. We want you to purposefully explore the tension between seeking to adapt mindfulness to the client's cultural identities and the concerns raised by various communities about the diffusion of mindfulness as it is used for therapeutic goals.

Here are potential questions to consider: What are your own personal values regarding cultural appropriation? How did our definition of appropriation and the ideas we presented in Chapter 3 fit for you? What ideas, concerns, or rebuttals arose for you? To what extent do you resonate with calls to "recontextualize" mindfulness (Lomas, 2017) within the traditions from which it was derived? Considering our running case example, are you generally okay with the approach Curtis took? What are the potential risks and advantages of having a more explicit conversation about the Buddhist roots of mindfulness?

Activity 7.8: Use Metaphors. Sometimes metaphors can give us a way to clarify how we think about abstract concepts, such as deciding how to integrate different values in therapy. Here, we provide two examples of metaphors; you can then think of your own.

The first example comes from a clinician we interviewed, among others. One of the last questions we asked of each person we interviewed was what they thought about the critiques related to the cultural appropriation of mindfulness. One therapist mentioned that she thinks about the difference between borrowing, sharing, or stealing a resource with another person or group. *Borrowing* implies that one has engaged in some sort of process to gain permission to use something, including a willingness to submit to any requests about appropriate use (e.g., norms to return the object in as good or better shape and take responsibility for any damage done to the object). *Sharing* implies a person has willingly given another person equal access to using the object, often with certain conditions of respectful use (e.g., norms regarding who can use what as well as when and how potential conflicts might be resolved). In contrast, *stealing* occurs when someone takes something as their own without permission or acknowledgment. As such, one feels no obligation to remain accountable to another person or group regarding how the object is used.

A second example is from current book author D. D. as he was starting to think about the issue. He thought of norms for preserving and protecting U.S. natural parks (e.g., Grand Canyon, Yosemite), places of stunning beauty that, thankfully, someone had the foresight to protect from the typical processes of development that mainly operate on the logic of profit building. To protect a national park, someone consecrated the space for certain uses. They allowed widespread use of the space, but to preserve the land, they set rules to protect the land (e.g., no cutting down trees, hunting, doing anything that would severely disrupt the natural ecosystem). National parks get thousands of visitors per day, so without these protections, the land would deteriorate within a few years. Perhaps a similar set of principles is needed to allow the use of mindfulness while also seeking to consecrate its use and avoid the exploitation that might result if market forces are left completely untethered by careful and considerate social norms.

Now, see if you can think of your own metaphor. Then use it to answer the following questions. From a systemic perspective, what if you were president of your major professional organization, such as the American Psychological Association or one of its divisions? Imagine you met with key leaders of Buddhism within the United States and also around the world. What do you think they would ask of our profession in terms of maintaining a respectful and mutually beneficial relationship? What are some things we could do as an act of good faith to indicate a willingness to express appreciation and gratitude for sharing cultural traditions that have the potential to help a lot of people? How can we demonstrate a desire and willingness to limit our negative impact on society and the future of Buddhism within the United States?

CONCLUSION

For clients from marginalized groups, it is important to show a willingness and responsiveness to collaborate in developing a treatment plan. This principle is probably true for all clients but especially for clients who may have good reason to wonder whether the institution of psychotherapy is aligned with their cultural worldview.

In the present chapter, we worked to illustrate practically how cultural humility can function like a social oil that helps reduce the wear and tear of cultural differences on the therapy relationship. But to this point, we focused largely on clients as individuals. In the next chapter, we add yet another layer of complexity by considering the client as a committed member of a spiritual community.

8

Earning Trust With Spiritual Communities

For most of this book, we have focused on the cultural humility of the individual therapist as well as how cultural humility shows up in the interpersonal relationship between therapist and client. This focus has been intentional, given that an abundance of research has found that an individual therapist's cultural humility is critical in (a) developing a strong working alliance with clients and (b) providing clients the opportunity to work on symptom improvement (e.g., Hook, Davis, Owen, & DeBlaere, 2017; Hook, Davis, Owen, Worthington, & Utsey, 2013). When working to adapt mindfulness interventions in therapy, especially with religious or spiritual clients, engaging with cultural humility is essential.

In this chapter, however, we return to a theme first discussed in Chapter 6. We suggested that for clients who identify as religious or spiritual, it might be helpful to ask key orienting questions. For example: (a) Are members of your religious or spiritual community, such as a spiritual leader, a potential resource for you in trying to address this problem? (b) Is there someone you can talk to about religious or spiritual matters as they relate to this problem? (c) Is there anything that I can do to help you access such resources? (d) Would it be helpful if I consulted with your spiritual leader? At the time, we simply suggested that it would be good to be willing to ask these questions. We said little about what to do if the client said *yes* to some or all of these questions and wanted coordination of care with their religious or spiritual leaders.

http://dx.doi.org/10.1037/0000156-008
Mindfulness-Based Practices in Therapy: A Cultural Humility Approach, by D. Davis, C. DeBlaere, J. N. Hook, and J. Owen

As we discuss in the present chapter, these questions are important. We broaden the focus and hone in on what it might look like to earn trust within various communities. We focus on earning trust within religious or spiritual communities, although the principles discussed in this chapter can be applied to other types of communities with established authorities and power structures. First, we discuss our thoughts and assumptions about engaging with the various contexts and communities that clients find themselves in, vis-à-vis the therapy relationship. Second, we discuss the importance of bringing this conversation to the multicultural community. Third, we give a brief historical overview that may provide insight into the collaboration struggles between professional psychology and religious or spiritual communities. Fourth, we discuss the concept of religious or spiritual authority and how it relates to what happens in therapy. Fifth, we discuss possible barriers to keep in mind when working with religious or spiritual communities. We wrap up the chapter with our suggestions for successful collaboration and engagement with religious or spiritual communities.

Activity 8.1: Explore Attitudes Toward Christianity. An important caveat for this chapter is that much of the theory and research on collaboration with religious or spiritual leaders has historically focused on Christianity. While writing this chapter, we considered that many of our readers may experience ambivalence related to the role of Christianity as a structure of power within the United States and particularly how this power has made it more difficult for some groups to flourish. Recent polling data have suggested that around 70% of people in the United States identify with a Christian group (Pew Research Center, n.d.). The second most common group includes people who do not identify with a religious identity (approximately 23%, which appears to be a growing population, particularly among younger U.S. Americans; Pew Research Center, n.d.). Around 6% of Americans identify with another religious group (1.9%, Jewish; .9%, Muslim; .7%, Buddhist; .7%, Hindu; and .3%, Other World Religions; Pew Research Center, n.d.).

We encourage you to examine your attitudes and beliefs about Christian religious leaders; notice whatever comes up for you. Christianity is a diverse religion with a variety of subgroups that may experience marginalization based on misalignment with dominant values within the United States. For example, a member of the Church of Jesus Christ of Latter-day Saints who is seeking a counselor in Salt Lake City may have a different experience than a member of that church who is seeking a counselor in New York City or Atlanta, Georgia. Likewise, many Protestant denominations have divisions that correspond with the history of racism within the United States. Go to http://www.pewforum.org/religious-landscape-study and examine the religious groups that you are most likely to encounter in your local region. Are there any religious communities for which you have particularly positive or negative associations? Are there any groups with which you are unfamiliar?

CLIENTS IN CONTEXT

As therapists, we often tend to focus on what happens in the therapy relationship. For example, if we see our clients once per week, we put a lot of time, energy, and focus on what happens during our 50-minute session. We think about helpful interventions or directions to pursue. We might watch video footage with our supervisor and question our decision points, or we might consider other courses of action. We might tune into our reactions to our client and analyze countertransference. These are important things to consider. And it makes sense that we focus on these activities because the therapy hour is our primary mode of contact with our clients.

However, it also is important to consider that our face-to-face time with our clients composes a small part of their daily lives. If the average person is awake 16 hours per day, the therapy hour composes less than 1% of the client's waking hours each week. That's not a lot of time! In line with this reality, the common factors approach to counseling has estimated that characteristics of the client and factors outside of therapy account for about 40% of client improvement (S. D. Miller, Duncan, & Hubble, 1997). Almost half of client improvement has absolutely nothing to do with the therapist or what happens in the therapy room.

This is part of the reason why it is important to consider the client's larger context. A good therapist knows that to create the conditions that will better support change, he must leverage the little bit of time spent with a client to align with other strengths in the client's life. Likewise, the therapist must apply this leverage to help remove barriers that are interfering with change. For clients who are religious or spiritual, an important part of this context involves their engagement with a religious or spiritual community.

Those who work with children or adolescents know that it is difficult to help a client who has weak support from parents or the larger family system. Good therapy requires systemic thinking and systemic approaches. Similarly, work with clients is contextualized within the client's broader community. It is important to take this information into consideration when contemplating how you might work to implement mindfulness interventions with a particular client.

Activity 8.2: Apply Mindfulness and Meditation Practices to a Current Client. Think about one of your current clients. Perhaps think about a client with whom you think it might be helpful to integrate mindfulness and meditation practices. Consider the four key aspects of client improvement according to the common factors approach: (a) client and extratherapeutic factors, (b) therapy model and techniques, (c) client expectancy, and (d) relationship factors. Think about the level of improvement your client has made in therapy thus far. (If this is a new client, think about the improvement you would like to see for the client.) Next, using the following grid, do this: For each of the four key aspects of client improvement, give each a percentage for how much you think that factor contributed (or will contribute) to your client's overall improvement. Make sure your percentages add up to 100%.

Factors that may influence therapy outcomes	Estimated percentage
Client and extratherapeutic factors	
Therapy model and techniques	
Client expectancy	
Relationship factors	
Total	100%

In their research, S. D. Miller et al. (1997) gave the following estimates for the factors that influence client improvement: client and extratherapeutic factors, 40%; therapy model and techniques, 15%; client expectancy, 15%; and relationship factors, 30%. What reactions do you have to their breakdown? How did your estimated breakdown compare with the breakdown of S. D. Miller et al.? What do you think of their estimate that client and extratherapeutic factors accounted for almost half of client improvement? Based on your experience, do you think this estimate is too high, too low, or about right? When you consider your client, what client factors are present that might contribute to his or her improvement in therapy? What extratherapeutic factors are present?

Continue to think about your current client, but now specifically consider his or her religious or spiritual identity. Does your client have religious or spiritual supports outside of therapy that might contribute to his or her improvement? How might you help your client access his or her religious or spiritual supports outside of therapy? Is there anything that might hold you back from helping the client access his or her religious or spiritual supports outside of therapy?

THE IMPORTANCE OF PARTNERING WITH RELIGIOUS OR SPIRITUAL LEADERS

Our profession generally values several major goals that require exceptional commitment and the ability to identify and remove key structural barriers. Some of these goals include reducing physical and mental health disparities and making society more just for marginalized groups, such sexual or gender minorities. Frankly, it is hard for us to imagine an effective response to such pervasive problems that does not involve partnering with religious or spiritual leaders and communities. Why do we say that?

Alignment With Current Ethical Commitments

Our primary reason is that not collaborating with religious or spiritual leaders does not align with our current ethical commitment to society. Clergy currently serve a large portion of the population in terms of "treatment-seeking individuals." Some have described religious leaders as the front lines of the mental health profession (Smith, Riding-Malon, Aspelmeier, & Leake, 2018), given that those leaders have a large number of people under their care and maintain relationships with people for long stretches compared with the more transitory role of psychotherapists under the structures of managed care. Religious or spiritual leaders are allied mental health professionals in every respect. Many people prefer to see a religious or spiritual leader over a counselor or psychologist. Also, for people engaged in a religious or spiritual community, clergy are on the front lines of mental health because they make referrals to trusted professionals. They not only see people for a few sessions but also may play an important role in people's lives across major life transitions (e.g., marriage, parenthood, empty nesting, retirement, death of a spouse or partner). Indeed, our ethical guidelines state that it would be negligent care to not consult with an allied mental health professional regarding someone's medical history (American Psychological Association [APA] Ethics Code Standard 3.09, Cooperation With Other Professionals; APA, 2017).

Clergy vary widely in their roles. Some may offer abundant counseling services themselves (sometimes at an unsustainable pace that leads to burnout). Likewise, their boundaries around time and family life are less circumscribed than for the role of psychotherapists. Furthermore, the training process varies widely. Some religious or spiritual traditions do not require graduate education. For those who attend seminary or divinity school, they may receive minimal training in counseling services, and some models prioritize short-term approaches to triage distress in a session or two before referring to another allied mental health professional.

It is important for therapists to fully review all ethical considerations before collaborating or consulting with religious or spiritual leaders. Some situations may warrant greater caution. For example, if a client identifies as LGBTQ+ and has not disclosed this identity to the broader community, plus attends a church that denounces same-sex relationships, the client might appropriately have reservations about giving consent for you to contact the religious or spiritual leader. In such cases, you have an opportunity to engage in an important conversation about the client's relationships within the religious or spiritual community and leader.

Taken together, the state recognizes religious or spiritual leaders with an ordination process, and they are granted similar privileges (and public trust), responsibility, and accountability as mental health professionals in counseling and psychology. Therefore, it could be seen as a major lapse in professional integrity when therapists fail to coordinate care with religious or spiritual figures who may have or may be currently conducting counseling or similar services in the client's life.

A System of Potent Force in People's Lives

Religion or spirituality remains an important force in many people's lives. Even though higher education does exert a secularizing force on people, and many young people are showing signs of greater ambivalence about organized religion, religion or spirituality remains a potent force in society on the order of government, family, and educational systems. For mental health professionals interested in promoting systemic change, this is a system that requires us to take a "seat at the table." Systems don't change much when people abandon their posts. Even if we have left or have never engaged in organized religion, it would be difficult to seek societal change without engaging effectively with religious or spiritual communities.

For example, for people invested in becoming allies for African Americans, it should stand out that this racial and ethnic group is more religious (85% have reported that religion is very important in their lives) compared with other racial groups (White, 60%; Asian Americans, 44%; Latinx, 56%; Newport, 2006). For people invested in supporting sexual minorities, it should stand out that a large number of sexual minorities are born into homes with theologically conservative families, and they face tremendous and dangerous barriers to developing a sense of integrity between their religious beliefs and their sexual orientation (Fontenot, 2013).

Taken together, we are concerned about the gap: Our Ethics Code (APA, 2017) seems to promise the general public that we will work well with allied professionals, and yet, historically, we have not followed through on this commitment in the area of collaborating with religious or spiritual leaders. We also have a commitment, especially as counseling psychologists, to engaging systems that influence the lives of marginalized groups, and religious or spiritual systems are a major force in the lives of many groups, including especially African Americans, Latinx, and sexual minorities born into religious or spiritual families. Yet, many psychotherapists report that they do not seek to coordinate care with religious or spiritual leaders. We wonder if it is possible to be good allies to marginalized groups, such as racial or ethnic minorities or sexual minorities, without investing some energy in forming strong relationships with the primary systems, such as religious or spiritual organizations, that affect their lives.

A BRIEF HISTORY OF PSYCHOLOGY AND RELIGION OR SPIRITUALITY

We offer a few tentative guesses that require examining the broader context of the relationship between psychology and clergy. Psychotherapists may feel cautious or reticent about helping clients access their religious or spiritual supports outside of therapy and may shy away from connecting with religious or spiritual communities or leaders. It is important to understand this caution or reticence within the context of the historical relationship between psychology and religion or spirituality.

Historically, the relationship between psychology and religion or spirituality has been tumultuous. Many of the men who founded psychology questioned the value of religion or spirituality and even criticized religion and spirituality as harmful to its followers (e.g., Freud, 1928/1961b; Skinner, 1953). Other influential psychologists had more positive and hopeful views of religion (e.g., James, 1985; Jung, 1968). Still, the field of professional psychology operated mostly independently from religion or spirituality throughout most of the 20th century. Perhaps part of the reason for this separation was that psychologists tended to be much less religious than the general population of clients whom they served (Shafranske & Malony, 1990).

Although psychologists remained less religious than the general population (Delaney, Miller, & Bisonó, 2007), the overall attitudes of psychology toward religion or spirituality appeared to shift and become more positive toward the end of the 20th century. In our perspective, there were two primary reasons for this shift. First, research began to accumulate showing that religion or spirituality was associated with positive physical and mental health outcomes (Koenig, McCullough, & Larson, 2001; W. R. Miller & Thoresen, 2003). Scientific evidence challenged pathologizing views of religion or spirituality. Based on this evidence, psychologists began to view religion or spirituality as a resource or source of support that people could turn to in times of difficulty or trouble. Also, religion or spirituality began to be viewed as a protective factor for preventing physical and mental illness.

The second reason for this shift was an increased valuing of multicultural counseling and diversity as well as a broadening of the identities that were considered under the multicultural umbrella. In the 1970s and 1980s, psychologists began to recognize that racial and ethnic minorities were not getting their needs met in counseling. This realization led to a series of articles that outlined what it meant to be multiculturally competent with diverse clients (D.W. Sue, Arredondo, & McDavis, 1992; D.W. Sue et al., 1982). At first, the multicultural counseling movement focused primarily on race and ethnicity. However, as the movement grew and developed, it expanded to include other aspects of diversity (APA, 2003), including religion and spirituality (Hook, Worthington, & Davis, 2012). Intersectional theories have continued to support the importance of attending to clients as wholistic beings rather than dividing the human up into parts (Boyd-Franklin, 2010; Cole, 2009).

In recent years, these shifts have led to an increase in psychological research on religion or spirituality. For example, several organizations now focus on psychological research of religion or spirituality (e.g., Division 36 of APA: Society for the Psychology of Religion and Spirituality). The APA journal *Psychology of Religion and Spirituality* was launched in 2009 (Piedmont, 2009), and another APA journal, *Spirituality in Clinical Practice*, began in 2014. The research base for intervention studies focused on a treatment adapted to a client's religious or spiritual commitments has expanded rapidly (Captari et al., 2018; Hook et al., 2010; Worthington, Hook, Davis, & McDaniel, 2011). This increased focus and attention on religion and spirituality was part of the impetus to write this book on adapting mindfulness interventions to spiritually diverse and marginalized clients.

Activity 8.3: Ask Questions for Self-Exploration. Consider the following questions regarding your experiences and attitudes regarding religion or spirituality. What is your background and experiences regarding religion or spirituality? Were you religious growing up? Were your parents religious or spiritual? Were your early experiences of religion or spirituality predominantly positive, negative, or mixed? How did your spirituality grow, develop, or change over time? What were some of the major turning points in your religious or spiritual development (e.g., conversion, deconversion)?

How would you describe your current views toward religion and spirituality? Are they predominantly positive, negative, or neutral? How do you view the relationship between psychology and religion or spirituality? Are they more separate or more collaborative? If you view the relationship between psychology and religion or spirituality to be more collaborative, do you view this relationship to be more egalitarian or more hierarchical? If you view the relationship as more hierarchical, do you place psychology in a position of authority over religion or spirituality, or do you place religion or spirituality in a position of authority over psychology?

EXPLORATION OF RELIGIOUS OR SPIRITUAL COMMUNITY AND AUTHORITY

For religious or spiritual clients, especially those who are strongly committed, their relationship to their religious or spiritual community, including their religious or spiritual authority, represents a significant personal context (Worthington, 1988). For some religious or spiritual clients, their relationship to their religious or spiritual community and authority is one of the most important and influential aspects of their lives. What this means is that it is important to explore the extent to which the activities and techniques used in therapy align with the client's religious or spiritual beliefs and values. Often these beliefs and values have their origins in one's religious or spiritual community and authority.

It follows then that one's religious or spiritual community can have a powerful influence on one's beliefs, values, and attitudes, especially those pertaining to religion or spirituality. First, a selection effect usually operates when individuals choose to become involved with a religious or spiritual community. Because a variety of such communities are available, especially for privileged religious groups, individuals often choose a church that aligns with their beliefs, values, attitudes, and preferences. For example, especially in larger cities, individuals can choose a congregation that is large or small, liberal or conservative, or homogenous or diverse. Religious or spiritual minorities may have fewer options. For example, Atlanta, Georgia, where the current book's authors D. D. and C. D. live, has more than 1,000 places of worship, but most of them are Christian (especially Protestant, Catholic, or Eastern Orthodox). Nearly 120,000 Jewish people are in the greater Atlanta area (it's the ninth-largest Jewish community in the United States; Ukeles & Miller, 2007). All of Georgia has only 52,000 Muslims in around 70 mosques and only 15,000 Hindus in around 18 temples (Association of Statisticians of American Religious Bodies, 2012).

Once a person becomes involved in a religious or spiritual community, the community itself can have a powerful effect on maintaining the status quo in regard to one's beliefs, values, and attitudes. When individuals engage with people who believe similarly, they receive consensual validation for their own beliefs (Vail et al., 2010). The opposite is also true: If a person holds an attitude that is discrepant from the dominant position, it can be difficult to maintain a minority position. Group acceptance (or not) can be a powerful motivator to stay in line. Thus, as theories of intersectionality have gained prominence in multicultural psychology, we have paid particular attention to groups that may experience marginalization within religious communities, such as gay Black men or women in theologically conservative communities.

Similarly, one's religious or spiritual authority can have a powerful influence on one's beliefs, values, and behaviors. Religious or spiritual authority often takes one of three forms: a person or group of people, a sacred text, or a tradition (Worthington, 1988). First, religious or spiritual authority often shows up in the form of a person or group of people, such as the Dalai Lama, a cherished spiritual leader for many people in the United States who are committed to or are exploring Buddhism or other Eastern spiritual perspectives. In many churches, congregants are encouraged to come under the authority of the religious leaders. Sometimes this recognition of authority is even mandated to be part of the group (e.g., become a member). Religious leaders may even have power to discipline members within the congregation for violating community norms.

Consider the following case example of the influence of religious or spiritual authority in a person's life.

Case Example: Judy

Judy is a 31-year-old, White, cisgender woman who lives in the Southwestern United States. She identifies as Southern Baptist, and her religious identity is her most important and salient identity. She attends a large church (around 1,000 members across several services) about 20 minutes away from where she lives. To become a member of the church, Judy was required to attend a 6-week class that covered information about the core beliefs and values of the church. At the end of the course, attendees decided whether to become members of the church. She signed a document indicating she agreed with the church's core beliefs and values so that she could become a member. As part of this agreement, Judy also consented to tithe regularly (i.e., give 10% of her income to the church) and regularly attend a small group. Judy committed to viewing the church leaders as her spiritual authority, which included involvement in a remediation process if Judy's behavior was discrepant from the core expectations of church members.

How do you see religious or spiritual authority showing up in Judy's life? If you were Judy's therapist, what questions might you ask to better understand the role of religious or spiritual authority in her life? If you were thinking about introducing a mindfulness exercise or practice in your work with Judy, what questions might you ask when introducing the exercise or practice? How might you work to understand Judy's perspective or level of openness to using mindfulness in therapy? Can you start to imagine how your work with Judy might be challenging to navigate if her local church has potential qualms about engagement with mindfulness?

Second, religious or spiritual authority often shows up in the form of a sacred text. Given the prominence of Judeo-Christian religions, many therapists may have some familiarity with the Bible and the different canons of Jews (e.g., Torah), Muslims (Qur'an), and Christians (Old and New Testaments). Some religious people may view the Bible as inerrant (i.e., without errors or mistakes) and infallible (i.e., incapable of error). Even if people have lower standards, they may still view their sacred text as the most important authority in their life.

Third, the religious tradition is often viewed as a form of religious or spiritual authority. For example, within Buddhism, the various traditions have different texts considered to be part of the canon. Or within Judaism, there is the Torah, which both Christianity and Islam also view as sacred. Different aspects of Judaism (e.g., conservative, liberal, orthodox, reformed) have different ways of understanding the history of Judaism and relating to sacred texts. For example, within Judaism, the Talmud documents rabbis having conversations about how to interpret the Torah. In a way, religious or spiritual individuals and groups advocate for a type of historical humility and are wary of individuals who advocate for quick change that disregards the long historical tradition of the church.

Imagine you are counseling Tracy, a 19-year old, White, cisgender, female client at the college counseling center (see box).

Case Example: Tracy

Tracy presents with high levels of anxiety. She feels nervous and jumpy in most situations and has had difficulty adjusting to college and making friends. Although she was an above-average student in high school, she has been struggling to adjust to her college-level classes, and is getting a mix of Bs and Cs in her courses. Last semester, she received a D in biology. Concerned about her grades (as well as her overall well-being), Tracy's parents talked with her about moving home and attending the local community college instead.

As therapy has progressed, you have wondered whether Tracy would benefit from mindfulness exercises. You have been learning about mindfulness and meditation in therapy and have incorporated, with good results, mindfulness with a few other clients. However, when you bring up the idea of mindfulness in therapy, Tracy hesitates, which is unusual because she usually is open about her thoughts and feelings in therapy. When you ask Tracy about her hesitation, she says, "I'm just not sure about all that mindfulness and meditation stuff. My family is religious—very religious. But I am not. It was not a good fit, and I'm afraid of getting back into all that mess." Although you haven't talked about religion much in therapy, you know from your intake paperwork that Tracy identifies as agnostic.

How would you respond to Tracy's statement? How might you respond to Tracy's statement with cultural humility? What questions would you want to ask about her experiences with religious or spiritual community and religious or spiritual authority? How might you ask these questions?

Activity 8.4: Explore Sources of Existential Authority. Take a few minutes and consider the sources of authority in your own life. Maybe religion or spirituality is important to you, and you connect with the sources of religious or spiritual authority discussed earlier in the chapter. But even if you are not religious or spiritual, you likely have certain sources of authority that have had an important influence on your beliefs, values, and attitudes about existential issues (e.g., where people came from, what happens after people die, what kinds of activities are worth pursuing to provide a sense of meaning or purpose, how you seek to find sources of social connection). For example, maybe you strongly value the opinion of a particular family member or political leader and have modeled your beliefs, values, and attitudes after that person. Perhaps a certain book, news source, or type of ideology has been influential in your development. Try to come up with the three most important sources of authority in your own life. List these three sources of authority along with a brief description of each.

Pair up with someone for this next exercise. If you're working through this book in a group or class, this is a great opportunity to connect with someone in your group. Plan to spend about an hour discussing your experiences in the authority exercise. Take turns being the talker and the listener. First, have the talker briefly share his or her three most important sources of authority. Second, have the listener ask questions about the talker's experience. Remember to be culturally humble, even if you disagree with the talker's sources of authority. The goal is to be curious, to explore, and to try to understand in a deeper way. After a few minutes of questions and exploration, switch roles and have the other person share his or her most important sources of authority. Repeat the process of asking questions and listening.

What was the partner discussion exercise like for you? Were your sources of authority similar or different from those of your discussion partner? Was it difficult to remain culturally humble when asking questions and listening? When your discussion partner was asking you questions, how culturally humble were they? What behaviors indicated high or low cultural humility?

BARRIERS TO WORKING WITH RELIGIOUS OR SPIRITUAL COMMUNITIES AND AUTHORITIES

It is important to consider how to develop relationships and work with religious or spiritual communities and authorities. However, before we begin to discuss how to do this well, it is important to consider four key barriers to effective relationship building and collaboration with religious or spiritual communities and authorities: poor relationship development, value misalignment, cultural mistrust, and lack of cultural humility.

Poor Relationship Development

The first key barrier involves a failure to apply basic relationship development skills to one's work with religious or spiritual communities and authorities. Many psychologists simply don't take the time and make the effort to work on their relationships with religious or spiritual communities and authorities. In any relationship, closeness and trust usually develop slowly over time. Relationships deepen as people go through life together and face experiences and hardships together. This pattern is especially true for religious or spiritual communities that may have reason to mistrust the motives of mental health professionals for engaging their community. For example, despite positive rhetoric, there is a sordid history of abuse when psychologists have engaged racial and ethnic minority communities, and additional abuses (e.g., overly prescribing medication for attention-deficit/hyperactivity disorder to young African American boys; Saulsberry, Bansa, DeFrino, & Dallas, 2017) continue to fray trust. Building relationships with religious or spiritual communities and authorities is a process that takes time and effort. If you don't take the time to get to know and engage with religious or spiritual communities and authorities, it will be impossible to develop a strong working relationship.

Unfortunately, many psychologists struggle to develop these kinds of relationships. As previously discussed, psychologists tend to be less religious or spiritual than the general population (Delaney et al., 2007; Shafranske & Malony, 1990), which may contribute to a lack of interest in developing these relationships. Also, some psychologists may harbor negative attitudes about religion or spirituality and view religion or spirituality as harmful, which could decrease motivation to connect with religious or spiritual communities and authorities. But this first point cannot be emphasized enough. If you want to develop trust with religious or spiritual communities and authorities, you have to do the hard and persistent work to build professional and personal relationships and connections. People may want to see you show up for a while before they will treat you like a trusted member of the community. If we act like strangers who rarely if ever show up, then we should not be surprised to be greeted like strangers—with caution.

Value Misalignment

In some cases, religious or spiritual communities and authorities may sense a value misalignment between the goals of psychology and the goals of their congregation, which can be a barrier to developing a strong relationship. Research in this area has focused almost exclusively on theologically and politically conservative Christian leaders. For example, Chaddock and McMinn (1999) conducted a study of 137 evangelical Christian clergy and psychologists who were APA members and asked them about values that were important for effective collaboration with individuals from the other profession. Clergy and psychologists differed on the importance of several values; the largest differences were for the importance of shared evangelical values, regulated sexuality, religious or spiritual values, and forgiveness—with clergy rating each value as more important.

This potential for differences in political values is likely amplified by the political polarization that has occurred over the past several decades (Abramowitz & Saunders, 2008). Value misalignment may be especially likely when psychologists and religious or spiritual communities and authorities hold different political viewpoints. Because psychology has historically placed a strong emphasis on more liberal political values and social justice (Vera & Speight, 2003), a common value misalignment occurs when more liberal psychologists try to engage with more conservative religious or spiritual communities and authorities. For example, recent research has documented that religious leaders who were more politically conservative were more likely to perceive higher levels of barriers to integrating psychology into church ministry (Hodge, Hook, Davis, & McMinn, 2018). And recent estimates have suggested an approximately 17:1 ratio of political liberals to conservatives in clinical psychology, and these proportions are likely even more unbalanced within counseling psychology (for a review, see Duarte et al., 2015). Political homogeneity is common because work often attracts people with shared values. However, it is important to recognize and own the potential limitations this lack of ideological diversity may have in our pursuit of engaging some religious or spiritual communities.

It is also important to consider assumptions regarding political diversity of certain groups. For example, racial and ethnic minority communities may exhibit strong political loyalty (e.g., perhaps caused by Democrats' greater emphasis on social issues related to seeking equity for marginalized groups) while still possessing values that might otherwise be classified as more conservative (e.g., Davis et al., 2016). Such issues have gained greater prominence in research on multiple marginalization. For example, gay Black men may experience marginalization within both the White sexual minority and gay communities and within African American religious communities. Therefore, especially when our own professional community has strong ideological commitments that affect our composition, it is crucial to cultivate cultural humility to earn trust and engage with religious or spiritual communities and authorities that may hold different ideological values.

More politically moderate or conservative psychologists may be in a unique position to form bridges of trust with more conservative religious or spiritual groups because of some shared values. Likewise, it may be easier for more politically liberal psychologists to engage with more liberal religious or spiritual communities and authorities. Our profession has generally done a poor job connecting with religious or spiritual racial and ethnic minority communities (e.g., Boyd-Franklin, 2010). We have a reputation for using the relationships to get grants but not sticking around to invest in communities. As some have noted, some racial and ethnic minority people (particularly African Americans, Latinx, and some Asian groups, e.g., Koreans) fall into a group that is both strongly religious or spiritual but also generally politically liberal. In terms of moral values, these groups may not hold a similar pattern of values as White liberals, and complex skills are required to earn trust with religious or spiritual communities from some of these groups. So, given our limitations (e.g., difficulty attracting racial or ethnic minority people and people of faith, in general), we have our work cut out for us to address these challenges to collaboration.

Related to mindfulness and meditation specifically, religious or spiritual leaders may have different levels of value alignment or misalignment with the idea of integrating mindfulness into therapy. For example, a conservative Christian religious or spiritual leader might be skeptical of integrating material that has its roots in another religious tradition. Other religious or spiritual leaders might feel positively toward mindfulness and meditation exercises, as long as they are contextualized within the individual's own religious tradition (e.g., religious adaption). Still other religious or spiritual leaders might express more openness to using techniques from different traditions, as long as they are useful to the client.

Activity 8.5: Explore Reactions to Religious or Spiritual Values. Think about how your core values line up (or don't) with various religious or spiritual values. First, consider areas of similarity or overlap. What are key values that you hold that some religious or spiritual communities and authorities also hold? Second, consider areas of difference or disagreement. What are key values that you hold that differ from those held by religious or spiritual communities and authorities? (We recognize that religious or spiritual communities and authorities are quite diverse, but write whatever comes to mind.) Can you think of any value differences that might apply to the main topic of this book, implementing mindfulness interventions in therapy? Write down any possible value differences that come up for you.

Maybe you struggled with this exercise because you aren't familiar with the core values of various religious or spiritual communities and authorities. What is one step you could take to better understand the core values of religious or spiritual communities and authorities?

Cultural Mistrust

A third barrier that can disrupt engagement and collaboration between psychologists and religious or spiritual communities and authorities is a lack of trust. This lack likely flows from the prior barriers regarding value differences and a lack of investment in ongoing relationships and partnerships. Historically, our professions have treated each other more like competitors than allied mental health professions—which is characteristic of the various subfields of mental health and is perhaps amplified by the different sources of authority (i.e., primary reliance on science versus primary reliance on sacred text and cultural tradition).

In their research on clergy and psychologist collaboration, McMinn, Chaddock, Edwards, Lim, and Campbell (1998) found that lack of trust was one of the key obstacles to successful collaboration. Mistrust of psychologists and religious leaders has not been researched in depth, but cultural research in other contexts has explored this topic more deeply. For example, in their exploration of cultural mistrust of African Americans toward White people, Terrell and Terrell (1981) argued that the history of mistreatment of African Americans by White people has led African Americans to develop a generalized mistrust of White people. Although certainly not as extreme, perhaps the historical disdain of psychology toward religion or spirituality has caused certain religious or spiritual communities to develop cultural mistrust toward the field of psychology as a whole. Thus, it may take more time, effort, and energy for psychologists to develop trust with some religious or spiritual communities and authorities.

Lack of Cultural Humility

A fourth barrier that can inhibit the development of positive relationships with religious or spiritual communities and authorities is a lack of cultural humility (Hook et al., 2017). Any strong moral conviction comes with a potential for feeling morally superior to others. If psychologists believe that their viewpoint is correct and that certain religious or spiritual perspectives are inherently backward or problematic, successful relationship building will be difficult if not impossible. We are in a sociopolitical climate that promotes disdain toward ideological enemies. Cultural humility focuses on how we handle our own feelings of moral hostility and refuse to allow blame to obscure our responsibility to treat other people with respect.

When we amplify moral hostility toward ideological enemies, no matter how justified the outrage, we potentially become part of the problem. We do not say this from a place of naive experience. Each coauthor of the current book has witnessed extremely terrible and painful abuses of religious or spiritual authority, both personally and professionally. We assume most readers have painful stories, too. These hurtful memories make it even more important that we remember our commitment to serve a pluralistic public. If we want to have integrity to the values of inclusion and openness to the other, then we cannot tolerate contemptuous attitudes and disdain to fester under any circumstances. It is essential to work through some of these negative attitudes, either in consultation or personal therapy, so they do not negatively affect our work with clients or our ability to engage religious or spiritual leaders or family members.

Activity 8.6: Explore Personal Experiences With Religious or Spiritual Authority. How often do you engage with religious or spiritual communities or religious or spiritual authorities? Have your experiences been mostly positive, mostly negative, or a mix of positive and negative? If your engagement has been minimal, what do you think that lack of engagement is about? Think about the four barriers discussed earlier. Which barrier tends to stop you from developing successful relationships with religious or spiritual communities and authorities? What is one step you could take to address this barrier in your work?

HOW TO FORM COLLABORATIVE RELATIONSHIPS WITH RELIGIOUS OR SPIRITUAL LEADERS

Now that we have a sense of the key barriers to positive engagement with religious or spiritual communities and authorities, where do we go from here? How can we take steps to positively engage with religious or spiritual communities and authorities, especially when we have clients who are religious or spiritual?

Be Aware of Your Own Religious or Spiritual Attitudes

It's essential to do some work to explore your own attitudes and experiences regarding religion or spirituality (Hook et al., 2012). This is especially true if you have had negative or traumatic experiences with religion or spirituality or hold negative attitudes toward religious or spiritual individuals and beliefs and values. Take time to take stock in your religious or spiritual history and development. Explore past hurts or struggles. Consider your relationships with religious or spiritual communities and authorities. Think about your past work with religious or spiritual clients or clients who presented with religious or spiritual issues. It may be helpful to spend time thinking and journaling about these issues. If certain hot button issues come up for you, it is important to discuss these issues in consultation, supervision, or personal therapy. We began some of this work in Chapter 5, and continuing this work will be a lifelong process.

Develop Relationships With Religious or Spiritual Leaders

To develop successful collaborative relationships with religious or spiritual leaders, it is important to do the legwork and be consistent over time. Relationships develop with stable engagement over the long haul. It is tough to rush things like trust and comfort. Reach out to religious or spiritual leaders in your community. Ask if you can take them out to lunch. Visit their congregations. Be curious about their mission and what they are doing in the community. Explore areas of shared interest. For example, most religious or spiritual leaders have challenges related to diversity, but they may have different ways of understanding these issues and attempting to bridge differences. Find areas to cultivate interest and a sense that you have something to learn from the leader's expertise. See if there are ways that you can help them in reaching their goals. Try to understand where they are coming from and what they are hoping to accomplish. Develop mutually reciprocal relationships. See how you can help them, and also see how they can help you.

Explore Convergent and Divergent Values

As you take steps to form new relationships, you likely will find areas of convergence and divergence in values. That is okay. It is unrealistic to think that your values will align completely. You are different people with different histories and backgrounds. Start by finding common ground and stick with it awhile. Amplifying differences is no way to deepen a friendship at first. But if some of your relationships ever deepen into closer friendships, it may be extremely fruitful to eventually explore areas of value difference and be respectful of each other's differences. Have conversation be the goal rather than conversion of the other person to your point of view.

Explore Acceptability (or Not) of Various Mindfulness-Related Interventions

When it comes to mindfulness and meditation interventions, explore their acceptability. When discussing mindfulness, it can be helpful to walk through the goal of the mindfulness activity as well as details about what the activity involves. It may be that the name of the intervention (e.g., Vipassana meditation) might invoke concerns about involvement in a particular religious practice that might differ from one's religious or spiritual background. Yet, when you discuss the details of the actual practice, it may seem more acceptable. It also might be possible to adapt the intervention to be more aligned with the religious or spiritual viewpoint of the particular client. For example, many meditation interventions can be adapted by changing the content or phrase of the meditation to something more aligned with the client's religious or spiritual perspective. When exploring the acceptability of various mindfulness-related interventions, note that some religious or spiritual individuals may be unwilling to engage in certain activities. Ethics requires us to refrain from pressuring clients to participate in activities against their will. As such, cultural humility may require us to change strategies or techniques that are more acceptable to particular clients.

The case example gives a practical example of what it might look like to consult with a religious leader.

Case Example: Oscar and Hector

As a therapist in training, Oscar, a 29-year-old who identifies as Mexican, cisgender man, and heterosexual, is consulting with Hector, a 51-year-old, Mexican, cisgender man who has not disclosed his sexual orientation. Hector is a Catholic priest. Oscar is not religious, but has decided to consult with Hector about a client who attends his parish.

OSCAR: Thanks for meeting with me again today, Father.

HECTOR: Absolutely. Glad to do it. I know the importance of mental health treatment, and I have a lot of respect for what you do day in and day out.

OSCAR: I appreciate your saying that, and I feel the same way. I know many of my clients are struggling with religious or spiritual issues, and for many of them, their psychological problems intersect with important aspects of their faith. As you know, I have a client who attends your parish and has given me permission to speak with you about a few things. I wanted to learn more about your perspective on mindfulness meditation, which, as you may have heard, has become very popular within psychology.

HECTOR: Sure, go ahead.

OSCAR: Well, a lot of my clients struggle with anxiety, and for many of them, I have found it helpful to use mindfulness techniques. Mindfulness techniques cover a broad range of activities, but basically they help the client to focus their attention to the present moment instead of letting it jump around. Most clients seem to get a lot out of it, but I have also heard secondhand that some clients may wonder about how mindfulness fits in with their faith. So, although

I generally think mindfulness can be helpful, I have been a little hesitant to use it with clients whom I know have a strong religious or spiritual identity. The part I am not sure how to deal with is that the inspiration for therapeutic approaches to mindfulness is from the Buddhist traditions of meditation. Many of the approaches being used have attempted to teach similar principles and practices with secular language, but I am not sure how to make sure that the way I present mindfulness supports the client's faith. In your role, what is your perspective of mindfulness techniques?

HECTOR: That's an interesting question. Thanks for asking. The first thing I think is important to point out is that the Catholic faith is very diverse. We do have a centralized authority with the Pope, but as a group, Catholics have a wide range of beliefs. For this reason, every client situation will be different. So, I can only speak for myself, and it is important to keep that in mind. But for me personally, I have appreciated the interest in mindfulness within our parish because it has led to a fruitful resurgence of interest in other contemplative practices within Catholicism. Of course, we tend to tie meditation and prayer more closely together, but some of the attentional practices are quite similar, such as focusing on the breath or some other center of attention or perhaps allowing a more open and free-form style of monitoring one's awareness. Although it is rarer for people to stay engaged with a long-term commitment to investing large amounts of time in meditation, when people do make such a commitment, I have seen transformative results. So, I regularly invest in supporting structures at my parish that can support devotional life.

Do you have any reactions to the conversation between Oscar and Hector? Do you think Oscar engaged with cultural humility? If you were Oscar, is there anything you might have said differently to be more culturally humble?

Share "Authority" Over the Client

It is important to remember that we have limited power over our clients and that, ultimately, our clients are in charge of their therapy and the direction they wish to go. Some psychologists may feel uncomfortable when a client has a religious or spiritual community or authority that exercises power over the client's choices and life direction. This may be especially true when we see our client experiencing marginalization within her religious or spiritual community. It may even sometimes feel as if the client has another "therapist" who may be steering her in a different direction than you think the client should go. With some religious or spiritual clients, it may be necessary to share the authority. Although the client may respect your opinion on a particular issue, she may weigh the view of her religious or spiritual community or authority more heavily. Instead of getting drawn into a power struggle, it will probably work better to engage with humility. Our authority as a therapist should be tempered relative to the client's self-determination and valued relationships and community.

Explore Sources of Authority in the Client's Life

It can be helpful to have a conversation about the sources of authority in the client's life. Explore where the client looks for guidance in regard to life directions, goals, and personal decisions. Depending on the particular client, this may even be a fruitful area of focus for therapy. Remember, the goal is not to influence or undercut the client's religious or spiritual community or authority; rather, it is to honestly discuss and explore how the client would like to live his or her life and where the client wants to look for direction and help.

Activity 8.7: Connect With a New Religious or Spiritual Leader. If this all remains conceptual and hypothetical, we seriously wonder how much growth is possible. So, it is time to commit to moving beyond the hypothetical. It's important to take real and practical steps that would make a difference. So, for this activity, we want you to reach out to a religious or spiritual leader in your community. Try to connect with someone who works in a different religious tradition than one you identify with. Discuss mental health and the needs of that leader's community. Before you engage, put cultural humility in the front of your mind. Ask questions, be curious, and seek first to understand. If you feel it fits the level of trust and intimacy in the relationship, ask about the religious or spiritual leader's perspective on mindfulness interventions. Or ask about other areas of potential shared interest, such as how the leader handles ideological diversity within the community. Ask about potential points of alignment or misalignment between the mindfulness practices and the religious or spiritual leader's religious values. After the conversation, spend time thinking and journaling about the experience. What did you learn? Did you engage in a culturally humble manner? Is there anything you wish you would have done differently? Could this be a relationship that you could continue to develop in the future?

The following case illustrates one way that a counselor might try to respond with an attitude of cultural humility to the client's spiritual concerns.

Case Example: Victor and Jinhi

In his private practice, Victor (45-year-old, White, cisgender man) is working with Jinhi (40-year-old, biracial [Asian and White], cisgender woman) on a pattern of problems in her dating relationships. She has never married and has had few romantic relationships over the course of her life. However, she wants to date more and hopes to get married someday. This dialogue is from their 10th session.

VICTOR: Last week you mentioned you had joined an online dating service. How has that been going?

JINHI: Well, to be honest, I haven't really done much with it. I feel so nervous about putting my personal information out there, so I've been having trouble creating my profile.

VICTOR: Hmm, okay. Tell me more about the nervousness.

JINHI: Well, anyone could be out there, you know? I've had friends who have been approached by some real crazy people. My friend Brooke even had a guy send her a really vulgar message. I'm not sure what I would do if something like that happened.

VICTOR: I see. So there's a potential for some bad things to happen if you were to step forward into trying online dating.

JINHI: Yes! It's a big unknown. I know I need to do it and put myself out there, but who knows what might happen? I might get rejected. Or, worse, I might not get any messages or anyone interested in me.

VICTOR: Yes, there does seem like there are a lot of possibilities. Last time, we talked about some things you could try when you are feeling anxious. Do you remember?

JINHI: Yes, the mindfulness stuff!

VICTOR: Did you try any of those strategies when you found yourself being nervous about online dating?

JINHI: Well, I thought about it. But to be honest, it felt a little weird to me. I didn't really say this last time we talked, but I'm not really religious. So, I'm not sure that the meditation stuff will really work for me.

VICTOR: Well, meditation certainly has its roots in Buddhism, so it's okay if you want to try other things. I have had clients who are from different religions or no religion find mindfulness helpful. For the ones who did not want anything to do with organized religion, they were sometimes able to try mindfulness with what they called a "no strings attached" kind of approach. Many liked it—but some did not. I do get the sense that you may fear that mindfulness somehow has a hidden tie to religion or at least spirituality. Do you want to try it to see how it feels to you, or should we try something else?

JINHI: Let me think about it, and I'll get back to you at next week's session. I am not quite sure yet. I hope that is okay.

What is your initial reaction about how Victor engaged with Jinhi, particularly around Jinhi's concerns about the mindfulness intervention Victor suggested? What would you say after Jinhi's last comment? How could Victor have responded to Jinhi's concerns in a more culturally humble manner? Now imagine that instead of being nonreligious, Jinhi identified as Buddhist, and her concern was focused on the cultural appropriation of mindfulness techniques in mainstream psychology. How could Victor have responded? Or, what if, instead of being nonreligious, Jinhi identified as a conservative Christian, and her concern was focused on potential social consequences of her friends, family, and pastor's finding out that she's "exploring other religions." What might cultural humility look like in this situation?

CONCLUSION

As therapists, we generally spend most of our time and energy thinking about what happens in the therapy hour. However, clients do not exist in a vacuum. Context is an incredibly important aspect of clients' lives and greatly affects the course of therapy. For religious or spiritual clients, it is important to consider the potential influence of their spiritual community.

Collaboration between psychologists and clergy has had a tumultuous history marked by seasons of not working well together. We discussed several barriers to effective relationship development and collaboration with religious or spiritual communities and authorities as well as helpful next steps for developing healthy working relationships. When using mindfulness with clients with a strong religious or spiritual identity, it is crucial to think systemically and express cultural humility through a willingness to play well with other people who play a formative role in the client's life.

9

Integrating Mindfulness in the Real World

We wrote this book with the idea of practical application in mind. Throughout the book so far, we have attempted to provide examples and activities that can help you apply the multicultural orientation (MCO) framework to the integration of mindfulness in therapy. However, we suspect many readers may still have lingering doubts about how to integrate contemplative practices into therapy with clients. Some of this comfort and preparedness will come with time, experience, and additional training. This knowledge will not be something you fully possess until you begin to seek out new professional experiences and obtain feedback about those experiences from clients, peers, and supervisors. Nonetheless, as we close this book, we thought we could begin to model what this contextualization might look like through developing a story about a supervision session among several therapists who are, to some degree, using mindfulness in their clinical work.

Therefore, we decided to end the book with a group supervision session. As we prepared to write this chapter, we interviewed a variety of clinicians using mindfulness in their practice. We draw loosely on some of the issues that came up during these interviews. This story is something of an amalgam of the tensions and issues they raised. So, we hope that some of the concerns of our group might partially reflect some of your concerns as you seek to integrate mindfulness into your practice while you also attend to issues of spiritual and cultural diversity. Our intention in writing this chapter is to

http://dx.doi.org/10.1037/0000156-009
Mindfulness-Based Practices in Therapy: A Cultural Humility Approach, by D. Davis, C. DeBlaere, J. N. Hook, and J. Owen

present more real-world examples of issues that might arise and how they may be addressed. In particular, we illustrate the major principles of the MCO framework: cultural humility, cultural comfort, and cultural opportunities in the context of integrating mindfulness practice in therapy. One tenet we highlight is cultural opportunities. We have found that therapists sometimes struggle with identifying what actually constitutes a cultural opportunity (e.g., Melissa, a doctoral-level student introduced later). Consequently, we explicitly present missed versus addressed cultural opportunities. We also identify when connecting with a spiritual leader may be helpful and when cultural discomfort can disrupt the working alliance (e.g., Kim, a doctoral-level student introduced later). Through this supervision session, we hope to help you see the ways in which our own process of engaging mindfulness practice in therapy can parallel the process of developing as a culturally humble therapist. To be done well, both processes require openness, present focus, self-awareness, and oftentimes consultation.

The authors of the present book are represented in the group supervisor. As we noted at the beginning of the book, the four of us have distinct cultural identities, including different spiritual journeys (and salience of spiritual identity), as well as varying degrees of experience holding certain privileged or marginalized identities. We thought the mock supervision session might be a way to give voice to our differing perspectives. Despite wanting to leave room for cultural differences, it was interesting that—despite differences in identity, primary theoretical approach, and how we integrate mindfulness into therapy—our interjections, responses, and general approach were quite similar. The convergence could be due to our shared commitment to the principles and values of the MCO framework, including integration of curiosity, openness, other-orientedness, and a valuing of differing perspectives in our work with clients.

GROUP DESCRIPTION

The supervision group comprises four doctoral-level students in a counseling psychology PhD program. The supervision group is part of a curriculum on integrating contemplative practices into therapy. Thus, a focus of the group is discussion of issues relevant to using contemplative practice in therapy. The group members include the following:

- Chris: A 30-year-old, African American, gay, cisgender man, Chris is in his fourth year in the doctoral program. He identifies as Methodist and often integrates his religious identity into his clinical work with clients. Chris is currently completing a practicum in a university counseling center.
- Kim: A 27-year-old, Latina, heterosexual, cisgender woman, Kim is in her second year in the doctoral program. She identifies as atheist. Kim is currently completing a practicum at a Veterans Affairs hospital.

- Becca: A 28-year-old, Palestinian American, heterosexual, genderqueer person, Becca is in their first year in the doctoral program. Becca was raised in a Muslim household but does not currently practice any faith. Becca is currently completing a practicum at a community mental health center.
- Melissa: A 24-year old, White, heterosexual, cisgender woman, Melissa is in her second year in the doctoral program. She identifies as Jewish. Melissa is currently completing her practicum at the university career resource center.

The instructor, Cheri, identifies as a 49-year-old, Asian American, heterosexual, cisgender woman. She identifies as spiritual but not religious. What follows is a portion of the transcript of one supervision session that occurred during Week 6 of a 15-week semester. Interspersed in the dialogue are commentary and interpretations from the current book authors as well as opportunities to reflect on the content of the supervision session. If it would be helpful and would enhance your experience, find four colleagues to role-play this session with you.

SESSION 6

CHERI: Welcome, everyone. Why don't we begin with a general check-in? Also, please share any client issues you hope that we can discuss during today's supervision.

BECCA: I can start. I had a pretty good week this week. I'm still struggling with the transition to a doctoral program. I'm not used to juggling so many different things at once: my research, coursework, practicum, and making time for my partner. I feel so stressed most of the time.

CHERI: That definitely sounds stressful. You started your check-in by saying you were doing pretty good, but it sounds like maybe you are feeling overwhelmed with everything. I think saying we're fine or pretty good when we're really actually struggling some is one of the ways that we disconnect from our present moment and feelings. Does that fit for you?

BECCA: Yeah, I definitely do that. It's just easier. I don't really feel like I have the time to feel things. If I do, I tend to feel really stressed and kind of shut down.

CHERI: You know, I'll bet that is something some of your clients do too. I think a lot of us fear that our emotions will overwhelm us, so we avoid them. I think this is one of the places where mindfulness or other contemplative practices can be so helpful in our work with clients—and also for us as we try to stay present to ourselves, as we sit with our clients. With mindfulness, we can learn to sit with our emotions without judgment, and over time, we see that we can experience emotions without them overwhelming us. Have you been practicing mindfulness?

BECCA: Not really. I know that I should, but I just don't feel like I have the time.

CHERI: Well, that's pretty typical and probably something our clients feel too. For the rest of the group: How do you make the time to practice mindfulness or help your clients to make the time?

CHRIS: I struggle with that too, Becca, so you are definitely not alone. I think I try to go easy on myself, but I also know I'm more likely to fit mindfulness practice into my day when I schedule it in. I sometimes find that funny—that I'm scheduling in mindfulness—but that's what works for me.

CHERI: I really appreciate what you shared, Chris. Whether you meant to or not, you modeled one of the most important aspects of mindfulness: nonjudgmental awareness. You mentioned that you think it's funny that you have to schedule it in, which represents a negative judgment, but immediately followed that statement with one that was more kind and accepting: "but it works for me." That's the type of thing that we're trying to help our clients do. We want them to shift from places of judgment to places of acceptance.

Authors' comments: Many people struggle with self-criticism. It is just part of their normal stream of consciousness and way of engaging life. In this section of dialogue, you see how Cheri used Becca's check-in to make explicit the parallel process that is occurring. That is, similar to what these supervisees likely observe with their clients, Becca is minimizing their (Becca's) feelings and not using mindfulness in their life with intention. It is important to recognize these moments as opportunities to model normalization of these challenges. In addition, Cheri was able to use what Chris shared to further illustrate the intention of mindfulness to note feelings and judgments and then let them go. Moreover, Cheri makes explicit that she is doing this. These are all helpful interventions to make in the moment with clients.

As the supervision session continues, others participate in the check-in. The supervisees are beginning to share challenges they experienced with grounding themselves in session with their clients that were due either to their client's or their own anxiety. Let's rejoin the group:

MELISSA: So, yeah, school stuff is fine, but my practicum is still a struggle. I had this one client come in, a Korean international student, who was just really rigid. He came in anxious and was so intent on figuring out all the things that he would need to do to change his major. I mean, I can help him with that, but his anxiety was so tough for me. It occurred to me that practicing some mindfulness with him could be helpful, but I ended up feeling so anxious with him that I went into advising mode and just printed out a bunch of information for him and sent him to the registrar's office. I feel frustrated that I didn't respond differently.

KIM: I get that feeling. I have a woman that I am working with who is really tough for me. She identifies as Latina too and was honorably discharged from the Air Force a few years ago. She was admitted to the VA [Veterans Affairs] domiciliary for long-term care after considering suicide. She's about 40 years old, I think, and a real perfectionist. She is so perfectionistic that she's become frozen in life. She tells me that if she can't do something perfectly, she can't do it at all. It's becomes debilitating for her. She is Catholic and shared that she finds prayer helpful, but she also said that she is losing hope. It's hard to sit with her in this. I also wonder if I should disclose that I'm atheist. I'm afraid that will hurt our connection if I do, but I also get the sense that she assumes we share the same faith.

CHERI: It sounds like you both had client experiences this week where it became difficult for you to feel grounded in your sessions. Melissa, I hear you saying that you began feeling anxious, and, Kim, I hear you saying that, at some point in your session, you started to feel afraid about your ability to connect with your client. Am I hearing you both correctly?

MELISSA: Yes, I think so.

KIM: Yeah, I think that fits. But I was also starting to feel nervous about my ability to help this person. She is having a really tough time, and I'm only a second-year student. What if I can't help her?

CHERI: If you're willing, let's just take 5 minutes to practice mindfulness. We will simply focus on our breath as we have done in other sessions. [*The group does 5 minutes of mindful breathing.*] Okay, come back to the group. Melissa. What do you notice?

MELISSA: I notice that I feel calmer, actually. I also notice that I had a hard time focusing, but it felt good to stop thinking about my client for a moment and try to focus on my breath.

CHERI: What about you, Kim?

KIM: I think I actually feel more anxious. I wasn't able to focus on my breath at all.

CHERI: Okay, and what does that tell you about where you are right now?

KIM: It tells me that I'm more anxious than I even realized.

CHERI: Hmm. So, although it was uncomfortable, you still increased your awareness. Does that sound, right?

KIM: Yes, it does.

CHERI: I think if you can connect this experience to your work with your client, that might be helpful. Mindfulness isn't always about feeling good. It is more about being present. When we are more grounded in our feelings and understanding as therapists, we tend to be able to intervene with our clients more effectively. Sitting with a client and being aware that you feel anxious is better than intervening with your client without that awareness. When we aren't self-aware, some of our interventions can be about meeting our needs more than those of our clients. Melissa, even if you don't use mindfulness with your clients in every session, it might be helpful for *you* to take a few moments to practice mindfulness before or between sessions. That said, I do want to check something out. Was there anything about what we just did that felt uncomfortable?

MELISSA: No, not at all.

CHERI: So, we see that a mindfulness intervention doesn't require a significant preamble to be effective. Sometimes, we just need to do it. Does that make sense? Perhaps when you are feeling anxious with a client, using a mindfulness intervention can benefit you both in the moment. And, even if it doesn't center your client, it may be enough that it centers you.

Authors' comments: In the last dialogue exchange, Cheri again used the process of the here and now to illustrate the parallels between what the supervisees and their clients are presenting with and the ways in which a mindfulness intervention can be helpful. As a therapist, you can do something similar with your clients. In the moments of therapy in which judgmental thinking occurs or anxiety is amplified, you could use mindfulness in the moment to allow clients to engage and become aware of their thoughts and feelings in ways that can be healing.

Activity 9.1: Engage in Cultural Opportunities. Given the focus of our book, did you notice any cultural opportunities in the last segment of dialogue? What could engaging those opportunities have looked like? Before we revisit that section and consider alternatives, take time to write down the cultural opportunities you observed. In addition, consider how you think you would have advised these trainees to move forward with those issues.

Now, let's revisit that section and consider alternatives:

MELISSA: So, yeah, school stuff is fine, but my practicum is still a struggle. I had this one client come in, a Korean international student, who was just really rigid. He came in anxious and was so intent on figuring out all the things that he would need to do to change his major. I mean, I can help him with that, but his anxiety was so tough for me. It occurred to me that practicing some mindfulness with him could be helpful, but I ended up feeling so anxious with him that I went into advising mode and just printed out a bunch of information for him and sent him to the registrar's office. I feel frustrated that I didn't respond differently.

CHERI: I hear you saying that anxiety was really present for both you and the client in your session, Melissa. Can you tell us more about that?

MELISSA: I guess. I think it was just that he was so intense, and I could tell he was super high-achieving.

CHERI: Uh-huh, and you also mentioned that he was really rigid. How did you make that assessment of him?

MELISSA: Well, he didn't seem particularly friendly. He just came in, told me what he needed, and expected me to help him. I felt a lot of pressure.

CHERI: I think feeling pressure can be pretty normal as a therapist, especially in a career resource center, where there can be some pretty circumscribed roles for career counselors. One thing I notice, though, is that you have had a lot of clients who have come in with a specific purpose and may not have been the most talkative, and you have not described them in the same way. What do you think about that?

MELISSA [*thinks for a long moment*]: I am not sure I know.

CHERI: Ah, good. Being not sure is okay. Do you have any guesses? Maybe we can explore some possibilities together as a group.

MELISSA: Well, I don't love anxious people. I also think I sometimes find men to be more abrupt and direct than women, and I don't always like that.

CHERI: Okay, what else?

MELISSA: It feels super weird to say this, but this client is the first Korean student that I've worked with.

CHERI: Okay, so you've mentioned that anxiety can be tough for you to engage as a therapist, mentioned some gender dynamics you don't like, and an ethnic identity that is new for you to work with. Those are all potentially salient issues and identities for the client but also for you in working with the client. I'm going to repeat back some of the ways you described your client: rigid, intense, super high-achieving, anxious about academics, less emotionally expressive. What do those sound like to you?

MELISSA [*appears increasingly uncomfortable*]: They sound like stereotypes about Asian people, if I'm being honest. This feels so terrible [*becomes tearful*].

CHERI: Melissa, can you share about your tears?

MELISSA [*becomes more tearful*]: I feel so bad. This is so embarrassing. I mean, we do so much training to not be prejudiced, and I think I may have been.

CHERI: I understand feeling badly. We have all said or done things as therapists that we wish we could have said or done differently. In this case, some of those things may have been related to some cultural stereotypes that we, as a society, hold about Asian people. Although, feeling bad is normal and okay, the intention of this class and your training is to help you grow as a therapist. These are learning opportunities, and you can do better next time. So, let's think about how you will go about doing better next time. What can you take away from this interaction?

Activity 9.2: Learn From Cultural Mistakes. How would you answer Cheri's final question? We all make missteps, cultural or otherwise, and it is important to learn from those moments. We all have internalized prejudicial attitudes about different cultural identities. It is impossible to exist in oppressed systems and not internalize those attitudes and biases, but how do we as therapists keep from acting on those attitudes in subtle and sometimes not so subtle ways? Take a few moments to discuss this question with a trusted colleague or journal about your thoughts. What do you think?

Now, think of a time when you made a mistake with a client. If this has ever involved the use of mindfulness, use that example. If not, just think of a time when you had a cultural difficulty with a client and realized that you had done something to contribute to the problem. Discuss the example with a trusted colleague or supervisor. What did you do to learn from the experience? Do you have any concrete evidence that you took responsibility for the problem and did things to make it less likely to happen again?

Here's another possibility: Now, let's consider Kim's client and the potential cultural opportunities present. If you recall, earlier in the practicum session, Kim shared the following about her experiences with a Latina client who is struggling with perfectionism:

KIM: I get that feeling. I have a woman that I am working with who is really tough for me. She identifies as Latina too and was honorably discharged from the Air Force a few years ago. She was admitted to the VA [Veterans Affairs] domiciliary for long-term care after considering suicide. She's about 40 years old, I think, and a real perfectionist. She is so perfectionistic that she's become frozen in life. Basically, she says that if she can't do something perfectly, she can't do it at all. It's become debilitating for her. She is Catholic and shared that she finds prayer helpful, but she also said that she is losing hope. It's hard to sit with that. I also wonder if I should disclose that I'm atheist. I'm afraid she won't connect with me if I do.

CHERI: That sounds like so much to sit with, Kim. You shared a lot of different things about this client, all of which feel important, but is there a particular place you'd like to start?

KIM: Well, I actually think that mindfulness could be really helpful for this client. With her level of perfectionism, I think helping her to identify her thoughts without judgment would be huge. Also, I think helping her to be more present with her feelings would be really good.

CHERI: Great. Sounds like you have some direction already, but you still sound hesitant. What is that hesitancy about?

KIM: There are probably a few things. First, when I introduce mindfulness meditation to clients, I usually try to acknowledge its Buddhist roots, and I'm a little nervous to do that with this client. She grew up in a Catholic family in Louisiana, so she's pretty conservative. I'm not sure how she's going to feel about mindfulness.

CHERI: That's seems like a reasonable concern to have. How have others dealt with this with their clients?

CHRIS: Well, for me, being Christian has been a mixed bag as a gay, African American man, but I think one thing I have found helpful is that I consider meditation to be similar to prayer. I actually had my friend say to me that she thinks of prayer as talking to God and meditation as listening. I really like that. I don't know if you would feel comfortable saying that to your client or not, but I've found that helpful when talking to people in my church about meditation.

KIM: I think I could do that. I mean, we already talked about how she finds prayer helpful. Maybe I can add this in. I still feel nervous about it, though.

BECCA: Is there a chaplain or someone at the VA [Veterans Affairs] you can talk to about how to approach it?

KIM: Hmm, there is, actually. I haven't ever gone to meet her, but I know other therapists have consulted with her, and I've heard good things.

BECCA: So, maybe consult with her and see what she says. She may run into similar questions from clients more often and may have a new way of thinking about it.

KIM: Yeah, that sounds good. I can do that.

CHERI: You know, Kim, one thing that we haven't talked about yet is your atheist identity in all of this. You mentioned it earlier as something you wonder about disclosing. How does that contribute to some of your fears about working with this client?

KIM: Well, we're both Latina women, so we have some shared connection. I know my client was actually really happy to be assigned to a woman of color. I think I might be the first therapist she's had that has been Latina, which feels cool. I know I really appreciated having a Latina therapist in the past. I also grew up in Houston. It's not Louisiana, but I went to Louisiana a bunch as a kid with my family, so she and I have connected over that too. That said, there aren't a lot of Latina atheists around. Most atheists I know are White men. My family has a really hard time with the fact that I'm atheist. We don't talk about it. They still expect me to go to church, and when I'm home, I do. It feels fake and weird, and I hate it, but I do it. So, I guess I'm ready for her to judge me for my identity. I am also afraid to disappoint her in a certain way. She seems to really connect with me, and I feel kind of bad potentially sharing something that might make her feel distant from me.

MELISSA: Thanks so much for sharing that, Kim. That sounds like a pretty scary thing for you to share.

KIM: Oh, it is. Do you know there is some kind of poll out there that says that almost half of Americans wouldn't vote for an atheist person as president? They would vote for almost any other identity more. Needless to say, I just don't tell most people. It's not worth it.

CHERI: Wow, that is really telling isn't it? Yet, with this client, you think it might be important to say something. Why?

KIM: Well, I want to be honest.

CHERI: Any other reasons?

KIM: Hmm. [*Thinks for around 10–15 seconds and begins to tear up.*] I'm worried that I might not be connecting in a genuine way with her since her religious identity is so important to her. Like, she might be assuming things about me or my religious background that aren't true.

CHERI: Those are some important reasons. I hear you saying you want to be authentic and genuine with your client. I also get the sense that you really care for this client and that the strong connection you described her having toward you goes both ways, which is wonderful. That said, I don't think I've heard or observed you do or say one thing that has not been affirming of your client's religious identity. I think it is always important when we are considering self-disclosure to be clear about who the self-disclosure is for: us or our client. Sometimes, it can be a little of both, but regardless, it's critical that we be clear about our intention. Who do you think you would be serving if you self-disclosed?

Activity 9.3: Discern Cultural Opportunities. Consider the previous dialogue. How would you answer that final question? Who do you think would benefit most from Kim's self-disclosure? Do you think that it is important for Kim to self-disclose at all? How would you supervise Kim to proceed? Respond to these questions with a colleague or in your journal.

As the supervision session continues, other supervisees in the group share about their clients:

BECCA: So, I'm starting to use the biofeedback clinic that we have at my site. It's interesting because I am constantly surprised about how much our bodies can tell us about what's going on for us emotionally, even when we are trying to contain how we feel.

CHERI: Is there a client you are thinking of as you say that?

BECCA: Yes. I was working with a young Black man this week. It was my third session with him. He's a college student here but didn't want to be seen on campus. Anyway, he said he wanted to work on his anxiety, but he seemed pretty flat affectwise in our first two sessions. So, last session, I took him to the biofeedback room and had him do some mindfulness breathing. I introduced the idea by sharing how mindfulness has been shown to be really effective with helping people with anxiety. I said that one way it does this is by helping us to be more aware of our thoughts and the judgments that might go along with those. He said he liked the idea and would like to know how to control his attention more. Plus, our biofeedback machines are just neat! People actually see what they're feeling.

CHERI: How did it go?

BECCA: Well, I started by just asking him to focus on his breath and to bring his attention back to his breath when his mind wandered. He looked calm and was doing the breathing, but the machines were showing elevated everything. It was striking to see the contrast.

Finally, I stopped and asked him what was coming up for him. He didn't answer for a while, but when he did, he said he had been thinking of the Black male student who had been killed by a police officer near campus. Do you all remember that? It happened about a month ago, which also happens to be when my client started to feel anxious.

CHRIS: Racial trauma is real.

BECCA: I literally saw that with my client. I guess I wonder if there is more I should be doing? My client shared that it was really helpful for him to see the response in his body, so that's something, I guess. But I wonder if I can be doing more with mindfulness in this situation.

CHERI: It sounds like mindfulness helped your client be more aware of his present moment, which is one goal. I wonder what you may have asked about the judgments or feelings he had related to the thoughts. What theory are you drawing from in your work with this client? I know you usually use interpersonal theory, but is that what you're using here?

BECCA: He didn't say much about his thoughts beyond saying that he had memories of other recent shootings. Most of the session was spent setting up. He told me about these memories at the end of the session. I didn't have time to do much. All I could think of to do was thank him for sharing what he did, and we scheduled for next week. I agree that asking those questions will be helpful. In terms of theory, I do usually use interpersonal theory, and I think I still will, but I also might introduce some ACT [acceptance and commitment therapy] elements too.

KIM: You may want to read some of the literature on racial trauma. And there are actually meditations focused on healing racial trauma. Maybe those could be helpful.

BECCA: There are?! Yes, I think those would definitely be helpful.

CHERI: Those are great suggestions, everyone. A few of my colleagues use mindfulness meditation as a way of addressing racial trauma, and one thing they have shared is that sometimes noting the thoughts is not enough. They have said that loving-kindness meditations can help provide more affirmation of the person—not just awareness of the painful experiences.

Activity 9.4: Engage Intersectionality. What are your thoughts on this case? How do you see integrating mindfulness into a treatment plan with this client? This segment of the supervision session did not explore the intersection of Becca's identities with those of her client. Consider how this exploration may have occurred. If you were the supervisor, how would you engage that dialogue? Perhaps role-play this interaction. If this were your client, how would your identities intersect and how could this intersection impact your therapy work?

We proceed with the final segment of the supervision session:

CHERI: So, I recognize that we are getting close to the end of our time together for this week. Does anyone else have anything else they would like to share?

CHRIS: Well, if it's okay with everyone, I'd like to share a few things that felt went well for me this week. After really trying to integrate contemplative practice into my work and questioning how that was going, I feel like I had some moments this week that make me think I might be doing okay, which feels really good to be able to say.

FELLOW SUPERVISEES [*respond in unison*]: Sure.

BECCA: That might be a nice way to end, actually. It can be nice to be reminded that this is a process and that we can look forward to some wins too.

CHRIS: Cool! So, you all remember that couple that I am seeing at the counseling center? They're married and have been for a couple of years now. The husband, John, feels like his wife, Laurel, is really passive and doesn't engage him. Laurel acknowledges this but still has a hard time being more assertive. Well, this Tuesday when I saw them, I had them discuss an argument that they had over the past week. As they were talking about it, John started to raise his voice, and Laurel started to shut down. So, basically, the interaction was replaying as it had when they had originally fought. I tried what we talked about in supervision last time and asked them to both stop and take a few minutes to focus on their breath. Then, I asked each of them to focus on their emotions. John mentioned feeling frustrated as usual, but Laurel shared that she was feeling scared—like she wanted to run away. What was really nice was that John responded in a much more compassionate way. He said he didn't realize that Laurel felt afraid. He thought that she was just being indecisive or pulling away. They both said that taking a few minutes to just focus on the breath and then focus on their emotions was helpful. That was so neat for me to hear, and I think it was encouraging to see a breakthrough in their understanding of one another. So, their homework for the next week is to stop, focus on the breath, focus on their emotion, and then share that emotion when they begin to argue. We'll see how it goes.

KIM: That sounds like it went really well, Chris.

CHRIS: Thanks. Yeah, I'm glad that this worked out. To be honest, I was kind of running out of ideas of what to do, so it was a relief that mindfulness helped them to have a bit more understanding of each other.

CHERI: Something I appreciate about what you shared Chris is that the intervention didn't need to be a long, drawn out process—that slowing down the session for just a few moments was enough to get this couple out of their communication rut. I think that's a helpful reminder for us all. Mindfulness interventions don't need to be long, drawn out demonstrations. I mean, sometimes a longer practice is called for, and it can be helpful. But, it's also important to remember that briefer interventions can be effective. Thanks for sharing, Chris.

CHRIS: No problem [*smiles*]. Actually, if it is okay, I'd like to share one more example.

CHERI: Yeah, if the group is okay with that. we have a few more minutes. [*Group nods.*]

CHERI: Okay then. Go ahead, Chris.

CHRIS: Well, you all know that I am a member of our pastoral counseling team at my church. As part of that, I developed a stress management workshop for members. Basically, it's a workshop on mindfulness. We discuss what stress is, what it can do to us physically and mentally, and then I teach some mindfulness approaches. I think a lot of people in my church are aware of counseling and psychologists, but I wouldn't say that there is blanket trust, so I was wondering if people would even show. I mean it is a predominately Black church, so it's not like mental health is something we discuss a lot. Still, like 20 people signed up, and 15 people actually attended. It was really great!

KIM: I know it's been hard for you to integrate your different identities, so that does sound really cool. How did you get buy-in, you think?

CHRIS: Well, first I just named the things that I thought might be barriers—like this might feel controversial or that mindfulness might feel incongruent or even offensive to their values.

CHERI: It sounds like you anticipated their hesitations and joined with the group.

CHRIS: Yeah, I guess I did. And, it really helped. They didn't have to pretend to not have concerns. I also used examples from scripture of contemplative practice. Like, I discussed how the Holy Spirit is described as breath, and people really connected with that. We also talked about radical acceptance and how there are so many examples in the Bible of how acceptance, even radical acceptance, can be really strengthening. I was surprised at how much people engaged the conversation. People actually requested another session, so I think I may do a series.

MELISSA: I can tell you are really excited. That's nice to see.

CHRIS: Thanks. Yes, it felt good.

CHERI: Okay, well, we are about out of time. Thanks for sharing so much today, everyone. I'll see you all next week.

Activity 9.5: Takeaways and Plan of Action. What stood out to you most about this supervision session? What aspects of the supervision session did you find most challenging, and which one were you able to relate to most easily? In the last segment, Chris discussed modifying his approach to discussing mindfulness to his audience. Practice how you would introduce mindfulness in your own practice. Now, consider an audience with whom you feel hesitation about broaching the subject of mindfulness. What makes you hesitate? Now think of ways that you may present mindfulness practice with this group.

CONCLUSION

Over the course of this book, we attempted to lay a path of deeper understanding of how to use cultural humility and other MCO constructs to integrate mindfulness practice into therapy in ways that are authentic to your values and respectful of the identities, beliefs, and values of your clients. In

Part I of the book, we shared our personal impetus for writing this book and the contextual issues we hoped to engage (Chapter 1), described popular mindfulness approaches in psychology and some of the related research (Chapter 2), engaged a current multicultural debate regarding the use of mindfulness in therapy (Chapter 3), discussed an MCO approach to mindfulness (Chapter 4), and developed enhanced cultural comfort for spiritual diversity (Chapter 5).

In Part II, we attempted to provide more nuts and bolts approaches to applying cultural humility, cultural comfort, and cultural opportunities in the actual work of therapy from assessment (Chapter 6), to development of a treatment plan (Chapter 7), and then connection with religious and spiritual communities that may enhance your ability to work with spiritual diversity (Chapter 8). The present chapter provided actual examples of how others have attempted to address issues that have arisen in their work with clients when they use mindfulness—both personally and with their clients.

The following are takeaway points for your consideration:

- We still don't know a great deal about the effectiveness and impact of mindfulness-based interventions (MBIs) across diverse cultural identities. More research is needed to better comprehend potential adverse reactions and potential differences in effectiveness and implementation needed by various identities (e.g., gender, race, level of education, religious or spiritual identity, political orientation). Until more is understood, it is essential that therapists use the tenets of MCO (i.e., cultural humility, cultural comfort, and cultural opportunities) to promote client well-being and best practice.

- Cultural considerations are critical in the integration of MBIs into therapy. These considerations can be explored well before a client enters into therapy. For example, therapists should develop a plan for integrating mindfulness practice (or not) into their work with clients. This plan can include developing a sound and culturally responsive intake form and providing multiple opportunities for clients to engage in the process of their therapy through the use of assessments and open-ended questions. As therapists, we should endeavor to not only accept but invite the influence of our clients in their therapy experience, including the integration of MBIs.

- As we use MCO tenets in our work with clients, it remains important to be vigilant to the threats to culturally humble practice. These threats can include an unexamined adherence to theoretical orthodoxy and scientism.

- Practicing as a culturally humble therapists is a lifelong, career-long process. To nurture this process, it is important to (a) develop a cultural network of diverse personal and professional colleagues that both support and challenge our values and perspectives, (b) seek a global perspective, and (c) step outside of our comfort zones to extend our cultural span and increase our cultural comfort with regard to difference.

As we noted at the outset (i.e., in Chapter 1), this is not the kind of book in which we could take a definitive and rigid stance on the issues present with the use of mindfulness practice in psychology. The issues are too complex and contextual. Nevertheless, we hope that this book keeps an important conversation going about attempting to balance competing values. We hold different perspectives in tension and, in this way, also hope to model the virtue of cultural humility that is the foundation of this book. Perhaps this dialogue can eventually lead to greater investment in resources that not only expand treatment uses of mindfulness but document and enrich the cultural traditions of Buddhism within the United States. Furthermore, these decisions have different implications for groups, especially racial or ethnic minorities, that historically have been underserved by the mental health professions.

We leave you with one thought that can potentially help harmonize tensions we raised in this book. We wonder if it is possible, under a value of cultural humility, for our field to keep growing its ability to act on the logic of need (i.e., focus on the areas of greatest need) rather than affinity (i.e., focus on our own salient identities). For anyone to have a chance to make this shift, that person must develop greater awareness about the intersections of identity and how power functions within all cultural groups and identities. The writing of this book represents our efforts to apply cultural humility and MCO to a complex topic. It is our hope that it has been of service to you as you begin or progress in your own cultural humility journey as a therapist.

REFERENCES

Abramowitz, A. I., & Saunders, K. L. (2008). Is polarization a myth? *Journal of Politics, 70,* 542–555. http://dx.doi.org/10.1017/S0022381608080493

Adler, N. J., & Aycan, Z. (2018). Cross-cultural interaction: What we know and what we need to know. *Annual Review of Organizational Psychology and Organizational Behavior, 5,* 307–333. http://dx.doi.org/10.1146/annurev-orgpsych-032117-104528

Alsubaie, M., Abbott, R., Dunn, B., Dickens, C., Keil, T. F., Henley, W., & Kuyken, W. (2017). Mechanisms of action in mindfulness-based cognitive therapy (MBCT) and mindfulness-based stress reduction (MBSR) in people with physical and/or psychological conditions: A systematic review. *Clinical Psychology Review, 55,* 74–91. http://dx.doi.org/10.1016/j.cpr.2017.04.008

Amanatullah, E. T., & Morris, M. W. (2010). Negotiating gender roles: Gender differences in assertive negotiating are mediated by women's fear of backlash and attenuated when negotiating on behalf of others. *Journal of Personality and Social Psychology, 98,* 256–267. http://dx.doi.org/10.1037/a0017094

Amanatullah, E. T., Morris, M. W., & Curhan, J. R. (2008). Negotiators who give too much: Unmitigated communion, relational anxieties, and economic costs in distributive and integrative bargaining. *Journal of Personality and Social Psychology, 95,* 723–738. http://dx.doi.org/10.1037/a0012612

Amanatullah, E. T., & Tinsley, C. H. (2013). Punishing female negotiators for asserting too much . . . or not enough: Exploring why advocacy moderates backlash against assertive female negotiators. *Organizational Behavior and Human Decision Processes, 120,* 110–122. http://dx.doi.org/10.1016/j.obhdp.2012.03.006

American Psychiatric Association. (2013). *Diagnostic and statistical manual of mental disorders* (5th ed.). Washington, DC: Author.

American Psychological Association. (2003). Guidelines on multicultural education, training, research, practice, and organizational change for psychologists. *American Psychologist, 58,* 377–402. http://dx.doi.org/10.1037/0003-066X.58.5.377

American Psychological Association. (2017). *Ethical principles of psychologists and code of conduct* (2002, Amended June 1, 2010, and January 1, 2017). Retrieved from http://www.apa.org/ethics/code/index.aspx

Ashton, M. C., Lee, K., & de Vries, R. E. (2014). The HEXACO Honesty-Humility, Agreeableness, and Emotionality factors: A review of research and theory. *Personality and Social Psychology Review, 18,* 139–152. http://dx.doi.org/10.1177/1088868314523838

Association of Statisticians of American Religious Bodies. (2012). U.S. religion census: Religious congregations & membership study, 2010 [Data file]. Retrieved from http://www.thearda.com/download/download.aspx?file=U.S.%20Religion%20Census%20Religious%20Congregations%20and%20Membership%20Study,%202010%20(State%20File).XLSX

A-Tjak, J. G., Davis, M. L., Morina, N., Powers, M. B., Smits, J. A., & Emmelkamp, P. M. (2015). A meta-analysis of the efficacy of acceptance and commitment therapy for clinically relevant mental and physical health problems. *Psychotherapy and Psychosomatics, 84,* 30–36. http://dx.doi.org/10.1159/000365764

Baer, R., & Nagy, L. M. (2017). Professional ethics and personal values in mindfulness-based programs: A secular psychological perspective. In L. M. Monteiro, J. F. Compson, & F. Musten (Eds.), *Practitioner's guide to ethics and mindfulness-based interventions* (pp. 87–111). Cham, Switzerland: Springer International. http://dx.doi.org/10.1007/978-3-319-64924-5_4

Baer, R. A., Smith, G. T., & Allen, K. B. (2004). Assessment of mindfulness by self-report: The Kentucky inventory of mindfulness skills. *Assessment, 11,* 191–206. http://dx.doi.org/10.1177/1073191104268029

Baer, R. A., Smith, G. T., Hopkins, J., Krietemeyer, J., & Toney, L. (2006). Using self-report assessment methods to explore facets of mindfulness. *Assessment, 13,* 27–45. http://dx.doi.org/10.1177/1073191105283504

Barnard, P. J., & Teasdale, J. D. (1991). Interacting cognitive subsystems: A systemic approach to cognitive-affective interaction and change. *Cognition and Emotion, 5,* 1–39. http://dx.doi.org/10.1080/02699939108411021

Benish, S. G., Quintana, S., & Wampold, B. E. C. (2011). Culturally adapted psychotherapy and the legitimacy of myth: A direct-comparison meta-analysis. *Journal of Counseling Psychology, 58,* 279–289. http://dx.doi.org/10.1037/a0023626

Bernal, G., Bonilla, J., & Bellido, C. (1995). Ecological validity and cultural sensitivity for outcome research: Issues for the cultural adaptation and development of psychosocial treatments with Hispanics. *Journal of Abnormal Child Psychology, 23,* 67–82. http://dx.doi.org/10.1007/BF01447045

Betancourt, J. R., Green, A. R., Carrillo, J. E., & Ananeh-Firempong, O., II. (2003). Defining cultural competence: A practical framework for addressing racial/ethnic disparities in health and health care. *Public Health Reports, 118,* 293–302. http://dx.doi.org/10.1093/phr/118.4.293

Binder, J. L., & Strupp, H. H. (1997). "Negative process": A recurrently discovered and underestimated facet of therapeutic process and outcome in the individual psychotherapy of adults. *Clinical Psychology: Science and Practice, 4,* 121–139. http://dx.doi.org/10.1111/j.1468-2850.1997.tb00105.x

Bingaman, K. A. (2011). The art of contemplative and mindfulness practice: Incorporating the findings of neuroscience into pastoral care and counseling. *Pastoral Psychology, 60,* 477–489. http://dx.doi.org/10.1007/s11089-011-0328-9

Bishop, S. R., Lau, M., Shapiro, S., Carlson, L., Anderson, N. D., Carmody, J., . . . Devins, G. (2004). Mindfulness: A proposed operational definition. *Clinical Psychology: Science and Practice, 11,* 230–241. http://dx.doi.org/10.1093/clipsy.bph077

Blanc, A. K. (2001). The effect of power in sexual relationships on sexual and reproductive health: An examination of the evidence. *Studies in Family Planning, 3,* 189–213. http://dx.doi.org/10.1111/j.1728-4465.2001.00189.x

Bluth, K., Roberson, P. N. E., & Girdler, S. S. (2017). Adolescent sex differences in response to a mindfulness intervention: A call for research. *Journal of Child and Family Studies, 26,* 1900–1914. http://dx.doi.org/10.1007/s10826-017-0696-6

Bodenlos, J. S., Strang, K., Gray-Bauer, R., Faherty, A., & Ashdown, B. K. (2017). Male representation in randomized clinical trials of mindfulness-based therapies. *Mindfulness, 8,* 259–265. http://dx.doi.org/10.1007/s12671-016-0646-1

Bowen, M. (1976). Theory in the practice of psychotherapy. In P. J. Guerin (Ed.), *Family therapy: Theory and practice* (pp. 42–90). New York, NY: Gardner Press.

Boyd-Franklin, N. (2010). Incorporating spirituality and religion into the treatment of African American clients. *Counseling Psychologist, 38,* 976–1000. http://dx.doi.org/10.1177/0011000010374881

Britton, W. B., Shahar, B., Szepsenwol, O., & Jacobs, W. J. (2012). Mindfulness-based cognitive therapy improves emotional reactivity to social stress: Results from a randomized controlled trial. *Behavior Therapy, 43,* 365–380. http://dx.doi.org/10.1016/j.beth.2011.08.006

Brown, C. G. (2017). Ethics, transparency, and diversity in mindfulness programs. In L. M. Monteiro, J. F. Compson, & F. Musten (Eds.), *Practitioner's guide to ethics and mindfulness-based interventions* (pp. 45–85). Cham, Switzerland: Springer International. http://dx.doi.org/10.1007/978-3-319-64924-5_3

Brown, K. W., Creswell, J. D., & Ryan, R. M. (2015). *Handbook of mindfulness: Theory, research, and practice.* New York, NY: Guilford Press.

Brown, K. W., & Ryan, R. M. (2003). The benefits of being present: Mindfulness and its role in psychological well-being. *Journal of Personality and Social Psychology, 84,* 822–848. http://dx.doi.org/10.1037/0022-3514.84.4.822

Captari, L. E., Hook, J. N., Hoyt, W., Davis, D. E., McElroy-Heltzel, S. E., & Worthington, E. L., Jr. (2018). Integrating clients' religion and spirituality within psychotherapy: A comprehensive meta-analysis. *Journal of Clinical Psychology, 74,* 1938–1951. http://dx.doi.org/10.1002/jclp.22681

Cashwell, C. S., & Watts, R. E. (2010). The new ASERVIC competencies for addressing spiritual and religious issues in counseling. *Counseling and Values, 55,* 2–5. http://dx.doi.org/10.1002/j.2161-007X.2010.tb00018.x

Castonguay, L. G., Goldfried, M. R., Wiser, S., Raue, P. J., & Hayes, A. M. (1996). Predicting the effect of cognitive therapy for depression: A study of unique and common factors. *Journal of Consulting and Clinical Psychology, 64,* 497–504. http://dx.doi.org/10.1037/0022-006X.64.3.497

Cavanagh, K., Strauss, C., Forder, L., & Jones, F. (2014). Can mindfulness and acceptance be learnt by self-help? A systematic review and meta-analysis of mindfulness and acceptance-based self-help interventions. *Clinical Psychology Review, 34,* 118–129. http://dx.doi.org/10.1016/j.cpr.2014.01.001

Chaddock, T. P., & McMinn, M. R. (1999). Values affecting collaboration among psychologists and evangelical clergy. *Journal of Psychology and Theology, 27,* 319–328. http://dx.doi.org/10.1177/009164719902700404

Chiesa, A., & Serretti, A. (2011). Mindfulness based cognitive therapy for psychiatric disorders: A systematic review and meta-analysis. *Psychiatry Research, 18,* 441–453. http://dx.doi.org/10.1016/j.psychres.2010.08.011

Clarke, T. C., Black, L. I., Stussman, B. J., Barnes, P. M., & Nahin, R. L. (2015). Trends in the use of complementary health approaches among adults: United States, 2002–2012. *National Health Statistics Reports, 79,* 1–16.

Clement, S., Schauman, O., Graham, T., Maggioni, F., Evans-Lacko, S., Bezborodovs, N., . . . Thornicroft, G. (2015). What is the impact of mental health-related stigma on help-seeking? A systematic review of quantitative and qualitative studies. *Psychological Medicine, 45,* 11–27. http://dx.doi.org/10.1017/S0033291714000129

Cole, E. R. (2009). Intersectionality and research in psychology. *American Psychologist, 64,* 170–180. http://dx.doi.org/10.1037/a0014564

Constantine, M. G., Lewis, E. L., Conner, L. C., & Sanchez, D. (2000). Addressing spiritual and religious issues in counseling African Americans: Implications for counselor training and practice. *Counseling and Values, 45,* 28–38. http://dx.doi.org/10.1002/j.2161-007X.2000.tb00180.x

Constantine, M. G., & Sue, D. W. (2005). *Strategies for building multicultural competence in mental health and educational settings.* Hoboken, NJ: Wiley.

Cook, J. M., Biyanova, T., Elhai, J., Schnurr, P. P., & Coyne, J. C. (2010). What do psychotherapists really do in practice? An Internet study of over 2,000 practitioners. *Psychotherapy, 47,* 260–267. http://dx.doi.org/10.1037/a0019788

Cornish, M. A., Wade, N. G., & Post, B. C. (2012). Attending to religion and spirituality in group counseling: Counselors' perceptions and practices. *Group Dynamics: Theory, Research, and Practice, 16,* 122–137. http://dx.doi.org/10.1037/a0026663

Craigie, M. A., Rees, C. S., Marsh, A., & Nathan, P. (2008). Mindfulness-based cognitive therapy for generalized anxiety disorder: A preliminary evaluation. *Behavioural and Cognitive Psychotherapy, 36,* 553–568. http://dx.doi.org/10.1017/S135246580800458X

Crenshaw, K. (1989). Demarginalizing the intersection of race and sex: A Black feminist critique of antidiscrimination doctrine, feminist theory, and antiracist politics. *University of Chicago Legal Forum, 1989*(1), Article 8.

Cross, W. E., Jr. (1991). *Shades of Black: Diversity in African-American identity.* Philadelphia, PA: Temple University Press.

Dahlsgaard, K., Peterson, C., & Seligman, M. E. (2005). Shared virtue: The convergence of valued human strengths across culture and history. *Review of General Psychology, 9,* 203–213. http://dx.doi.org/10.1037/1089-2680.9.3.203

Davis, D. E., DeBlaere, C., Owen, J., Hook, J. N., Rivera, D. P., Choe, E., . . . Placeres, V. (2018). The multicultural orientation framework: A narrative review. *Psychotherapy, 5,* 89–100. http://dx.doi.org/10.1037/pst0000160

Davis, D. E., Hook, J. N., Worthington, E. L., Jr., Van Tongeren, D. R., Gartner, A. L., Jennings, D. J., II, & Emmons, R. A. (2011). Relational humility: Conceptualizing and measuring humility as a personality judgment. *Journal of Personality Assessment, 93,* 225–234. http://dx.doi.org/10.1080/00223891.2011.558871

Davis, D. E., Rice, K., Hook, J. N., Van Tongeren, D. R., DeBlaere, C., Choe, E., & Worthington, E. L., Jr. (2015). Development of the Sources of Spirituality Scale. *Journal of Counseling Psychology, 62,* 503–513. http://dx.doi.org/10.1037/cou0000082

Davis, D. E., Rice, K., Van Tongeren, D. R., Hook, J. N., DeBlaere, C., Worthington, E. L., Jr., & Choe, E. (2016). The moral foundations hypothesis does not replicate well in Black samples. *Journal of Personality and Social Psychology, 110,* e23–e30. http://dx.doi.org/10.1037/pspp0000056

DeBlaere, C., Zelaya, D. G., Bowie, J. A., Chadwick, C. N., Davis, D. E., Hook, J. N., & Owen, J. (2018). *Multiple microaggressions and racial/ethnic minority women in counseling: A mediational model.* Manuscript in preparation.

Delaney, H. D., Miller, W. R., & Bisonó, A. M. (2007). Religiosity and spirituality among psychologists: A survey of clinician members of the American Psychological Association. *Professional Psychology: Research and Practice, 38,* 538–546. http://dx.doi.org/10.1037/0735-7028.38.5.538

DeLuca, S. M., Kelman, A. R., & Waelde, L. C. (2018). A systematic review of ethnoracial representation and cultural adaptation of mindfulness- and meditation-based interventions. *Psychological Studies, 63,* 117–129. http://dx.doi.org/10.1007/s12646-018-0452-z

DeRubeis, R. J., Cohen, Z. D., Forand, N. R., Fournier, J. C., Gelfand, L. A., & Lorenzo-Luaces, L. (2014). The Personalized Advantage Index: Translating research on prediction into individualized treatment recommendations. A demonstration. *PLoS One, 9,* e83875. http://dx.doi.org/10.1371/journal.pone.0083875

Dimidjian, S., & Segal, Z. V. (2015). Prospects for a clinical science of mindfulness-based intervention. *American Psychologist, 70,* 593–620. http://dx.doi.org/10.1037/a0039589

Dobkin, P. L., Irving, J. A., & Amar, S. (2012). For whom may participation in a mindfulness-based stress reduction program be contraindicated? *Mindfulness, 3,* 44–50. http://dx.doi.org/10.1007/s12671-011-0079-9

Dreher, G. F., & Cox, T. H., Jr. (1996). Race, gender, and opportunity: A study of compensation attainment and the establishment of mentoring relationships. *Journal of Applied Psychology, 81,* 297–308. http://dx.doi.org/10.1037/0021-9010.81.3.297

Dreyfus, G. (2011). Is mindfulness present-centred and non-judgmental? A discussion of the cognitive dimensions of mindfulness. *Contemporary Buddhism, 12,* 41–54. http://dx.doi.org/10.1080/14639947.2011.564815

Drinane, J. M., Owen, J., Adelson, J. L., & Rodolfa, E. (2016). Multicultural competencies: What are we measuring? *Psychotherapy Research, 26,* 342–351. http://dx.doi.org/10.1080/10503307.2014.983581

Drinane, J. M., Owen, J., & Tao, K. W. (2018). Cultural concealment and therapy outcomes. *Journal of Counseling Psychology, 65,* 239–246. http://dx.doi.org/10.1037/cou0000246

Drinane, J. M., Winderman, K., Roberts, T. S., Frierson Freeman, V., & Wang, Y. (2019). *Sexual identity disparities within therapist caseloads in a university counseling center.* Manuscript submitted for publication.

Duarte, J. L., Crawford, J. T., Stern, C., Haidt, J., Jussim, L., & Tetlock, P. E. (2015). Political diversity will improve social psychological science. *Behavioral and Brain Sciences, 38,* e130. http://dx.doi.org/10.1017/S0140525X14000430

Eckel, M. D. (2010). Is Buddhist environmentalism a contradiction in terms? How much is enough? In R. K. Payne (Ed.), *How much is enough? Buddhism, consumerism, and the human environment* (pp. 161–170). New York, NY: Wisdom.

Ericsson, K. A., Prietula, M. J., & Cokely, E. T. (2007, July–August). The making of an expert. *Harvard Business Review*, pp. 114–121, 193.

Exline, J. J., Pargament, K. I., Grubbs, J. B., & Yali, A. M. (2014). The Religious and Spiritual Struggles Scale: Development and initial validation. *Psychology of Religion and Spirituality, 6*, 208–222. http://dx.doi.org/10.1037/a0036465

Feldman, G., Greeson, J., & Senville, J. (2010). Differential effects of mindful breathing, progressive muscle relaxation, and loving-kindness meditation on decentering and negative reactions to repetitive thoughts. *Behaviour Research and Therapy, 48*, 1002–1011. http://dx.doi.org/10.1016/j.brat.2010.06.006

Fiske, S. T. (2001). Effects of power on bias: Power explains and maintains individual, group, and societal disparities. In A. Y. Lee-Chai & J. A. Bargh (Eds.), *The use and abuse of power: Multiple perspectives on the causes of corruption* (pp. 181–193). New York, NY: Psychology Press.

Fletcher, L., & Hayes, S. C. (2005). Relational frame theory, acceptance and commitment therapy, and a functional analytic definition of mindfulness. *Journal of Rational-Emotive & Cognitive-Behavior Therapy, 23*, 315–336. http://dx.doi.org/10.1007/s10942-005-0017-7

Fontenot, E. (2013). Unlikely congregation: Gay and lesbian persons of faith in contemporary U.S. culture. In K. I. Pargament, J. J. Exline, & J. W. Jones (Eds.), *APA handbook of psychology, religion, and spirituality: Vol. 1. Context, theory, and research* (pp. 617–633). Washington, DC: American Psychological Association. http://dx.doi.org/10.1037/14045-034

Foronda, C., Baptiste, D.-L., Reinholdt, M. M., & Ousman, K. (2016). Cultural humility: A concept analysis. *Journal of Transcultural Nursing, 27*, 210–217. http://dx.doi.org/10.1177/1043659615592677

Foster, R. P. (1998). The clinician's cultural countertransference: The psychodynamics of culturally competent practice. *Clinical Social Work Journal, 26*, 253–270. http://dx.doi.org/10.1023/A:1022867910329

Fowers, B. J., Anderson, A. R., Lefevor, G. T., & Lang, S. (2015). Beyond harms: Exploring the individual and shared goods of psychotherapy. *Counseling Psychologist, 43*, 380–392. http://dx.doi.org/10.1177/0011000014568202

Frank, J. D., & Frank, J. B. (1993). *Persuasion and healing: A comparative study of psychotherapy*. Baltimore, MD: Johns Hopkins University Press.

Fredrickson, B. L., Cohn, M. A., Coffey, K. A., Pek, J., & Finkel, S. M. (2008). Open hearts build lives: Positive emotions, induced through loving-kindness meditation, build consequential personal resources. *Journal of Personality and Social Psychology, 95*, 1045–1062. http://dx.doi.org/10.1037/a0013262

Freud, S. (1961a). The dissolution of the Oedipus complex. In J. Strachey (Ed. & Trans.), *The standard edition of the complete psychological works of Sigmund Freud* (Vol. 19, pp. 171–180). London, England: Hogarth. (Original work published 1924)

Freud, S. (1961b). A religious experience. In J. Strachey (Ed. & Trans.), *The standard edition of the complete psychological works of Sigmund Freud* (Vol. 4, pp. 167–172). London, England: Hogarth Press. (Original work published 1928)

Friedlander, M. L. (2015). Use of relational strategies to repair alliance ruptures: How responsive supervisors train responsive psychotherapists. *Psychotherapy, 52*, 174–179. http://dx.doi.org/10.1037/a0037044

Fuertes, J. N., & Brobst, K. (2002). Clients' ratings of counselor multicultural competency. *Cultural Diversity & Ethnic Minority Psychology, 8*, 214–223. http://dx.doi.org/10.1037/1099-9809.8.3.214

Fuertes, J. N., Stracuzzi, T. I., Bennett, J., Scheinholtz, J., Mislowack, A., Hersh, M., & Cheng, D. (2006). Therapist multicultural competency: A study of therapy dyads. *Psychotherapy, 43,* 480–490. http://dx.doi.org/10.1037/0033-3204.43.4.480

Gawande, A. (2009). *The checklist manifesto: How to get things right.* New York, NY: Viking.

Geller, S. M., & Greenberg, L. S. (2002). Therapeutic presence: Therapists' experience of presence in the psychotherapy encounter. *Person-Centered and Experiential Psychotherapies, 1,* 71–86. http://dx.doi.org/10.1080/14779757.2002.9688279

Geller, S. M., & Greenberg, L. S. (2012). *Therapeutic presence: A mindful approach to effective therapy.* Washington, DC: American Psychological Association. http://dx.doi.org/10.1037/13485-000

Geller, S. M., & Porges, S. W. (2014). Therapeutic presence: Neurophysiological mechanisms mediating feeling safe in therapeutic relationships. *Journal of Psychotherapy Integration, 24,* 178–192. http://dx.doi.org/10.1037/a0037511

Gladwell, M. (2008). *Outliers: The story of success.* New York, NY: Little, Brown.

Godfrin, K. A., & van Heeringen, C. (2010). The effects of mindfulness-based cognitive therapy on recurrence of depressive episodes, mental health and quality of life: A randomized controlled study. *Behaviour Research and Therapy, 48,* 738–746. http://dx.doi.org/10.1016/j.brat.2010.04.006

Gotink, R. A., Chu, P., Busschbach, J. J. V., Benson, H., Fricchione, G. L., & Hunink, M. G. M. (2015). Standardised mindfulness-based interventions in healthcare: An overview of systematic reviews and meta-analyses of RCTs. *PLoS ONE, 10,* e0124344. http://dx.doi.org/10.1371/journal.pone.0124344 (Retraction published 2019, *PLoS ONE, 14,* e0215608. http://dx.doi.org/10.1371/journal.pone.0215608)

Gottman, J. M., & Driver, J. L. (2005). Dysfunctional marital conflict and everyday marital interaction. *Journal of Divorce & Remarriage, 43,* 63–77. http://dx.doi.org/10.1300/J087v43n03_04

Goyal, M., Singh, S., Sibinga, E. M. S., Gould, N. F., Rowland-Seymour, A., Sharma, R., . . . Haythornthwaite, J. A. (2014). Meditation programs for psychological stress and well-being: A systematic review and meta-analysis. *JAMA Internal Medicine, 174,* 357–368. http://dx.doi.org/10.1001/jamainternmed.2013.13018

Graham, J., Haidt, J., & Nosek, B. A. (2009). Liberals and conservatives rely on different sets of moral foundations. *Journal of Personality and Social Psychology, 96,* 1029–1046. http://dx.doi.org/10.1037/a0015141

Grant, A. (2015, October 9). Can we end the meditation madness? *The New York Times.* Retrieved from http://www.nytimes.com/2015/10/10/opinion/can-we-end-the-meditation-madness.html/

Greenberg, J. (2002). Who stole the money, and when? Individual and situational determinants of employee theft. *Organizational Behavior and Human Decision Processes, 89,* 985–1003. http://dx.doi.org/10.1016/S0749-5978(02)00039-0

Greenberg, J., Pyszczynski, T., & Solomon, S. (1986). The causes and consequences of a need for self-esteem: A terror management theory. In R. F. Baumeister (Ed.), *Public self and private self* (pp. 189–212). New York, NY: Springer. http://dx.doi.org/10.1007/978-1-4613-9564-5_10

Greenberg, J. R., & Mitchell, S. A. (1983). *Object relations in psychoanalytic theory.* Cambridge, MA: Harvard University Press.

Griffith, J. L. (2006). Managing religious countertransference in clinical settings. *Psychiatric Annals, 36,* 196–203.

Gu, J., Strauss, C., Bond, R., & Cavanagh, K. (2015). How do mindfulness-based cognitive therapy and mindfulness-based stress reduction improve mental health and wellbeing? A systematic review and meta-analysis of mediation studies. *Clinical Psychology Review, 37,* 1–12. http://dx.doi.org/10.1016/j.cpr.2015.01.006 (Corrigendum published 2016, *Clinical Psychology Review, 49,* 119. http://dx.doi.org/10.1016/j.cpr.2016.09.011)

Hall, G. C. N., Hong, J. J., Zane, N. W. S., & Meyer, O. L. (2011). Culturally competent treatments for Asian Americans: The relevance of mindfulness and acceptance-based psychotherapies. *Clinical Psychology: Science and Practice, 18,* 215–231. http://dx.doi.org/10.1111/j.1468-2850.2011.01253.x

Hanley, A. W., Abell, N., Osborn, D. S., Roehrig, A. D., & Canto, A. I. (2016). Mind the gaps: Are conclusions about mindfulness entirely conclusive? *Journal of Counseling & Development, 94,* 103–113. http://dx.doi.org/10.1002/jcad.12066

Hanley, A. W., Warner, A. R., Dehili, V. M., Canto, A. I., & Garland, E. L. (2015). Washing dishes to wash the dishes: Brief instruction in an informal mindfulness practice. *Mindfulness, 6,* 1095–1103. http://dx.doi.org/10.1007/s12671-014-0360-9

Harrington, A., & Dunne, J. D. (2015). When mindfulness is therapy: Ethical qualms, historical perspectives. *American Psychologist, 70,* 621–631. http://dx.doi.org/10.1037/a0039460

Hayes, A. M., & Feldman, G. (2004). Clarifying the construct of mindfulness in the context of emotion regulation and the process of change in therapy. *Clinical Psychology: Science and Practice, 11,* 255–262. http://dx.doi.org/10.1093/clipsy.bph080

Hayes, S. (2006, January 11). *The six core processes of ACT.* Retrieved from https://contextualscience.org/the_six_core_processes_of_act

Hayes, S. C. (2002). Buddhism and acceptance and commitment therapy. *Cognitive and Behavioral Practice, 9,* 58–66. http://dx.doi.org/10.1016/S1077-7229(02)80041-4

Hayes, S. C., Luoma, J. B., Bond, F. W., Masuda, A., & Lillis, J. (2006). Acceptance and commitment therapy: Model, processes and outcomes. *Behaviour Research and Therapy, 44,* 1–25. http://dx.doi.org/10.1016/j.brat.2005.06.006

Hayes, S. C., Strosahl, K. D., & Wilson, K. G. (2012). *Acceptance and commitment therapy.* New York, NY: Guilford Press.

Henretty, J. R., & Levitt, H. M. (2010). The role of therapist self-disclosure in psychotherapy: A qualitative review. *Clinical Psychology Review, 30,* 63–77. http://dx.doi.org/10.1016/j.cpr.2009.09.004

Hess, E. D., & Ludwig, K. (2017). *Humility is the new smart: Rethinking human excellence in the smart machine age.* Oakland, CA: Berrett-Koehler.

Hickey, W. S. (2010). Meditation as medicine: A critique. *Cross Currents, 60,* 168–184. http://dx.doi.org/10.1111/j.1939-3881.2010.00118.x

Hodge, A., Hook, J. N., Davis, D. E., & McMinn, M. (2018). *Attitudes of religious leaders toward integrating psychology and church ministry.* Denton: University of North Texas.

Hofmann, S. G., Sawyer, A. T., Witt, A. A., & Oh, D. (2010). The effect of mindfulness-based therapy on anxiety and depression: A meta-analytic review. *Journal of Consulting and Clinical Psychology, 78,* 169–183. http://dx.doi.org/10.1037/a0018555

Hölzel, B. K., Lazar, S. W., Gard, T., Schuman-Olivier, Z., Vago, D. R., & Ott, U. (2011). How does mindfulness meditation work? Proposing mechanisms of action from a conceptual and neural perspective. *Perspectives on Psychological Science, 6,* 537–559. http://dx.doi.org/10.1177/1745691611419671

Hook, J. N., Davis, D., Owen, J., & DeBlaere, C. (2017). *Cultural humility: Engaging diverse identities in therapy.* Washington, DC: American Psychological Association. http://dx.doi.org/10.1037/0000037-000

Hook, J. N., Davis, D. E., Owen, J., Worthington, E. L., Jr., & Utsey, S. O. (2013). Cultural humility: Measuring openness to culturally diverse clients. *Journal of Counseling Psychology, 60,* 353–366. http://dx.doi.org/10.1037/a0032595

Hook, J. N., Farrell, J. E., Davis, D. E., DeBlaere, C., Van Tongeren, D. R., & Utsey, S. O. (2016). Cultural humility and racial microaggressions in counseling. *Journal of Counseling Psychology, 63,* 269–277. http://dx.doi.org/10.1037/cou0000114

Hook, J. N., Worthington, E. L., Jr., & Davis, D. E. (2012). Religion and spirituality in counseling. In N. A. Fouad, J. A. Carter, & L. M. Subich (Eds.), *APA handbook of counseling psychology: Vol. 2. Practice, interventions, and applications* (pp. 417–432). Washington, DC: American Psychological Association. http://dx.doi.org/10.1037/13755-017

Hook, J. N., Worthington, E. L., Jr., Davis, D. E., Jennings, D. J., II, Gartner, A. L., & Hook, J. P. (2010). Empirically supported religious and spiritual therapies. *Journal of Clinical Psychology, 66,* 46–72. http://dx.doi.org/10.1002/jclp.20626

Hoshmand, L. T. (2005). Narratology, cultural psychology, and counseling research. *Journal of Counseling Psychology, 52,* 178–186. http://dx.doi.org/10.1037/0022-0167.52.2.178

Huey, S. J., Jr., Tilley, J. L., Jones, E. O., & Smith, C. A. (2014). The contribution of cultural competence to evidence-based care for ethnically diverse populations. *Annual Review of Clinical Psychology, 10,* 305–338. http://dx.doi.org/10.1146/annurev-clinpsy-032813-153729

Imel, Z. E., Baldwin, S., Atkins, D. C., Owen, J., Baardseth, T., & Wampold, B. E. (2011). Racial/ethnic disparities in therapist effectiveness: A conceptualization and initial study of cultural competence. *Journal of Counseling Psychology, 58,* 290–298. http://dx.doi.org/10.1037/a0023284

Ivey, A. E., D'Andrea, M., Ivey, M. B., & Simek-Morgan, L. (2007). *Counseling and psychotherapy: A multicultural perspective* (6th ed.). Boston, MA: Allyn & Bacon.

Jacoby-Senghor, A. S., Sinclair, S., & Shelton, J. N. (2016). A lesson in bias: The relationship between implicit racial bias and performance in pedagogical contexts. *Journal of Experimental Social Psychology, 63,* 50–55. http://dx.doi.org/10.1016/j.jesp.2015.10.010

James, W. (1985). *The varieties of religious experience: A study in human nature.* Cambridge, MA: Harvard University Press. (Original work published 1902)

Jennings, P. A. (2016). Mindfulness-based programs and the American public school system: Recommendations for best practices to ensure secularity. *Mindfulness, 7,* 176–178. http://dx.doi.org/10.1007/s12671-015-0477-5

Jung, C. G. (1968). *Psychology and alchemy. The collected works of C. G. Jung* (R. F. C. Hull, Trans; 2nd ed., Vol. 12). Princeton, NJ: Princeton University Press.

Kabat-Zinn, J. (1982). An outpatient program in behavioral medicine for chronic pain patients based on the practice of mindfulness meditation: Theoretical considerations and preliminary results. *General Hospital Psychiatry, 4,* 33–47. http://dx.doi.org/10.1016/0163-8343(82)90026-3

Kabat-Zinn, J. (2011). Some reflections on the origins of MBSR, skillful means, and the trouble with maps. *Contemporary Buddhism, 12,* 281–306. http://dx.doi.org/10.1080/14639947.2011.564844

Kabat-Zinn, J. (2017). Too early to tell: The potential impact and challenges—ethical and otherwise—inherent in the mainstreaming of dharma in an increasingly dystopian world. *Mindfulness, 8,* 1125–1135. http://dx.doi.org/10.1007/s12671-017-0758-2

Kang, C., & Whittingham, K. (2010). Mindfulness: A dialogue between Buddhism and clinical psychology. *Mindfulness, 1,* 161–173. http://dx.doi.org/10.1007/s12671-010-0018-1

Kearney, D. J., McDermott, K., Malte, C., Martinez, M., & Simpson, T. L. (2012). Association of participation in a mindfulness program with measures of PTSD, depression and quality of life in a veteran sample. *Journal of Clinical Psychology, 68,* 101–116. http://dx.doi.org/10.1002/jclp.20853

Kernberg, O. F. (1976). *Object-relations theory and clinical psychoanalysis.* New York, NY: Aronson.

Kerr, M. E., & Bowen, M. (1988). *Family evaluation.* New York, NY: Norton.

Khusid, M. A., & Vythilingam, M. (2016). The emerging role of mindfulness meditation as effective self-management strategy, Part 1: Clinical implications for depression, post-traumatic stress disorder, and anxiety. *Military Medicine, 181,* 961–968. http://dx.doi.org/10.7205/MILMED-D-14-00677

Kirsch, I., Wampold, B., & Kelley, J. M. (2016). Controlling for the placebo effect in psychotherapy: Noble quest or tilting at windmills? *Psychology of Consciousness: Theory, Research, and Practice, 3,* 121–131. http://dx.doi.org/10.1037/cns0000065

Kivlighan, D. M., III, Adams, M. C., Drinane, J. M., Tao, K. W., & Owen, J. (2019). Construction and validation of the Multicultural Orientation Inventory–Group Version. *Journal of Counseling Psychology, 66,* 45–55. http://dx.doi.org/10.1037/cou0000294

Kline, K. V., Hill, C. E., Morris, T., O'Connor, S., Sappington, R., Vernay, C., . . . Okuno, H. (2018). Ruptures in psychotherapy: Experiences of therapist trainees. *Psychotherapy Research,* 1–13. http://dx.doi.org/10.1080/10503307.2018.1492164

Knabb, J. J., & Frederick, T. V. (2017). *Contemplative prayer for Christians with chronic worry.* New York, NY: Routledge. http://dx.doi.org/10.4324/9781315524658

Knabb, J. J., & Vazquez, V. E. (2018). A randomized controlled trial of a 2-week Internet-based contemplative prayer program for Christians with daily stress. *Spirituality in Clinical Practice, 5,* 37–53. http://dx.doi.org/10.1037/scp0000154

Koenig, H. G., McCullough, M. E., & Larson, D. B. (2001). *Handbook of religion and health.* New York, NY: Oxford University Press.

Krägeloh, C. U., Bergomi, C., Siegert, R. J., & Medvedev, O. N. (2018). Response shift after a mindfulness-based intervention: Measurement invariance testing of the Comprehensive Inventory of Mindfulness Experiences. *Mindfulness, 9,* 212–220. http://dx.doi.org/10.1007/s12671-017-0764-4

Kruger, J., & Dunning, D. (1999). Unskilled and unaware of it: How difficulties in recognizing one's own incompetence lead to inflated self-assessments. *Journal of Personality and Social Psychology, 77,* 1121–1134. http://dx.doi.org/10.1037/0022-3514.77.6.1121

Kuyken, W., Byford, S., Taylor, R. S., Watkins, E., Holden, E., White, K., . . . Teasdale, J. D. (2008). Mindfulness-based cognitive therapy to prevent relapse in recurrent depression. *Journal of Consulting and Clinical Psychology, 76,* 966–978. http://dx.doi.org/10.1037/a0013786

Kuyken, W., Warren, F. C., Taylor, R. S., Whalley, B., Crane, C., Bondolfi, G., . . . Dalgleish, T. (2016). Efficacy of mindfulness-based cognitive therapy in prevention of depressive relapse: An individual patient data meta-analysis from randomized trials. *JAMA Psychiatry, 73,* 565–574. http://dx.doi.org/10.1001/jamapsychiatry.2016.0076

Lannert, J. L. (1991). Resistance and countertransference issues with spiritual and religious clients. *Journal of Humanistic Psychology, 31,* 68–76. http://dx.doi.org/10.1177/0022167891314005

Lazarus, R. S., & Folkman, S. (1984). *Stress, appraisal, and coping.* New York, NY: Springer.

Leary, M. R., & Baumeister, R. F. (2000). The nature and function of self-esteem: Sociometer theory. *Advances in Experimental Social Psychology, 32,* 1–62. http://dx.doi.org/10.1016/S0065-2601(00)80003-9

Leigh, J., Bowen, S., & Marlatt, G. A. (2005). Spirituality, mindfulness and substance abuse. *Addictive Behaviors, 30,* 1335–1341. http://dx.doi.org/10.1016/j.addbeh.2005.01.010

Lilienfeld, S. O. (2007). Psychological treatments that cause harm. *Perspectives on Psychological Science, 2,* 53–70. http://dx.doi.org/10.1111/j.1745-6916.2007.00029.x

Lindahl, J. R., Kaplan, C. T., Winget, E. M., & Britton, W. B. (2014). A phenomenology of meditation-induced light experiences: Traditional Buddhist and neurobiological perspectives. *Frontiers in Psychology, 4,* 973. http://dx.doi.org/10.3389/fpsyg.2013.00973

Linehan, M. (2014). *DBT: Skills training manual.* New York, NY: Guilford Press.

Linehan, M. M. (1993). *Cognitive behavioral therapy of borderline personality disorder* (Vol. 51). New York, NY: Guilford Press.

Lomas, T. (2017). Recontextualizing mindfulness: Theravada Buddhist perspectives on the ethical and spiritual dimensions of awareness. *Psychology of Religion and Spirituality, 9,* 209–219. http://dx.doi.org/10.1037/rel0000080

Lomas, T., Etcoff, N., Van Gordon, W., & Shonin, E. (2017). Zen and the art of living mindfully: The health-enhancing potential of Zen aesthetics. *Journal of Religion and Health, 56,* 1720–1739. http://dx.doi.org/10.1007/s10943-017-0446-5

Lovett, I. (2015, October 14). Court rules "hot yoga" isn't entitled to copyright. *The New York Times.* Retrieved from http://www.nytimes.com/2015/10/15/us/court-rules-hot-yoga-isnt-entitled-to-copyright.html

Lustyk, M. K., Chawla, N., Nolan, R. S., & Marlatt, G. A. (2009). Mindfulness meditation research: Issues of participant screening, safety procedures, and researcher training. *Advances in Mind-Body Medicine, 24,* 20–30.

Ma, S. H., & Teasdale, J. D. (2004). Mindfulness-based cognitive therapy for depression: Replication and exploration of differential relapse prevention effects. *Journal of Consulting and Clinical Psychology, 72,* 31–40. http://dx.doi.org/10.1037/0022-006X.72.1.31

Mak, C., Whittingham, K., Cunnington, R., & Boyd, R. N. (2018). Efficacy of mindfulness-based interventions for attention and executive function in children and adolescents—A systematic review. *Mindfulness, 9,* 59–78. http://dx.doi.org/10.1007/s12671-017-0770-6

Malik, N. M., & Lindahl, K. M. (2004). System for coding interactions in dyads (SCID). In P. K. Kerig & D. H. Baucom (Eds.), *Couple observational coding systems* (pp. 173–188). Mahwah, NJ: Erlbaum.

Masuda, A. (Ed.). (2014). *Mindfulness and acceptance in multicultural competency: A contextual approach to sociocultural diversity in theory and practice.* Oakland, CA: New Harbinger.

Maxwell, S. E., Lau, M. Y., & Howard, G. S. (2015). Is psychology suffering from a replication crisis? What does "failure to replicate" really mean? *American Psychologist, 70,* 487–498. http://dx.doi.org/10.1037/a0039400

McCullough, M. E., & Willoughby, B. L. (2009). Religion, self-regulation, and self-control: Associations, explanations, and implications. *Psychological Bulletin, 135,* 69–93. http://dx.doi.org/10.1037/a0014213

McMinn, M. R., Chaddock, T. P., Edwards, L. C., Lim, B. R. K. B., & Campbell, C. D. (1998). Psychologists collaborating with clergy. *Professional Psychology: Research and Practice, 29,* 564–570. http://dx.doi.org/10.1037/0735-7028.29.6.564

Mercier, B., Kramer, S. R., & Shariff, A. F. (2018). Belief in God: Why people believe, and why they don't. *Current Directions in Psychological Science, 27,* 263–268. http://dx.doi.org/10.1177/0963721418754491

Miller, C. J., Elder, K., & Scavone, A. (2017). The feasibility of bringing mindfulness-based training to the university classroom. *Mindfulness, 8,* 1047–1054. http://dx.doi.org/10.1007/s12671-017-0680-7

Miller, S. D., Duncan, B. L., & Hubble, M. A. (1997). *Escape from Babel: Toward a unifying language for psychotherapy practice.* New York, NY: Norton.

Miller, W. R., & Thoresen, C. E. (2003). Spirituality, religion, and health. An emerging research field. *American Psychologist, 58,* 24–35. http://dx.doi.org/10.1037/0003-066X.58.1.24

Monteiro, L. M., Compson, J. F., & Musten, F. (Eds.). (2017). *Practitioner's guide to ethics and mindfulness-based interventions.* Cham, Switzerland: Springer International. http://dx.doi.org/10.1007/978-3-319-64924-5

Monteiro, L. M., Musten, R. F., & Compson, J. (2015). Traditional and contemporary mindfulness: Finding the middle path in the tangle of concerns. *Mindfulness, 6,* 1–13. http://dx.doi.org/10.1007/s12671-014-0301-7

Murdoch, L. (2013). *Daily life of Victorian women.* Santa Barbara, CA: Greenwood Press.

Newport, F. (2006, November 29). Religion most important to Blacks, women and older Americans [Bar graph]. Retrieved from http://www.gallup.com/poll/25585/ReligionMost-Important-Blacks-Women-Older-Americans.aspx

Norcross, J. C., & Lambert, M. J. (2018). Psychotherapy relationships that work III. *Psychotherapy, 55,* 303–315. http://dx.doi.org/10.1037/pst0000193

Norcross, J. C., Pfund, R. A., & Prochaska, J. O. (2013). Psychotherapy in 2022: A Delphi poll on its future. *Professional Psychology: Research and Practice, 44,* 363–370. http://dx.doi.org/10.1037/a0034633

Olano, H. A., Kachan, D., Tannenbaum, S. L., Mehta, A., Annane, D., & Lee, D. J. (2015). Engagement in mindfulness practices by U.S. adults: Sociodemographic barriers. *Journal of Alternative and Complementary Medicine, 21,* 100–102. http://dx.doi.org/10.1089/acm.2014.0269

Ossana, S. M., Helms, J. E., & Leonard, M. M. (1992). Do "womanist" identity attitudes influence college women's self-esteem and perceptions of environmental bias? *Journal of Counseling & Development, 70,* 402–408. http://dx.doi.org/10.1002/j.1556-6676.1992.tb01624.x

Öst, L.-G. (2014). The efficacy of acceptance and commitment therapy: An updated systematic review and meta-analysis. *Behaviour Research and Therapy, 61,* 105–121. http://dx.doi.org/10.1016/j.brat.2014.07.018

Owen, J. (2013). Early career perspectives on psychotherapy research and practice: Psychotherapist effects, multicultural orientation, and couple interventions. *Psychotherapy, 50,* 496–502. http://dx.doi.org/10.1037/a0034617

Owen, J., Adelson, J., Budge, S., Wampold, B., Kopta, M., Minami, T., & Miller, S. (2015). Trajectories of change in psychotherapy. *Journal of Clinical Psychology, 71,* 817–827. http://dx.doi.org/10.1002/jclp.22191

Owen, J., Drinane, J., Tao, K. W., Adelson, J. L., Hook, J. N., Davis, D., & Fookune, N. (2017). Racial/ethnic disparities in client unilateral termination: The role of therapists' cultural comfort. *Psychotherapy Research, 27,* 102–111. http://dx.doi.org/10.1080/10503307.2015.1078517

Owen, J., Drinane, J. M., Tao, K. W., DasGupta, D. R., Zhang, Y. S. D., & Adelson, J. (2018). An experimental test of microaggression detection in psychotherapy: Therapist multicultural orientation. *Professional Psychology: Research and Practice, 49,* 9–21. http://dx.doi.org/10.1037/pro0000152

Owen, J., Imel, Z., Adelson, J., & Rodolfa, E. (2012). "No-show": Therapist racial/ethnic disparities in client unilateral termination. *Journal of Counseling Psychology, 59,* 314–320. http://dx.doi.org/10.1037/a0027091

Owen, J., Leach, M. M., Wampold, B., & Rodolfa, E. (2011). Client and therapist variability in clients' perceptions of their therapists' multicultural competencies. *Journal of Counseling Psychology, 58,* 1–9. http://dx.doi.org/10.1037/a0021496

Owen, J., Tao, K. W., Drinane, J. M., Hook, J., Davis, D. E., & Kune, N. F. (2016). Client perceptions of therapists' multicultural orientation: Cultural (missed) opportunities and cultural humility. *Professional Psychology: Research and Practice, 47,* 30–37. http://dx.doi.org/10.1037/pro0000046

Owen, J. J., Tao, K., Leach, M. M., & Rodolfa, E. (2011). Clients' perceptions of their psychotherapists' multicultural orientation. *Psychotherapy, 48,* 274–282. http://dx.doi.org/10.1037/a0022065

Owens, B. P., Wallace, A. S., & Waldman, D. A. (2015). Leader narcissism and follower outcomes: The counterbalancing effect of leader humility. *Journal of Applied Psychology, 100,* 1203–1213. http://dx.doi.org/10.1037/a0038698

Ozawa-de Silva, B., & Dodson-Lavelle, B. (2011). An education of heart and mind: Practical and theoretical issues in teaching cognitive-based compassion training to children. *Practical Matters, 4,* 1–28.

Panos, P. T., Jackson, J. W., Hasan, O., & Panos, A. (2014). Meta-analysis and systematic review assessing the efficacy of dialectical behavior therapy (DBT). *Research on Social Work Practice, 24,* 213–223. http://dx.doi.org/10.1177/1049731513503047

Pargament, K. I., & Mahoney, A. (2005). Sacred matters: Sanctification as a vital topic for the psychology of religion. *International Journal for the Psychology of Religion, 15,* 179–198. http://dx.doi.org/10.1207/s15327582ijpr1503_1

Park, C. L., Currier, J. M., Harris, J. I., & Slattery, J. M. (2017). *Trauma, meaning, and spirituality: Translating research into clinical practice.* Washington, DC: American Psychological Association. http://dx.doi.org/10.1037/15961-000

Pew Research Center. (n.d.). Religious landscape study [Interactive map geography of religious affiliation]. Retrieved from http://www.pewforum.org/religious-landscape-study/#geography

Piedmont, R. L. (2009). Editorial. *Psychology of Religion and Spirituality, 1,* 1–2. http://dx.doi.org/10.1037/a0015253

Plante, T. G. (Ed.). (2010). *Contemplative practices in action: Spirituality, meditation, and health.* Santa Barbara, CA: Praeger.

Popper, K. R. (1974). Scientific reduction and the essential incompleteness of all science. In F. J. Ayala & T. Dobzhansky (Eds.), *Studies in the philosophy of biology* (pp. 259–284). London, England: Springer. http://dx.doi.org/10.1007/978-1-349-01892-5_16

Porges, S. W. (2011). *The polyvagal theory: Neurophysiological foundations of emotions, attachment, communication, self-regulation.* New York, NY: Norton.

Prilleltensky, I. (2008). The role of power in wellness, oppression, and liberation: The promise of psychopolitical validity. *Journal of Community Psychology, 36,* 116–136. http://dx.doi.org/10.1002/jcop.20225

Proulx, J., Croff, R., Oken, B., Aldwin, C. M., Fleming, C., Bergen-Cico, D., . . . Noorani, M. (2018). Considerations for research and development of culturally relevant mindfulness interventions in American minority communities. *Mindfulness, 9,* 361–370. http://dx.doi.org/10.1007/s12671-017-0785-z

Purdie-Vaughns, V., & Eibach, R. P. (2008). Intersectional invisibility: The distinctive advantages and disadvantages of multiple subordinate-group identities. *Sex Roles, 59,* 377–391. http://dx.doi.org/10.1007/s11199-008-9424-4

Purser, R., & Loy, D. (2013). Beyond McMindfulness. *HuffPost.* Retrieved from https://www.huffingtonpost.com/ron-purser/beyond-mcmindfulness_b_3519289.html

Purser, R. E. (2015). Clearing the muddled path of traditional and contemporary mindfulness: A response to Monteiro, Musten, and Compson. *Mindfulness, 6,* 23–45. http://dx.doi.org/10.1007/s12671-014-0373-4

Quaglia, J. T., Braun, S. E., Freeman, S. P., McDaniel, M. A., & Brown, K. W. (2016). Meta-analytic evidence for effects of mindfulness training on dimensions of self-reported dispositional mindfulness. *Psychological Assessment, 28,* 803–818. http://dx.doi.org/10.1037/pas0000268

Quaglia, J. T., Brown, K. W., Lindsay, E. K., Creswell, J. D., & Goodman, R. J. (2015). From conceptualization to operationalization of mindfulness. In K. W. Brown, J. D. Creswell, R. M. Ryan, K. W. Brown, J. D. Creswell, & R. M. Ryan (Eds.), *Handbook of mindfulness: Theory, research, and practice* (pp. 151–170). New York, NY: Guilford Press.

Racker, H. (1982). *Transference and counter-transference.* London, England: Karnak Books.

Rapgay, L., & Bystrisky, A. (2009). Classical mindfulness: An introduction to its theory and practice for clinical application. *Annals of the New York Academy of Sciences, 1172,* 148–162. http://dx.doi.org/10.1111/j.1749-6632.2009.04405.x

Rosales, A., & Tan, S.-Y. (2016). Acceptance and commitment therapy (ACT): Empirical evidence and clinical applications from a Christian perspective. *Journal of Psychology and Christianity, 35,* 269–275.

Rye, M. S., Pargament, K. I., Pan, W., Yingling, D. W., Shogren, K. A., & Ito, M. (2005). Can group interventions facilitate forgiveness of an ex-spouse? A randomized clinical trial. *Journal of Consulting and Clinical Psychology, 73,* 880–892. http://dx.doi.org/10.1037/0022-006X.73.5.880

Safran, J. D., & Kraus, J. (2014). Alliance ruptures, impasses, and enactments: A relational perspective. *Psychotherapy, 51*, 381–387. http://dx.doi.org/10.1037/a0036815

Safran, J. D., & Muran, J. C. (2006). Has the concept of the therapeutic alliance outlived its usefulness? *Psychotherapy, 43*, 286–291. http://dx.doi.org/10.1037/0033-3204.43.3.286

Sandage, S. J., & Shults, F. L. (2007). Relational spirituality and transformation: A relational integration model. *Journal of Psychology and Christianity, 26*, 261–269.

Santorelli, S. F. (2014). *Mindfulness-based stress reduction (MBSR): Standards of practice*. Retrieved from http://www.umassmed.edu/contentassets/24cd221488584125835e2eddce7dbb89/mbsr_standards_of_practice_2014.pdf

Saulsberry, A., Bansa, M., DeFrino, D., & Dallas, C. M. (2017). Skills and strategies of African American parents in the management of ADHD: A qualitative study. *Journal of Attention Disorders*, 1087054717727351. http://dx.doi.org/10.1177/1087054717727351

Saunders, S. M., Miller, M. L., & Bright, M. M. (2010). Spiritually conscious psychological care. *Professional Psychology: Research and Practice, 41*, 355–362. http://dx.doi.org/10.1037/a0020953

Schneider, A. (2003). On "appropriation": A critical reappraisal of the concept and its application in global art practices. *Social Anthropology, 11*, 215–229. http://dx.doi.org/10.1111/j.1469-8676.2003.tb00169.x

Segal, Z. V., Bieling, P., Young, T., MacQueen, G., Cooke, R., Martin, L., . . . Levitan, R. D. (2010). Antidepressant monotherapy vs sequential pharmacotherapy and mindfulness-based cognitive therapy, or placebo, for relapse prophylaxis in recurrent depression. *Archives of General Psychiatry, 67*, 1256–1264. http://dx.doi.org/10.1001/archgenpsychiatry.2010.168

Shafranske, E. P., & Malony, H. N. (1990). Clinical psychologists' religious and spiritual orientations and their practice of psychotherapy. *Psychotherapy, 27*, 72–78. http://dx.doi.org/10.1037/0033-3204.27.1.72

Shonin, E., Van Gordon, W., & Griffiths, M. D. (2014). The emerging role of Buddhism in clinical psychology: Towards effective integration. *Psychology of Religion and Spirituality, 6*, 123–137. http://dx.doi.org/10.1037/a0035859

Shults, F. L. R., & Sandage, S. J. (2006). *Transforming spirituality: Integrating theology and psychology*. Grand Rapids, MI: Baker Academic.

Sin, N. L., & Lyubomirsky, S. (2009). Enhancing well-being and alleviating depressive symptoms with positive psychology interventions: A practice-friendly meta-analysis. *Journal of Clinical Psychology, 65*, 467–487. http://dx.doi.org/10.1002/jclp.20593

Skinner, B. F. (1953). *Science and human behavior*. New York, NY: Simon & Schuster.

Smith, A. E., Riding-Malon, R., Aspelmeier, J. E., & Leake, V. (2018). A qualitative investigation into bridging the gap between religion and the helping professions to improve rural mental health. *Journal of Rural Mental Health, 42*, 32–45. http://dx.doi.org/10.1037/rmh0000093

Soto, A., Smith, T. B., Griner, D., Rodriguez, M. D., & Bernal, G. (2018). Cultural adaptions and therapist multicultural competence: Two meta-analytic reviews. *Journal of Clinical Psychology, 74*, 1907–1923. http://dx.doi.org/10.1002/jclp.22679

Sperry, L., & Stoupas, G. (2017). Incorporating mindfulness in secular and spiritually-oriented psychotherapy: Ethical concerns. *Spirituality in Clinical Practice, 4,* 152–154. http://dx.doi.org/10.1037/scp0000132

Stanley, C. A. (2006). Coloring the academic landscape: Faculty of color breaking the silence in predominantly White colleges and universities. *American Educational Research Journal, 43,* 701–736. http://dx.doi.org/10.3102/00028312043004701

Stratton, S. P. (2015). Mindfulness and contemplation: Secular and religious traditions in Western context. *Counseling and Values, 60,* 100–118. http://dx.doi.org/10.1002/j.2161-007X.2015.00063.x

Strauss, C., Cavanagh, K., Oliver, A., & Pettman, D. (2014). Mindfulness-based interventions for people diagnosed with a current episode of an anxiety or depressive disorder: A meta-analysis of randomised controlled trials. *PLoS One, 9,* e96110. http://dx.doi.org/10.1371/journal.pone.0096110

Sue, D. W. (2017). The challenges of becoming a White ally. *Counseling Psychologist, 45,* 706–716. http://dx.doi.org/10.1177/0011000017719323

Sue, D. W., Arredondo, P., & McDavis, R. J. (1992). Multicultural counseling competencies and standards: A call to the profession. *Journal of Counseling & Development, 70,* 477–486. http://dx.doi.org/10.1002/j.1556-6676.1992.tb01642.x

Sue, D. W., Bernier, J. E., Durran, A., Feinberg, L., Pedersen, P., Smith, E. J., & Vasquez-Nuttall, E. (1982). Position paper: Cross-cultural counseling competencies. *Counseling Psychologist, 10,* 45–52. http://dx.doi.org/10.1177/0011000082102008

Sue, D. W., Carter, R. T., Casas, J. M., Fouad, N. A., Ivey, A. E., Jensen, M., & Vazquez-Nutall, E. (1998). *Multicultural counseling competencies: Individual and organizational development* (Vol. 11). Thousand Oaks, CA: Sage.

Sue, D. W., & Sue, D. (2016). *Counseling the culturally diverse: Theory and practice* (7th ed.). New York, NY: Wiley.

Sue, S., Zane, N., Nagayama Hall, G. C., & Berger, L. K. (2009). The case for cultural competency in psychotherapeutic interventions. *Annual Review of Psychology, 60,* 525–548. http://dx.doi.org/10.1146/annurev.psych.60.110707.163651

Tao, K. W., Owen, J., Pace, B. T., & Imel, Z. E. (2015). A meta-analysis of multicultural competencies and psychotherapy process and outcome. *Journal of Counseling Psychology, 62,* 337–350. http://dx.doi.org/10.1037/cou0000086

Taylor, R. J., & Chatters, L. M. (2010). Importance of religion and spirituality in the lives of African Americans, Caribbean Blacks and non-Hispanic Whites. *Journal of Negro Education, 79,* 280–294.

Teasdale, J. D., Moore, R. G., Hayhurst, H., Pope, M., Williams, S., & Segal, Z. V. (2002). Metacognitive awareness and prevention of relapse in depression: Empirical evidence. *Journal of Consulting and Clinical Psychology, 70,* 275–287. http://dx.doi.org/10.1037/0022-006X.70.2.275

Teasdale, J. D., Segal, Z. V., Williams, J. M. G., Ridgeway, V. A., Soulsby, J. M., & Lau, M. A. (2000). Prevention of relapse/recurrence in major depression by mindfulness-based cognitive therapy. *Journal of Consulting and Clinical Psychology, 68,* 615–623. http://dx.doi.org/10.1037/0022-006X.68.4.615

Terrell, F., & Terrell, S. (1981). An inventory to measure cultural mistrust among Blacks. *Western Journal of Black Studies, 5,* 180–185.

Tervalon, M., & Murray-García, J. (1998). Cultural humility versus cultural competence: A critical distinction in defining physician training outcomes in multicultural education. *Journal of Health Care for the Poor and Underserved, 9,* 117–125. http://dx.doi.org/10.1353/hpu.2010.0233

Tinsley, C. H., Cheldelin, S. I., Schneider, A. K., & Amanatullah, E. T. (2009). Women at the bargaining table: Pitfalls and prospects. *Negotiation Journal, 25,* 233–248. http://dx.doi.org/10.1111/j.1571-9979.2009.00222.x

Tirch, D., Silberstein, L. R., & Kolts, R. L. (2015). *Buddhist psychology and cognitive-behavioral therapy: A clinician's guide*. New York, NY: Guilford Press.

Topor, A., Bøe, T. D., & Larsen, I. B. (2018). Small things, micro-affirmations and helpful professionals everyday recovery-orientated practices according to persons with mental health problems. *Community Mental Health Journal, 54,* 1212–1220. http://dx.doi.org/10.1007/s10597-018-0245-9

Tovote, K. A., Fleer, J., Snippe, E., Bas, I. V., Links, T. P., Emmelkamp, P. M., . . . Schroevers, M. J. (2013). Cognitive behavioral therapy and mindfulness-based cognitive therapy for depressive symptoms in patients with diabetes: Design of a randomized controlled trial. *BMC Psychology, 1,* 17. http://dx.doi.org/10.1186/2050-7283-1-17

Tovote, K. A., Schroevers, M. J., Snippe, E., Emmelkamp, P. M. G., Links, T. P., Sanderman, R., & Fleer, J. (2017). What works best for whom? Cognitive behavior therapy and mindfulness-based cognitive therapy for depressive symptoms in patients with diabetes. *PLoS ONE, 12,* e0179941. http://dx.doi.org/10.1371/journal.pone.0179941

Tracey, T. J., Wampold, B. E., Lichtenberg, J. W., & Goodyear, R. K. (2014). Expertise in psychotherapy: An elusive goal? *American Psychologist, 69,* 218–229. http://dx.doi.org/10.1037/a0035099

Trub, L., & Starks, T. J. (2017). Textual healing: Proof of concept study examining the impact of a mindfulness intervention on smartphone behavior. *Mindfulness, 8,* 1225–1235. http://dx.doi.org/10.1007/s12671-017-0697-y

Twenge, J. M. (2017). *iGen: Why today's super-connected kids are growing up less rebellious, more tolerant, less happy—and completely unprepared for adulthood—and what that means for the rest of us*. New York, NY: Atria Books.

Ukeles, J. B., & Miller, R. (2007). *Jewish community centennial study of greater Atlanta 2006*. Retrieved from the Jewish Federation of Greater Atlanta website: http://fedweb-assets.s3.amazonaws.com/fed-46/2/2006%2520Final%2520Community%2520Study%2520Report.pdf

United Nations General Assembly. (2007, October 2). *United Nations declaration on the rights of indigenous peoples: Resolution/adopted by the General Assembly* (A/RES/61/295). Retrieved from http://www.refworld.org/docid/471355a82.html

Vail, K. E., III, Rothschild, Z. K., Weise, D. R., Solomon, S., Pyszczynski, T., & Greenberg, J. (2010). A terror management analysis of the psychological functions of religion. *Personality and Social Psychology Review, 14,* 84–94. http://dx.doi.org/10.1177/1088868309351165

Valentine, S. E., Bankoff, S. M., Poulin, R. M., Reidler, E. B., & Pantalone, D. W. (2015). The use of dialectical behavior therapy skills training as stand-alone treatment: A systematic review of the treatment outcome literature. *Journal of Clinical Psychology, 71,* 1–20. http://dx.doi.org/10.1002/jclp.22114

Van Dam, N. T., van Vugt, M. K., Vago, D. R., Schmalzl, L., Saron, C. D., Olendzki, A., . . . Meyer, D. E. (2018). Mind the hype: A critical evaluation and prescriptive agenda for research on mindfulness and meditation. *Perspectives on Psychological Science, 13,* 36–61. http://dx.doi.org/10.1177/1745691617709589

Van Gordon, W., Shonin, E., & Griffiths, M. D. (2015). Towards a second generation of mindfulness-based interventions. *Australian and New Zealand Journal of Psychiatry, 49,* 591–592. http://dx.doi.org/10.1177/0004867415577437

van Stapele, N. (2014, March). Intersubjectivity, self-reflexivity and agency: Narrating about "self" and "other" in feminist research. *Women's Studies International Forum, 43,* 13–21.

Vera, E. M., & Speight, S. L. (2003). Multicultural competence, social justice, and counseling psychology: Expanding our roles. *Counseling Psychologist, 31,* 253–272. http://dx.doi.org/10.1177/0011000003031003001

Vieten, C., Scammell, S., Pilato, R., Ammondson, I., Pargament, K. I., & Lukoff, D. (2013). Spiritual and religious competencies for psychologists. *Psychology of Religion and Spirituality, 5,* 129–144. http://dx.doi.org/10.1037/a0032699

Volf, M. (1996). Theology, meaning, and power. In M. Volf, C. Krieg, & T. Kucharz (Eds.), *The future of theology: Essays in honor of Jürgen Moltmann* (pp. 98–113). Grand Rapids, MI: Eerdmans.

Wachtel, P. L. (2008). *Relational theory and the practice of psychotherapy.* New York, NY: Guilford Press.

Waelde, L. C., Thompson, J. M., Robinson, A., & Iwanicki, S. (2016). Trauma therapists' clinical applications, training, and personal practice of mindfulness and meditation. *Mindfulness, 7,* 622–629. http://dx.doi.org/10.1007/s12671-016-0497-9

Walsh, R., & Shapiro, S. L. (2006). The meeting of meditative disciplines and Western psychology: A mutually enriching dialogue. *American Psychologist, 61,* 227–239. http://dx.doi.org/10.1037/0003-066X.61.3.227

Wampold, B. E., Frost, N. D., & Yulish, N. E. (2016). Placebo effects in psychotherapy: A flawed concept and a contorted history. *Psychology of Consciousness: Theory, Research, and Practice, 3,* 108–120. http://dx.doi.org/10.1037/cns0000045

Wampold, B. E., & Imel, Z. E. (2015). *The great psychotherapy debate: The evidence for what makes psychotherapy work.* New York, NY: Routledge. http://dx.doi.org/10.4324/9780203582015

Wang, P. S., Aguilar-Gaxiola, S., Alonso, J., Angermeyer, M. C., Borges, G., Bromet, E. J., . . . Wells, J. E. (2007). Use of mental health services for anxiety, mood, and substance disorders in 17 countries in the WHO world mental health surveys. *Lancet, 370,* 841–850. http://dx.doi.org/10.1016/S0140-6736(07)61414-7

Wendt, D. C., Gone, J. P., & Nagata, D. K. (2015). Potentially harmful therapy and multicultural counseling: Extending the conversation. *Counseling Psychologist, 43,* 393–403. http://dx.doi.org/10.1177/0011000015576801

Whitcomb, D., Battaly, H., Baehr, J., & Howard-Snyder, D. (2017). Intellectual humility: Owning our limitations. *Philosophy and Phenomenological Research, 94,* 509–539. http://dx.doi.org/10.1111/phpr.12228

Williams, J. M. G., Fennell, M. J. V., Barnhofer, T., Crane, R., & Silverton, S. (2015). *Mindfulness-based cognitive therapy with people at risk of suicide: Working with people at risk of suicide.* New York, NY: Guilford Press.

Wilson, J. (2014). *Mindful America: Meditation and the mutual transformation of Buddhism and American culture.* New York, NY: Oxford University Press.

Worthington, E. L., Jr. (1988). Understanding the values of religious clients: A model and its application to counseling. *Journal of Counseling Psychology, 35,* 166–174. http://dx.doi.org/10.1037/0022-0167.35.2.166

Worthington, E. L., Jr., Hook, J. N., Davis, D. E., & McDaniel, M. A. (2011). Religion and spirituality. *Journal of Clinical Psychology, 67,* 204–214. http://dx.doi.org/10.1002/jclp.20760

Worthington, E. L., Jr., & Sandage, S. J. (2016). *Forgiveness and spirituality in psychotherapy: A relational approach.* Washington, DC: American Psychological Association. http://dx.doi.org/10.1037/14712-000

Yalom, I. D. (1980). *Existential psychotherapy* (Vol. 1). New York, NY: Basic Books.

INDEX

G

H

I

J

K

L

M

N

O

T

ABOUT THE AUTHORS

Don Davis, PhD, is an associate professor of counseling psychology, counselor education and practice, and mental health counseling at Georgia State University in Atlanta. His research interests focus on positive psychology, especially humility and related virtues. He also does research and writing on spirituality and its intersection with other identities in counseling. He teaches courses on leadership in positive psychology, group counseling, and appraisal and measurement, and also coordinates a doctoral track designed to prepare master's students to apply to doctoral programs in either counseling psychology or counselor education and practice. Dr. Davis has coedited or coauthored several books, including *Cultural Humility: Engaging Diverse Identities in Therapy* (2017); *Helping Groups Heal: Leading Groups in the Process of Transformation* (2017); and the *Handbook of Humility: Theory, Research, and Applications* (2017). He is an associate editor of *The Journal of Positive Psychology* and also serves on the editorial boards of the *Journal of Counseling Psychology* and *Spirituality in Clinical Practice.*

Cirleen DeBlaere, PhD, is an associate professor of counseling psychology at Georgia State University in Atlanta. Her research and professional interests focus on examining the experiences of individuals with marginalized identities. Her research has been published in premier journals in her field, such as the *Journal of Counseling Psychology, The Counseling Psychologist,* and *Psychology of Women Quarterly*. She has been recognized with several national awards, including the 2011 Outstanding *TCP [The Counseling Psychologist]* Major Contribution Award, 2012 Research on Psychotherapy With Women Award, 2012 Women of Color Psychologies Award, and 2018 Evelyn Hooker Award for Distinguished Contribution by an Ally. Dr. DeBlaere is invested in teaching, training, and service activities that manifest her investment in diversity and social justice issues. For instance, she currently serves as the vice president for diversity and public interest for the Society of Counseling Psychology (American Psychological Association, Division 17). Recently, she was awarded the Outstanding Early Career Professional Supervisor/Trainer Award from the Society of Counseling Psychology's Supervision and Training Section in recognition of her contributions to supervision and training. Dr. DeBlaere also cofounded and is the inaugural cochair of the Division on Asian Americans With Multiple Heritages of the Asian American Psychological Association. She serves or has served on multiple editorial boards as a member, including the *Journal of Counseling Psychology* and *Psychology of Women Quarterly*; and as an associate editor, including *The Counseling Psychologist, Psychology of Sexual Orientation and Gender Diversity,* and *Sex Roles: A Journal of Research.* She coauthored the book *Cultural Humility: Engaging Diverse Identities in Therapy* (2017).

Joshua N. Hook, PhD, is an associate professor of counseling psychology at the University of North Texas in Denton, where he teaches the graduate multicultural counseling course. He is a licensed clinical psychologist in Texas. Dr. Hook's professional interests include humility, religion and spirituality, and multicultural counseling. His research has been published in premier journals in his field, such as the *Journal of Counseling Psychology, The Counseling Psychologist, The Journal of Positive Psychology,* and *Psychology of Religion and Spirituality.* He has coedited or coauthored several books, including *Cultural Humility: Engaging Diverse Identities in Therapy* (2017); *Helping Groups Heal: Leading Groups in the Process of Transformation* (2017); and the *Handbook of Humility: Theory, Research, and Applications* (2017). He serves on several editorial boards, including the *Journal of Counseling Psychology, Psychology of Religion and Spirituality,* and *Spirituality in Clinical Practice.* In 2019, he won the Fritz & Linn Kuder Early Career Award for Distinguished Scientific Contributions to Counseling Psychology. He blogs regularly at http://www.JoshuaNHook.com.

Jesse Owen, PhD, is a professor of counseling psychology at the University of Denver in Colorado. His research interests focus on multicultural processes in psychotherapy, therapist expertise, and romantic relationships. He is an American Psychological Association fellow for the Society for the Advancement of Psychotherapy (SAP; Division 29), and he has been awarded the Early Career Awards for SAP and Division 17 (Counseling Psychology). He also has served as SAP's domain chair and representative for education and training, and is currently the treasurer. Dr. Owen has published more than 125 peer-reviewed publications, most of which focus on psychotherapy process and outcomes; he is the incoming editor for the journal *Psychotherapy*; and he coauthored the book *Cultural Humility: Engaging Diverse Identities in Therapy* (2017). In his small private practice in Denver, Dr. Owen focuses on individual and couple therapy as well as psychological assessment.